What People Are Say

T0278916

# Altered Perspectives

This collection of essays presents a clear, fascinating, and thoughtful introduction to the emerging field of the philosophy of psychedelics. New thoughts are mingled with those of established thinkers, including Spinoza, Hume, Kant, Schopenhauer, Bergson, and of course, William James — who can in many ways be considered the seminal thinker in this field. Yet the application of the psychedelic experience is not limited to Western figures: we are also introduced to Eastern styles of thinking, somewhat seemingly alien to us Westerners, as well as to alien phenomenology in the extraterrestrial sense — not to mention otherworldly aesthetics, causation, and modes of illumination. Nothing is beyond limit in this book that explores the outer limits of the mind.

**Peter Sjöstedt-Hughes**, philosopher, lecturer at the University of Exeter, and author of *Noumenautics* and *Modes of Sentience*

The essays in *Altered Perspectives* eruditely unpick philosophical entanglements from the many corners of psychedelia, and they entertain as much as they enlighten.

**Robert Dickins**, historian and founder of Psychedelic Press

Sam Woolfe reveals that there is a great deal of territory where philosophy and psychedelics overlap — a region he mines in surprising and insightful ways in these essays, with visits to history, spiritual traditions, and ethnobotany along the way. Destinations in this whirlwind tour are fascinating and far-flung — there are explorations of déjà vu, DMT jesters, plant spirits, unreadable languages, and the possibility that we can remember our own birth. But Woolfe's feet are firmly grounded. His open-mindedness is balanced with a good dose of scepticism.

**Cody Johnson**, author of *Magic Medicine: A Trip Through the Intoxicating History and Modern-Day Use of Psychedelic Plants and Substances*

# Altered Perspectives

## Critical Essays on Psychedelic Consciousness

# Altered Perspectives

## Critical Essays on Psychedelic Consciousness

Sam Woolfe

IFF
BOOKS

London, UK
Washington, DC, USA

# CollectiveInk

First published by iff Books, 2024
iff Books is an imprint of Collective Ink Ltd.,
Unit 11, Shepperton House, 89 Shepperton Road, London, N1 3DF
office@collectiveinkbooks.com
www.collectiveinkbooks.com
www.iff-books.com

For distributor details and how to order please visit the 'Ordering' section on our website.

Text copyright: Sam Woolfe 2023

ISBN: 978 1 80341 653 3
978 1 80341 652 6 (ebook)
Library of Congress Control Number: 2023946054

All rights reserved. Except for brief quotations in critical articles or reviews, no part of this book may be reproduced in any manner without prior written permission from the publishers.

The rights of Sam Woolfe as author have been asserted in accordance with the Copyright, Designs and Patents Act 1988.

A CIP catalogue record for this book is available from the British Library.

Design: Lapiz Digital Services

UK: Printed and bound by CPI Group (UK) Ltd, Croydon, CR0 4YY
Printed in North America by CPI GPS partners

We operate a distinctive and ethical publishing philosophy in all areas of our business, from our global network of authors to production and worldwide distribution.

# Contents

This book is dedicated to my parents.

Our normal waking consciousness ... is but one special type of consciousness, while all about it, parted from it by the filmiest of screens, there lie potential forms of consciousness entirely different. We may go through life without suspecting their existence; but apply the requisite stimulus, and at a touch they are there in all their completeness.... No account of the universe in its totality can be final which leaves these other forms of consciousness quite disregarded. How to regard them is the question — for they are so discontinuous with ordinary consciousness.

William James, *The Varieties of Religious Experience* (1902)

# Preface

The philosophy of psychedelics is a growing field, and for good reason. The psychedelic experience, much like philosophy, can instil in us radical shifts in perspective, related to everything that matters to us, and to many things we rarely (if ever) question or consider. The mind-altering, belief-challenging nature of philosophy aligns well with the psychedelic experience, in which these effects are felt more dramatically and viscerally. In a flash of illumination and insight, a particular idea one suspected was true can feel confirmed; a cherished perspective may, alternatively, be discarded; or perhaps a belief previously rejected or overlooked is adopted. These changes of mind may occur swiftly or slowly.

The question of whether to trust these psychedelic-induced insights is a topic that is relevant to epistemology. Many other areas of philosophy can shed light on certain aspects of the psychedelic experience. Each essay in this book focuses on one specific (and often very strange) visual, emotional, or mystical feature of psychedelic states. I analyse these phenomena mostly from philosophical perspectives but also refer to psychological, anthropological, and evolutionary angles — and weave in personal narratives — where relevant.

The psychedelic phenomena I attempt to interpret through these various lenses include seeing the self as an illusion, noetic experiences (feelings of profound insight), alien abduction-type experiences, the sublime (fear mixed with wonder), visions of alien symbols/writing, meetings with jester entities, the feeling of receiving messages from spirits, déjà vu, and existential joy. (These essays can be read as standalone texts, except for the two-part essay 'On Plant Spirits and Psychedelic Teleology'.)

The specific disciplines of philosophy that are pertinent and therefore applied in the following discussions are metaphysics, philosophy of mind, Buddhist philosophy, epistemology, aesthetics, and existentialism. And the philosophers whose ideas I draw on include Baruch Spinoza, Immanuel Kant, Arthur Schopenhauer, David Hume, William James, Friedrich Nietzsche, Rudolf Otto, Alfred North Whitehead, Henri Bergson, and Martin Buber, as well as contemporary thinkers like Peter Sjöstedt-Hughes. In addition, I explore and apply the theories of a number of prominent psychologists, including Carl Jung, Otto Rank, and Stanislav Grof.

My aim in these essays is to investigate certain psychedelic phenomena with a critical and sceptical outlook, as there are many experiences one can have on psychedelics that may lead to strong and certain conclusions about consciousness or reality but which nonetheless deserve scrutiny. This means we have to pay attention to truth-testing factors like consistency, logical reasoning, evidence, and, conversely, the absence of these factors in any arguments put forward.

Looking for the best explanations of psychedelic phenomena is a difficult and perhaps never-ending task, but it is still highly engaging and often fruitful. Even if this activity does not lead to any completely satisfactory conclusions, it can at least encourage a spirit of open-mindedness and intellectual humility, which are often seen as cornerstones of the psychedelic experience.

Here again we can see the interrelatedness of psychedelic states and philosophy; since both encourage an ethos of reflectiveness and a willingness to consider new ideas and challenge one's own, they can both improve each other. Psychonautical journeys can complement philosophical explorations, and vice versa. Honing skills of critical thinking and an understanding of particular systems of thought can lead to a kind of 'philosophical integration' — a post-psychedelic phase of interpreting psychedelic phenomena with a philosophical perspective in mind. This would enrich, deepen, and expand these experiences, which might otherwise just be compartmentalised as something intense and strange that happened on a particular day. (Of course, this is not to say that intense and strange subjective states aren't valuable and interesting in their own right.)

Throughout these essays, I attempt to present differing theories and the relative strengths and weaknesses of each, both in themselves and when used to interpret psychedelic states. While some essays involve a critique of a particular stance or a defence of another (based on perceived explanatory power), I see these discussions as very much ongoing. Ideas that feel sturdier and more defensible than others today may be modified — or even overturned — later on, based on that ever-complicated (and ever-evolving) interplay between experiential reality and the ideas we use to make sense of that reality.

I have called the title of this collection of essays *Altered Perspectives* because of this interplay — this relationship between experiences (specifically psychedelic experiences) and ideas. Varying one can change the other. We now know from scientific research that psychedelics can alter people's core metaphysical beliefs.[1] These essays will hopefully illustrate the manifold ways in which psychedelics can alter our perspectives — be they perceptual, emotional, ethical, existential, or metaphysical — as well as emphasise the mysterious nature of these profound changes in consciousness. Whether the deepest questions about how we experience reality (sober or altered) will ever be solved is uncertain. This might feel unsettling. But perhaps this *mystery of mystery* — or *meta-mystery* — can be embraced. After all, uncertainty is necessary for the adventure of ideas.

I would like to thank the publishing team at Iff Books for making this book a reality, with special thanks to Nick Welch for creating the brilliant cover design and Denise Smith for her meticulous copyediting. I also want to thank Peter Sjöstedt-Hughes, Robert Dickins, and Cody Johnson for taking the time to read my manuscript and share their thoughts; my parents for their constant support and encouragement; and all those who have read and commented on my work over the years — I deeply value the feedback and words of appreciation.

**Endnotes**

1.  Timmermann, C., Kettner, H., Letheby, C., Roseman, L., Rosas, F.E., and Carhart-Harris, R.L. (2021). 'Psychedelics alter metaphysical beliefs'. *Scientific Reports*, 11, Article: 22166.

# Chapter 1

# Mescaline Revelations: Hume, Buddhism, and the Illusory Self

One of the most interesting aspects of psychedelics is how they can attract one to — or concretise — certain philosophical ideas, theories, and systems. For example, in his essay 'The Subjective Effects of Nitrous Oxide' (1882), the psychologist William James wrote that the nitrous oxide trance provided him with "the conviction that Hegelism was true after all".[1] For me, a single experience with mescaline hydrochloride provided a visceral confirmation of Arthur Schopenhauer's theory of the will to live, his attendant views on compassion, and the moral worth of non-human animals.[2]

As with many other potentially valuable insights gained on psychedelics, these ideas matured and gained more meaning after a period of personal reflection. During this particular mescaline experience, a mixture of visual imagery, intuition, and perspective shift led to another philosophical insight: specifically about the illusory nature of the self. After some time spent digesting this, I was able to draw on a philosophical theory to better make sense of it. I then later discovered a separate (but connected) idea that further illuminated this experience as well as a subsequent journey with mescaline.

The first theory I used to interpret the experience, relating to the nature of the self, was David Hume's bundle theory of the self, while the second was the Buddhist model of the five skandhas. In this essay, I would like to describe the part of this mescaline experience in which my normal conception of the self was challenged, and how — through integration — I came to connect this experience with both the Humean and Buddhist perspectives on personal identity. I will also explore how a

1

later experience with mescaline helped me to better understand the juxtaposition of Hume's bundle theory with the Buddhist teaching on the five skandhas.

## The Centreless Self

During the peak of my mescaline experience, seemingly out of nowhere, I started to perceive meaningful imagery in my mind's eye. I was seeing a sequence of visual images of myself — specifically my facial expressions going through changes. Each facial expression was distinct, associated with a disposition, a feeling, a state of mind, or a particular quality of myself. These phantasmic impressions showed me morphing from deflated, gloomy, and negative to elated, upbeat, and positive. I could see an irritable version of myself, and a calmer version of myself.

Several variations manifested before the insight running through these images became clear: there was no core — no centre — *behind* any of these expressions. I seemed to be exploring all the different moods and personality traits that make up how I appear to myself, yet I could see no central identity that was common to all these changing states.

I was well aware, conceptually, of the idea that the self is illusory.[3] I had discovered cognitive scientists like Bruce Hood who claimed that everyone experiences a strong *sense* of self, but that beyond this experience, there is nothing we can identify *as* the self.[4] A useful analogy is the Kanizsa triangle, a perceptual illusion whereby we see a triangle, even though no triangle has been drawn. Our brain 'fills in the gaps', as it were. Hood states that our brain performs the same trick when it comes to our impression of the self. He describes the self as a useful narrative that connects our experiences, thoughts, and behaviours together, helping us to act in an advantageous way in the world.[5]

As a social animal that evolved in tight-knit groups in order to survive, a sense of self or personal identity can have adaptive value.[6] When cooperation becomes essential for survival, it is important to coordinate people's actions and strengthen interpersonal bonds. A sense of self may have been formed, in large part, through the internalisation of how members of a social group perceive and evaluate individuals. Coordination can then be facilitated when your self-concept aligns with how other members of the group perceive you as an individual. This feeling of a private self means that self-esteem and self-feelings (e.g. guilt, shame, embarrassment, and pride) can arise, both of which have social functions. Self-esteem can serve as a cue for your relative standing in the group (your status and role); it can indicate your level of loyalty, bravery, trustworthiness, kindness, and intelligence; and finally, it tells you how accepted you are by other group members. Self-feelings are useful too. For example, guilt motivates an individual to assure group members that he or she will adjust their behaviour in a favourable direction.

In this way, the self evolved out of the need for social approval, affiliation, and alliances. The Canadian psychologist Steven Pinker states, "It's to our advantage to be seen as brave, trustworthy, kind and so forth. We have the ability to float above ourselves and look down at ourselves, to play back tapes of our own behavior to evaluate and manipulate it. Knowing thyself is a way of making thyself as palatable as possible to others."[7]

This illusory self is real in the sense that it is an experience we have — and which we have all the time — but it is still nonetheless a story we have fabricated. As Virginia Woolf wrote in her diary, "We're splinters & mosaics; not, as they used to hold, immaculate, monolithic, consistent wholes."[8] As well as the scientific perspective on the self, I had come across the Buddhist notion of *anattā* ('non-self'), the doctrine that says there is no unchanging and permanent self underlying our experiences.

However, mescaline offered me a much deeper, experiential confirmation of this perennial idea. It felt plain to me that the self was truly centreless. In each sequence of visual imagery, I recognised a way of being that I would normally attach an identity to. Under the influence of mescaline, nonetheless, the mechanism of the mind that weaves the self into these states seemed to be temporarily halted. In each expression — showing my physical appearance, mood, personality, and way of being — I could no longer see a special, unique, solid identity. Nothing about my experiences of myself revealed an essential or distinct self underneath. I felt I was just a series of fleeting personas.

Even if I introspect and think of this 'me' as a constellation of thoughts and personality traits, this does not genuinely create a feeling of personal identity — an identity different from everyone else — that I normally experience in everyday life. Without the usual illusion of identity at play, day-to-day experiences seem more like ephemeral changes in tone, style, and colour. There is no essential substance that persists in these changes. What I am left with are changing patterns without a solid surface upon which the patterns appear.

Upon further reflection, this new, intuitive understanding of the self felt strongly connected to Hume's theory of personal identity, which the Scottish philosopher explicated in his work *A Treatise of Human Nature* (1738).

## Hume's Bundle Theory of the Self

*A Treatise of Human Nature* is one of Hume's most important and influential works. It stands out as a classic defence of philosophical empiricism (the theory that all knowledge ultimately originates from sense experience) and philosophical naturalism (the belief that only natural objects, laws, and forces exist, which thus entails disbelief in the supernatural). He expounds on his views on personal identity in Section VI of his treatise.

His conclusions arise out of his broader theory — bundle theory more generally — that considers all objects as mere collections (or bundles) of properties. In this way, a tree has properties such as greenness, the roughness of bark, branching patterns, being a type of plant, etc. — but there is no tree beyond these properties; there is no unifying substance called 'tree' that underlies the changes the tree goes through, or that exists separately from these properties. According to bundle theory, we cannot conceive of an object except in terms of its properties, and so the notion of a substance inherent to these properties is a fiction, with the self being included as one such figment of the imagination. This stands in opposition to substance theory, which posits that each object has a *bare particular*, an element that is distinct from — and can exist independently of — the object's properties. This bare particular is thought to be without any properties but still very much real (so not something abstract).

As a philosophical naturalist, Hume rejects the notion that there exists an immaterial soul that persists over time, and as an empiricist, he aims to explore the nature of the self using introspective experience, just as one often tends to do — either spontaneously or intentionally — in a psychedelic state. Through the lens of introspection, Hume concludes that the self is "nothing but a bundle or collection of different perceptions, which succeed each other with an inconceivable rapidity, and are in a perpetual flux and movement".[9]

This description certainly aligns with my experience of the self under the influence of mescaline. I saw properties of experience, succeeding one another, and constantly changing. If there was anything that I could pinpoint as the self, to be able to say *there I am*, it could only be a bundle of ever-changing properties. Yet this meant that the normal idea of an integrated and precise self really was just a mental projection, a useful conceptual category like the idea of a 'tree', which helps to make sense of the world and navigate through it, but which does not refer to anything substantial.

We have a tendency, Hume argues, to confound the idea of a "perfect identity" (a soul, self, or substance) with the idea of "a succession of related objects".[10] We mistakenly interpret "a distinct idea of several different objects existing in succession, and connected together by a close relation" as an "uninterrupted" identity.[11] For Hume, this "close relation" consists of "resemblance, contiguity, or causation".[12] But upon close examination, there is nothing about the relation between perceptions that really encapsulates our everyday feeling of selfhood. According to Hume, our tendency to confound identity with relation — to ascribe an identity to variable and interrupted objects — is what leads to the fiction of the self: "a fiction, either of something invariable and uninterrupted, or something mysterious and inexplicable".[13]

Again, in the succession of images of myself that I saw during this mescaline experience, there was no thread of personal identity connecting them all together. Moreover, I noticed that these changing bundles were marked by uncontrollability, unpredictability, and diversity. I did not feel there was a 'me' in control of these changing states. There was no sense that each variation was just a brief diversion away from a predictable self. And out of all the various bundles, none particularly stood out as strongly indicative of a singular identity. Indeed, Hume is keen to point out that we have no constant impression of the self:

It must be some one impression that gives rise to every real idea. But self or person is not any one impression, but that to which our several impressions and ideas are supposed to have a reference. If any impression gives rise to the idea of self, that impression must continue invariably the same through the whole course of our lives, since self is supposed to exist after that manner. But there is no impression constant and invariable. Pain and pleasure, grief and joy, passions and sensations succeed each other and never all exist at the same time. It cannot, therefore, be from any of these impressions or from any other that the idea of self is derived, and, consequently, there is no such idea.[14]

Elsewhere, Hume states that our selves are simply composed of different perceptions:

> For my part, when I enter most intimately into what I call *myself*, I always stumble on some particular perception or other, of heat or cold, light or shade, love or hatred, pain or pleasure. I never can catch *myself* at any time without a perception and never can observe anything but the perception. When my perceptions are removed for any time, as by sound sleep, so long am I insensible of myself and may truly be said not to exist. And were all my perceptions removed by death and could I neither think nor feel nor see nor love nor hate after the dissolution of my body, I should be entirely annihilated, nor do I conceive what is further requisite to make me a perfect nonentity.[15]

Here we can see both Hume's empiricism and naturalism at play. When the self is viewed solely from the point of view of perception — which is the ground of knowledge for the empiricist — we discover no unified or coherent self. In addition, Hume is arguing that upon physical death, we would be "entirely annihilated" — there would be no continuation of the self. In this way, examining the self during a psychedelic experience can be a way of bolstering philosophical naturalism, in that it becomes difficult to identify a supernatural self, an immaterial essence that is 'you' that can survive death. Instead, the bundle of properties making up the *sense* of 'you' can be described in purely natural terms, as awareness, a physical body, feelings, thoughts, habits, idiosyncrasies, and demeanours — all without supernatural connotations. When all these properties disappear, so too will the self.

I was somewhat familiar with Hume's bundle theory before my experiment with mescaline, but it was only after this psychedelic experience that I properly incorporated this idea into my worldview. This experience, which I suppose aligns with Hume's insistence on observing the mind, illustrated to me the insightfulness of introspection, a state of mind that is often stimulated and heightened during a psychedelic experience. However, seeing my 'self' from this different vantage point did not necessarily resolve the potential issues associated with Hume's theory.

For example, one of the most common and enduring responses to Hume's theory is as follows: If the 'I' is nothing more than a bundle of perceptions, then what is it that ties these perceptions together? Other bundle theorists, such as Bertrand Russell, postulated that a special relation called *compresence* (a *togetherness*) connects bundled properties to one another. This term refers to a relation that is usually considered ontologically primitive, special, and unanalysable. This relation holds between qualities experienced simultaneously — between qualities that overlap. In *Human Knowledge: Its Scope and Value* (1948), Russell notes that this overlapping or compresence "is not itself to be defined logically; it is an empirically known relation, having ... only an ostensive definition".[16]

We experience compresence when we experience different events together at the same time (such as an itch, the temperature outside, the greenness of the leaves, the sound of a dog barking, the smell of flowers, and so on). Likewise, we can experience this compresence in the context of the self when we experience the simultaneous presence of our physical appearance, emotions, thoughts, desires, interests, plans, etc. The existence of a bundle, including the bundle imagined as the self, also depends upon this relation of compresence. Simply enumerating properties does not constitute a bundle. Overlapping must be involved.

However, my mescaline experience relating to the self — and subsequent consideration of it — has not illuminated this notion of compresence in any definitive way. During my experience, I did not ponder *how* I experience perceptions simultaneously, nor did I question *why* this bundling relation should exist. Could a sense of self not have evolved or manifested *without* this bundling? Is it not possible to have all our perceptions alongside a fictitious self that is based on a separate and distinct perception? In addition, while I applied (without intending to) the kind of scepticism to the self that Hume also applied, I did not push this questioning of assumptions to its limits.

For instance, while I was able to visualise myself as nothing more than a bundle of qualities and a sequence of bundles, I did not know what qualities, if any, I could eliminate while still retaining my sense of self. This pertains to the ship of Theseus thought experiment, which asks us to question when, if at all, an object loses its identity through the gradual loss or replacement of its parts. If I were to eliminate my physical body, appearance, and expressions from the bundle, would I still feel a sense of personal identity? Would I lose just a degree of it? Is personal identity even something that we can feel degrees of (since such identity is felt, at least, to be fixed)? Then there is the question of whether some qualities in the bundle are more central to identity than others. Do personality traits have more identity-forming powers than moods, for example? Of course, the very fact that I am now asking such questions may not have even happened if it were not for the openness and novel thinking encouraged by my mescaline experience, so in that sense, it does have a real connection to these thought-provoking questions, which I am asking many years after the experience took place.

There are still other criticisms of Hume's bundle theory of the self that I do not feel my mescaline experience has helped to resolve, either in terms of the experience itself or in terms of how I have integrated it. The philosopher Nelson Pike, for instance, raises the following question:

> Given that the mind is simply a collection of experiences (as Hume said), by what principle shall we distinguish between the perceptions making up your mind and the perceptions making up mine? Providing an answer to this question is often taken to be the crucial problem confronting any advocate of the bundle theory of the self.[17]

Indeed, if I examine my mescaline-induced experience of the bundled self, what is the principle that allows me to section off 'my' supposed bundled self from someone else's? What is it that creates this sense of *belongingness*, which allows me to distinguish my fictitious self from that of others? In Hume's opinion, we find resemblance among our perceptions due to memory; we remember past perceptions, and this remembering allows us to connect our many varied and successive perceptions together. Through the "frequent placing of these resembling perceptions in the chain of thought", we gain the sense of "the continuance of one object".[18] Hume concludes that "the memory not only discovers the identity, but also contributes to its production, by producing the relation of resemblance among the perceptions. The case is the same whether we consider ourselves or others".[19]

We also see our successive perceptions connected by a cause-and-effect relation. Understanding this relation, whereby we see one perception leading to another, depends on the faculty of memory. Without memory, Hume believes, we would never be able to imaginatively construct a sense of self. And I can see the truth of this when I reflect upon my mescaline experience. While I may not have been recalling actual events when I was in a certain emotional state (since the images I was seeing seemed more creative), I can nonetheless recognise that these mescaline-induced images were, in some way, drawn from my memories. Furthermore, based on the assumption that I have unique memories of my perceptions and that my localised brain exclusively produces these memories, it makes sense that I will see my bundled self as distinct.

We can still question, however, whether there is an adequate criterion that allows us to divide perceptions into individual bundles. It is one thing to recognise that memory contributes to personal identity and quite another to understand why some perceptions are included in the bundled self but not others. For instance, I have memories linking together my perceptions of others and the world around me, but why does my sense of self often seem to exclude these perceptions? Under the influence of mescaline, I did not perceive in *myself* the qualities of inanimate objects, plants, animals, or other people; all of the qualities related to the self appeared to be restricted to the spatiotemporal boundaries of my physical body (and all the thoughts and moods demarcated by my body).

Of course, it is useful for the mind to delimit certain perceptions, with some belonging to the self and others relating to the rest of the world. The brain has evolved mechanisms to conjure up this convenient, illusory self,[20] and there is a neural basis that shapes boundaries between the self and others.[21] Nevertheless, it is also true that, under the influence of psychedelics, the neural networks contributing to the sense of self can be altered and the boundaries between self and others can dissolve.[22] Even if it is not clear what the exact principle is that divides perceptions into individual bundles, modern neuroscience and the experience of ego dissolution at least illustrate that this principle can be tampered with, changing — or completely breaking down — the boundaries of the bundled self. The malleability of the self and the possibility of having conscious experiences without it (in the state of ego dissolution) seem to bolster Hume's ideas on personal identity.

Pike does, nonetheless, stress another potential flaw with Hume's bundle theory. Hume claims to 'look within' and discover only a collection of perceptions in his self, but what is it that is doing the looking and the discovering? The same question equally applies to my altered state: When I was thinking about myself, did this thinking itself belong to this bundle known as the self or was it something of a different nature? Hume denies the existence of a transcendent ego, a self that is more than just a bundle of perceptions, but he seems to refer to this kind of ego when he writes about observing and thinking about the self. I, too, was examining and having realisations about the self. Was I a bundle experiencing itself (like looking in the mirror)? Was I a bundle looking at this separate bundle called the self? Or was I an observer that was not a bundle of perceptions?

It may be that 'looking within' does not require a sense of self, that this introspection (which is more than just mindful awareness) could be its own kind of bundle. Yet even if one views the sense of self from the point of view of mindfulness, which, unlike introspection, is non-analytical, it is difficult to ascertain whether such awareness is a bundle or not. The simple quality of noticing could be a distinct property rather than a bundle made up of multiple properties — but it is also possible to imagine the opposite.

While I have become more strongly convinced of Hume's theory, the mescaline experience and my later analysis of it have in no way ironed out all of the potential issues with this theory. This fleeting experience, nevertheless, has ended up inspiring many questions and avenues of thought, which appears to be one of the key lasting effects of psychedelics.[23] This experience did not provide me with a flawless revelation about the nature of the self, but it did provide a powerful conviction of a specific philosophical theory, similar to James's experiences with nitrous oxide.

Next, I would like to draw on the notion of the five skandhas, as taught in Buddhism, as this concept bears a striking resemblance to both Hume's bundle theory and my personal experiences with mescaline.

## The Five Skandhas

The five skandhas are elucidated in the Heart Sutra, one of the most important sutras (Buddhist scriptures) in Mahayana Buddhism. *Skandhas* in Sanskrit (or *khandhas* in Pali) can be translated as 'heaps', 'aggregates', 'collections', or 'groupings'. In the sutra, Avalokiteśvara — the Bodhisattva of Compassion — is addressing Śariputra, one of the disciples of the Buddha, and is describing how all phenomena are fundamentally empty, i.e. empty of fundamental essence. This Buddhist notion of emptiness is referred to as *śūnyatā*. Avalokiteśvara famously states in the sutra: "Form is emptiness, emptiness is form."[24] And he explains to Śariputra that the fundamental emptiness of phenomenal reality can be known through the five skandhas.

In Buddhism, the five skandhas constitute a person and their personality. They give rise to our sense of self. The Buddha also catalogued and detailed the five skandhas in the *Anattalakkhana Sutta* or the Discourse on the Not-Self Characteristic, found in the Pali Canon (the earliest and most complete collection of Buddhist scriptures). They are as follows:

1. Form (*Rupa* in Sanskrit): this refers to matter — something material that takes up physical space and can be perceived by the senses. Rupa includes the material form of our bodies.

2. Sensation (*Vedana*): this skandha refers to the physical or mental sensations we experience when our sensory faculties come into contact with objects in the external

world (according to Buddhism, the mind is included as one such sensory faculty). These sensations can be pleasant, unpleasant, or neutral.

3. Perception (*Samjna*): this is the faculty that recognises. It is what we might call thinking. This refers to our capacity to conceptualise and label things through our association of things with other things (e.g. I register and label a tree as a 'tree' because I associate it with my other experiences of trees). Context, too, features in perception, as we are able to recognise objects based on the context in which they exist (e.g. I recognise a dish as food because I see it served in a restaurant).

4. Mental formations (*Samskara*): these mental formations include all volitional actions, both good and bad. Buddhists interpret actions as mental formations because the mind precedes all actions: an impure mind precedes a certain way of speaking and acting (leading to suffering), while a pure mind precedes a different way of speaking and acting (leading to happiness). Samskara includes all the mental imprints and conditioning that objects trigger within us, a process that initiates action. Biases, prejudices, attitudes, interests, and predilections belong to this skandha.

5. Consciousness (*Vijnana*): this refers to awareness of an object and our ability to discern its components and aspects — and there are six types of consciousness, with each one consisting of one sensing faculty as its basis, along with a corresponding object. In Buddhism, these six faculties include the five sensory modalities we are familiar with (sight, hearing, taste, smell, and touch), plus the sense organ of the mind. One example of consciousness would be visual-awareness, which has the faculty of sight as its basis and a visual form as its object. For mental-awareness, the mind is the basis and an idea

or thought would be its object. Vijnana is dependent on the other skandhas.[25]

The Buddhist conception of the five skandhas aligns with both Hume's bundle theory and my mescaline-induced experience in some important ways. Firstly, the terms 'heap' and 'aggregate' are interchangeable with 'bundle'. Thus, both the Buddha and Hume are essentially viewing the self with the same kind of conceptual framework; both see the sense of self as made up of component parts. According to the Buddhist and Humean perspectives, these distinct parts are bundled together, and it is through this bundling that the sense of a single self is created.

Like Hume, the Buddha taught that there is no real self occupying either an individual skandha or the skandhas collected together. The Buddhist scholars Damien Keown and Charles S. Prebish write, "Canonical Buddhism teaches that the notion of a self is unnecessarily superimposed upon five collections or aggregates (*skandha*) of phenomena."[26] In the Discourse on the Not-Self Characteristic, the Buddha asks his followers, "Now, that which is impermanent, unsatisfactory, subject to change, is it proper to regard that as: 'This is mine, this I am, this is my self'?" To which the monks respond, "Indeed, not that, O Lord."[27] The Buddha rejected the notion of *atman* in Hindu philosophy, which refers to an individual's true self — their inner, unchanging self or soul. Atman is eternal and beyond identification with phenomena. In Buddhism, on the other hand, there is still no true self that exists apart from the five skandhas (the Sanskrit translation of anattā or 'non-self' is *anātman*, which means the opposite of atman).

Each skandha, and the five skandhas together, are characterised by śūnyatā; they are empty of any intrinsic, fixed essence. For this reason, they must be empty of true selfhood (anattā), as a self implies an unchanging essence. No self possesses the skandhas. No self underpins them. This selflessness or anattā also accords with the Buddhist concept of *anicca* (impermanence), which teaches that all things are impermanent and changing, so any feeling of fixity (including the sense of being a fixed 'me' or 'I') is illusory. Indeed, like everything else in phenomenal reality, the skandhas are temporary and conditioned. Just as in Hume's analysis, the skandhas are always in a state of flux. Indeed, Hume captures the essence of anicca and anattā in *A Treatise of Human Nature*, when he states,

> The mind is a kind of theatre, where several perceptions successively make their appearance; pass, re-pass, glide away, and mingle in an infinite variety of postures and situations. There is properly no *simplicity* in it at one time, nor *identity* in different; whatever natural propension we may have to imagine that simplicity and identity.[28]

## The Varieties of Introspection

It is curious to note here just how closely Hume converges with Buddhist thought. Hume never explicitly refers to Buddhism in his philosophical writings, nor is there any record of him speaking or writing about Buddhist philosophy in general. The first Western philosopher to take Buddhism seriously and incorporate its ideas into a philosophical system was Schopenhauer. While living in Weimar, Germany, in the early 1800s, Friedrich Majer — a historian of religion and acquaintance of Schopenhauer — introduced Schopenhauer to Eastern philosophy, which led him to read Hindu texts like the Upanishads and the Bhagavad Gita as well as the early Buddhist texts.

Schopenhauer said, "If I were to take the results of my philosophy as the standard of truth, I would have to consider Buddhism the finest of all religion", and at times he referred to himself as a "Buddhaist".[29] Schopenhauer was undoubtedly impressed by Buddhism, although he claims he formulated most of his ideas before ever coming across the religion (although this is questionable) and only later realised the similarities. Schopenhauer, in line with Buddhism, argued that life is characterised by suffering and that this suffering is rooted in desire. Perhaps Hume, too, independently developed a system of thought that had affinities with Buddhism, without exposure to it. After all, it is not unheard of for the same or similar philosophical ideas to emerge in times and places that are disconnected from each other. This is known as perennial wisdom, and it can be accessed in different ways, such as through meditation, introspection, or psychedelics. It does not matter whether introspection is of the Buddhist, Humean, or psychedelic variety — all these forms of introspection can lead to a singular truth, or the same realisation: the unreality of the self.

Nonetheless, Alison Gopnik — an affiliate professor of philosophy at the University of California, Berkeley — has pointed out that it is possible Hume made contact with Buddhist philosophical views,[30] potentially via the influence of Jesuit scholars at the Royal College of La Flèche in France. Charles Francois Dolu was a Jesuit missionary who resided at the Royal College from 1723–1740, a period that overlapped with Hume's stay. Dolu had extensive knowledge of other religions and cultures. Moreover, he had first-hand experience with Theravada Buddhism, as he was part of the second French embassy to Siam (now Thailand) in 1687–1688. Dolu was also acquainted with Ippolito Desideri, a Jesuit missionary who visited Tibet and studied Tibetan Buddhism from 1716–1721. This means it is at least possible that Hume heard about Buddhist ideas through conversations with Dolu.

Whether or not he did, it is still intriguing to note even further similarities between his philosophy and Buddhist thought. One correspondence we find is between Hume's introspective argument against the reality of the self and the Theravada

Buddhist practice of developing *vipassanā* ('insight' or 'clear-seeing'). The aim of developing vipassanā in meditation is to gain insight into the true nature of reality. This means understanding the truths of anicca, anattā, and *dukkha*. In Buddhism, anicca, anattā, and dukkha are known as the three marks of existence, which refers to the belief that all life is marked by impermanence, egolessness, and unsatisfactoriness (or suffering), respectively. The Mahayana tradition diverges from the older Theravada school of Buddhism through its emphasis on gaining insight into śūnyatā, the idea that all forms lack 'inherent existence', which is related to the concept of anattā. We can think of anattā as an aspect of śūnyatā since the former refers specifically to the emptiness of an essential self, whereas the latter encompasses the emptiness of a fixed essence in all things.

In any case, through vipassanā meditation (which allows one to discern conditioned phenomena), one can learn that anicca, anattā, and dukkha define the five aggregates. To practise vipassanā, you want to cultivate certain qualities of mind, including *sati* ('attention' or 'mindfulness'), which refers to the quality of paying attention to experiences without clinging to what is pleasant or feeling aversion to what is unpleasant. The Buddha's explanation of mindfulness and how to practise it is found in the *Satipatthana Sutta* (the Discourse on the Establishing of Mindfulness). The development of concentration (*samadhi*) is also conducive to insight. Concentration differs from mindfulness in that it requires forcing the mind to remain focused on a single object (such as the breath). It is a strongly effortful activity. Concentration can also be referred to as one-pointedness of mind.[31]

Mindfulness, in contrast, chooses the object of attention and simply notices when attention has gone astray. It involves effort too, but it is gentler in nature compared to concentration. Concentration does the real work of holding attention steady on a chosen object. It is through concentration that one develops *samatha* (meaning 'tranquillity': a calming and slowing of the mind). When the mind is calm, you will be able to see your experiences more clearly. Samadhi is a prerequisite for insight. By developing mindfulness, concentration, and calmness in tandem, you will be primed to understand the nature of the five aggregates.

The practice of vipassanā meditation may not necessarily be identical to the introspective awareness employed by Hume, but the qualities of mind involved in each are very closely related (vipassanā is a kind of introspection, after all). And both ways of looking inward yield the same result: the recognition that the self is a non-substantial collection of experiences. Another similarity between Buddhism and Hume is that the two are opposed to substance theory. Buddhism does not accept the existence of an underlying essential substance but instead, like Hume, views reality in terms of elements that are constantly combining and recombining.

While the specific categorisation and definition of the five skandhas may not fit my mescaline experience exactly, there are, nonetheless, some interesting parallels. For example, when seeing images of successive selves, a series of bundles, I could pick out distinct features or categories that made up the bundle, such as my physical body (rupa) and mental formations (samskara). I could see the variety of rupa (e.g. different kinds of facial expressions) and samskara (e.g. negative and positive states of mind). Like the five skandhas, the different qualities making up my sense of self were interrelated; particular thoughts, attitudes, and feelings correlated with certain physical expressions and demeanours. This experience also naturally helped to reinforce both the notions of anattā and anicca.

One of the noticeable differences between the five skandhas and Hume's bundle theory is that the former is more systematic, given how it acts as a system of classification, dividing the bundle we call the self into five distinct aspects. Hume, on the other hand, does not view the self in this systematic way but instead sees it more generally as a collection of many different perceptions. We can glean another key difference between the two philosophical theories when we look at the intentions that Hume and the Buddha had when presenting their ideas. While Hume was simply trying to enlighten the reader about the illusion of the self, the Buddha was drawing attention to this illusion because of the additional belief that the five skandhas cause us to suffer. According to the Buddha, gaining insight into this truth will help to liberate ourselves from suffering.

### The Illusion of the Self and Its Relation to Suffering

In Buddhism, the skandhas are also called the five aggregates of clinging (*Pañcupādānakkhandhā* in Pali) because they are attributes that we crave and cling to, and it is through this clinging that we experience dukkha (this concept is often translated as 'suffering', but it more broadly means 'unsatisfactoriness'). To understand this, we need to examine the Second Noble Truth of Buddhism, which states that the cause of suffering (or dukkha) is craving, attachment, and clinging. (Craving is not the only cause of suffering; Buddhists also recognise ignorance and hatred as causes, although craving is considered the principal and most obvious root of our discontent.)

The Buddha said that there are three types of craving (or *tanha* in Pali): "craving for sensual pleasure, craving for becoming, and craving for non-becoming".[32] It is clear what sensual pleasures would include (e.g. food and sex); 'craving for becoming', meanwhile, refers to the desire to become this or that (e.g. wanting to be rich, famous, and powerful), while 'craving for non-becoming' pertains to the wish to get rid of something (e.g. wanting to eliminate a certain physical or personal characteristic).

Craving causes suffering because of the truth of anicca —
anything we gain can be damaged, broken, lost, or stolen. Every
gain will always be temporary and subject to change. We suffer
when we want the things we have gained to be permanent.
When we have this mindset, losing what we possess brings
suffering, as does the fear of losing those things. Craving also
brings suffering in the following ways: we become dissatisfied
after not getting what we want, we become dissatisfied after
getting what we want but realising that it does not meet our
expectations, and we become dissatisfied after finding out that
the satisfaction of a craving is never enough (since fulfilling
one desire just causes others to arise). Hence, craving never
leads to lasting satisfaction. It instead makes feelings of
unsatisfactoriness (dukkha) inevitable. Schopenhauer, too,
emphasises this point when discussing his concept of the *will*
(a blind, unconscious kind of desire and striving that directs
our behaviour). In his magnum opus *The World as Will and
Representation* (1818), speaking of the will, he writes that

> its desires are unlimited, its claims inexhaustible, and every
> satisfied desire gives birth to a new one. No possible satisfaction
> in the world could suffice to still its craving, set a final goal to its
> demands, and fill the bottomless pit of its heart.[33]

We can now connect the relationship between craving and
suffering to the Buddhist conception of the self. Our cravings for
both becoming and non-becoming (the last two types of tanha)
often relate to our sense of self: we want to be a certain way and
also want to lose certain qualities. These cravings cause us to
suffer, however, because we do not feel satisfied until our self
is the way we want it to be. Moreover, the truth of anicca makes
the self a source of suffering because any state of becoming or
non-becoming that makes us happy is only temporary. When

we crave fleeting aspects of the self to stay the same, we are bound to be disappointed.

But the connection between selfhood and craving also runs much deeper than this. In order to cling to or crave something, you need two things: a clinger and something to cling to. You need to see the world as divided up into 'me' and 'the world separate from me'. Yet according to Buddhism, this notion of separation is illusory — and furthermore, it is because of this illusion that we crave and cling to things. The belief in a separate 'me' that must be promoted and indulged is what leads to insatiable craving. If we continue to see ourselves as an 'I' separate from the world, then craving — and therefore suffering — will continue. The nature of craving also encourages emotions like jealousy, hatred, and fear to arise, which cause others to suffer too (think of the harm that can result when you act from the place of these emotions).

Part of ending our suffering involves relinquishing our attachment to the skandhas. And we begin this process by overcoming our ignorance about them, by seeing through the illusion. In this way, the Buddhist outlook is both normative and soteriological. It is normative because it makes a value judgement about the illusory nature of the self; it postulates that our attachment to this illusion has undesirable outcomes. And the outlook is soteriological because it teaches a way of relating to the skandhas (non-attachment) that can save us from our suffering. Hume's account of the self, on the other hand, is simply descriptive. He does not claim that identifying with this bundle of perceptions leads to suffering; he merely states that this identification is mistaken.

## Evaluating Bundle Theory and the Five Skandhas, in Light of the Psychedelic Experience

Following a subsequent experience with mescaline, I have come to find much value in the normative and soteriological aspects of the five skandhas. During this powerful experience, I found myself joyously lost in an ecstatic state, with my subjective personal identity completely dissolved. At one point, however, I could see my sense of self in my mind's eye, like in the previous mescaline experience that I described earlier. Yet the image of this self appeared differently. This time I was looking at a negative self-image, based around deprecating and limiting beliefs about myself. This image appeared tiny and mirage-like, and as with all mirages, I was able to discover its insubstantiality. I let it disappear into nothingness, and upon this letting go, a feeling of bliss and peace washed over me.

The amalgamation of the five skandhas can also be referred to as the 'small self' or 'false self' — and these descriptions resonate strongly with this subsequent mescaline experience. I was able to view my self-image detachedly as an observer so that it appeared in the distance and separate from my conscious awareness. Normally, I am identified with this small self, which makes it feel close to me and undeniably real. During this experience, however, this sense of identity appeared as flimsy as a hologram. I no longer saw my habitual self as possessing the reality I thought it had. Moreover, I understood that this familiar sense of who I was, which had not been serving me well, was not something set in stone. It could be different. (Interestingly, the philosophers Chris Letheby and Philip Gerrans have argued that the therapeutic benefits of psychedelics stem from their ability to disrupt and revise maladaptive models of self.[34])

The psychological distress associated with the small self — and the relief accompanying its dissolution — underscores to me an advantage of the Buddhist perspective over Hume's. Buddhism supplements the insight about the fictitious nature of the self with wisdom about the inimical effects of clinging to this fiction. However, the application of this wisdom should not involve an intention to eradicate the sense of self. As is consistent with the Buddhist view on the cause of suffering, the point is not to get rid of the thing which one clings to but to refrain from clinging. Suffering arises not from the experience of pain, pleasure, or the self. It is caused by attachment to those experiences.

I have since tried to think of this mescaline experience in terms of the principle of non-attachment, which does not mean a lack of interest in positive or negative experiences or giving up those experiences; it means not allowing these experiences to own you. Practising non-attachment involves experiencing the self — and benefiting from this experience — without becoming ensnared by it. In daily life, if I find myself caught up in the concerns of the chattering, insecure ego, it is helpful to recall the image of my small self. This reimagining then recreates the same sense of spaciousness and detachment, and, in turn, the same feeling of unburdening myself.

To reiterate the point made at the beginning of this discussion, a sense of self has great utility. Belief and imagination work to fabricate the self because a more solid sense of identity allows us to live coherently and carry out activities. Hence, the normative and soteriological aspects of the five skandhas do not imply that one should reject the self in everyday life in order to alleviate suffering, only that one's *relation* to the self needs to change.

Connecting these lessons to my own ego-dissolving experience, the fruitful path to take seems to involve building and strengthening a healthy ego, so that all aspects of life — lived from the egoic standpoint — can be fulfilling. After all, viewing oneself, others, and the world through the lens of a negative and limiting ego will lead to negative and limiting experiences. At the same time, having a detached (but not indifferent) attitude towards this secure sense of self will stave off the dangers of clinging. This creates a balanced self that avoids the unnecessary extremes of both self-centredness and self-abnegation.

# Endnotes

1.  James, W. (1882). 'The Subjective Effects of Nitrous Oxide'. *Mind*, Volume 7.
2.  Woolfe, S. (2020). 'How Mescaline Helped Me to Better Understand Schopenhauer's Philosophy', Psychedelic Frontier, 11 September. http://psychedelicfrontier.com/mescaline-helped-understand-schopenhauer/
3.  Woolfe, S. (2013). 'The Illusion of the Self'. *Philosophy Now*, Issue 97.
4.  Hood, B. (2012). *The Self Illusion: Why There is No 'You' Inside Your Head*. London: Constable.
5.  Lehrer, J. (2012). 'The Self Illusion: An Interview With Bruce Hood', *Wired*, 25 May. https://www.wired.com/2012/05/the-self-illusion-an-interview-with-bruce-hood/
6.  Sedikides, C. and Skowronski, J. (2003). 'Evolution of the symbolic self: Issues and prospects' in *Handbook of Self and Identity*, pp. 594–609. Edited by Leary, M.R. and Tangney, J.P. New York: Guildford Press.
7.  Angier, N. (1997). 'Evolutionary Necessity or Glorious Accident? Biologists Ponder the Self', *New York Times*, 22 April. https://www.nytimes.com/1997/04/22/science/evolutionary-necessity-or-glorious-accident-biologists-ponder-the-self.html
8.  Woolf, V. (1924). *The Diary of Virginia Woolf, Volume II*, p. 314. Edited by Bell, A.O. London: Penguin, 1984.
9.  Hume, D. (1739). Part IV, Section VI: 'Of Personal Identity' in *A Treatise of Human Nature*. https://personal.lse.ac.uk/ROBERT49/teaching/ph103/pdf/Hume_1740_OfPersonalIdentity.pdf
10. Ibid.
11. Ibid.
12. Ibid.
13. Ibid.

14. Ibid.
15. Ibid.
16. Russell, B. (1948). *Human Knowledge: Its Scope and Limits*, p. 297. London: George Allen and Unwin.
17. Pike, N. (1967). 'Hume's Bundle Theory of the Self: A Limited Defense'. *American Philosophical Quarterly*, 4(2), pp. 159–165.
18. Hume, D. (1739). Part IV, Section VI: 'Of Personal Identity' in *A Treatise of Human Nature*. https://personal.lse.ac.uk/ROBERT49/teaching/ph103/pdf/Hume_1740_OfPersonalIdentity.pdf
19. Ibid.
20. Deleniv, S. (2018). 'The 'me' illusion: How your brain conjures up your sense of self', *New Scientist*, 5 September. https://www.newscientist.com/article/mg23931940-100-the-me-illusion-how-your-brain-conjures-up-your-sense-of-self/
21. Ereia, S., Hauser, T.U., Moran, R., Story, G.W., Dolan, R.J., and Kurth-Nelson, Z. (2020). 'Social training reconfigures prediction errors to shape Self-Other boundaries'. *Nature Communications*, 11(1), Article: 3030.
22. Briggs, S. (2021). 'Dissolving Ego Dissolution', MIND Foundation, 14 May. https://mind-foundation.org/ego-dissolution/
23. MacLean, K.A., Johnson, M.W., and Griffiths, R.R. (2011). 'Mystical Experiences Occasioned by the Hallucinogen Lead to Increases in the Personality Domain of Openness'. *Journal of Psychopharmacology'*, 25(11), pp. 1453–1461.
24. Anon (n.d.). *The Heart Sutra*. Translated by Pine, R. Berkeley, California: Counterpoint, 2006.
25. O'Brien, B. (2020). 'The Five Skandhas', Learn Religions, 25 August. https://www.learnreligions.com/the-skandhas-450192

26. Keown, D. and Prebish, C. (2009). *Encyclopedia of Buddhism*, p. 844. London: Routledge.

27. Mendis, N.K.G. (2010). 'The Discourse on the Not-Self Characteristic', Access to Insight, 13 June. https://www.accesstoinsight.org/tipitaka/sn/sn22/sn22.059.mend.html

28. Hume, D. (1739). Part IV, Section VI: 'Of Personal Identity' in *A Treatise of Human Nature*. https://personal.lse.ac.uk/ROBERT49/teaching/ph103/pdf/Hume_1740_OfPersonalIdentity.pdf

29. Abelsen, P. (1993). 'Schopenhauer and Buddhism'. *Philosophy East and West*, 43(2), pp. 255–278.

30. Gopnik, A. (2009). 'Could David Hume Have Known about Buddhism?: Charles François Dolu, the Royal College of La Flèche, and the Global Jesuit Intellectual Network'. *Hume Studies*, 35(1&2), pp. 5–28.

31. Gunaratana, B.H. (2011). *Mindfulness in Plain English*, 'Chapter 14'. https://www.vipassana.co.uk/meditation/mindfulness_in_plain_english_16.html

32. O'Brien, B. (2020). 'The Second Noble Truth', Learn Religions, 27 August. https://www.learnreligions.com/the-second-noble-truth-450092

33. Schopenhauer, A. (1818). *The World as Will and Representation*, Vol. 2, p. 573. Translated and edited by Norman, J., Welchman, A., and Janaway, C. Cambridge: Cambridge University Press, 2010.

34. Gerrans, P. and Letheby, C. (2017). 'Psychedelics work by violating our models of self and the world', *Aeon*, 8August. https://aeon.co/essays/psychedelics-work-by-violating-our-models-of-self-and-the-world

## Chapter 2

# Noetic Experiences and Spinoza's God

The feeling of gaining direct knowledge of something grand or important about reality is a common aspect of mystical experiences generally and psychedelic mystical states more specifically. This is known as a *noetic* experience, one of the four defining qualities of a mystical experience, as propounded by the American psychologist and philosopher William James in *The Varieties of Religious Experience* (1902). He describes this noetic quality as follows:

> Although so similar to states of feeling, mystical states seem to those who experience them to be also states of knowledge. They are states of insight into depths of truth unplumbed by the discursive intellect. They are illuminations, revelations, full of significance and importance, all inarticulate though they remain; and as a rule they carry with them a curious sense of authority for after-time.[1]

This 'Aha!' moment could relate to the individual's life or the nature of the universe itself. Briefly, the other three essential aspects of the mystical experience, according to James, are *ineffability*: "The subject of it immediately says that it defies expression, that no adequate report of its contents can be given in words", *transiency*: "Mystical states cannot be sustained for long", and *passivity*: "when the characteristic sort of consciousness once has set in, the mystic feels as if his own will were in abeyance, and indeed sometimes as if he were grasped and held by a superior power."[2] For James, ineffability and the noetic quality are the two necessary and sufficient conditions for a mystical experience, while transiency and passivity are subtler and not required (although they do often accompany this unique altered state of consciousness).

Since James's time, other philosophers and psychologists (e.g. Walter Stace, Walter Pahnke, and Ralph W. Hood) have developed further articulations of the mystical experience, adding in other defining characteristics, including spacelessness and timelessness, a feeling of sacredness or reverence, unity or interconnectedness, ego loss, and bliss or profound joy. Stace made a distinction between 'extrovertive' and 'introvertive' mystical experiences: he calls the former an experience of unity within the world, in which one is unified with the objects of perception,[3] whereas the latter is "an experience of unity devoid of perceptual objects; it is literally an experience of 'no-thing-ness'"[4] — a state of pure consciousness. These subsequent ideas on mysticism have gone on to influence psychedelic research: scales measuring mystical qualities (such as the Hood Mysticism Scale) have been applied to see if — and to what degree — people have a classic mystical experience following the ingestion of a psychedelic.[5]

## Noetic Experiences: A Common Feature of Mystical States

There is much debate within the philosophy of mysticism about what makes a certain experience *mystical*, and many researchers also take issue with the application of mysticism in psychedelic science.[6] However, for the sake of discussion, I will regard the noetic quality as a common aspect of the mystical psychedelic state, which is in keeping with James's thought, how the classic mystical experience is widely defined, and what many people report after their most profound experiences with psychedelics.

James himself reported that the noetic quality — the feeling of immense revelation — was a key part of his experiments with nitrous oxide. This compound is also known as 'laughing gas', a coinage that comes from the English chemist Humphry Davy, who also wrote about his nitrous oxide experiences, which left him with the conviction that Idealism was true: "[W]ith the most intense belief and prophetic manner, I exclaimed ... 'Nothing exists but thoughts! — the universe is composed of impressions, ideas, pleasures and pains!'"[7] In his 1882 essay 'The Subjective Effects of Nitrous Oxide', James writes,

> With me, as with every other person of whom I have heard, the keynote of the experience is the tremendously exciting sense of an intense metaphysical illumination. Truth lies open to the view in depth beneath depth of almost blinding evidence. The mind sees all the logical relations of being with an apparent subtlety and instantaneity to which its normal consciousness offers no parallel; only as sobriety returns, the feeling of insight fades, and one is left staring vacantly at a few disjointed words and phrases, as one stares at the cadaverous-looking snow peak from which the sunset glow has just fled, or at the black cinder left by an extinguished brand.[8]

In this essay, James mentions how he was inspired by the ideas expressed in *The Anaesthetic Revelation and the Gist of Philosophy* (1874), written by the American philosopher and poet Benjamin Paul Blood. The latter tried nitrous oxide and found himself experiencing states of consciousness and insights that metaphysical philosophers like Plato and Hegel were privy to. In the preface to his book *Pluriverse* (published posthumously in 1920), Blood states,

> It was in the year 1860 that there came to me, through the necessary [medical] use of anaesthetics, a Revelation or insight of the immemorial Mystery which among enlightened peoples still persists as the philosophical secret or problem of the world.... After fourteen years of this experience at

varying intervals, I published in 1874 "The Anaesthetic Revelation and the Gist of Philosophy," not assuming to define therein the purport of the illumination, but rather to signalize the experience, and in a résumé of philosophy to show wherein that had come short of it.[9]

He argued that the "anaesthetic revelation" he experienced was "primordial", "Adamic", and incommunicable (in keeping with James's ineffability requirement for mystical states).[10] He wrote to James, "Philosophy is past. It was the long endeavor to logicize what we can only realize practically or in immediate experience."[11] All who experimented with this psychoactive gas and similar drugs reported indescribable metaphysical illuminations, as James highlights. These other figures include Xenos Clark, Edmund Gurney, J.A. Symonds, and William Ramsay. Blood was a *pluralistic mystic* because he asserted that his mystical experiences were simply experiences; he did not tie them to a grand systematic doctrine like Hegelian philosophy.

In a poem from James about nitrous oxide, we find the following lines: "No verbiage can give it, because the verbiage is other," "And it fades! And it's infinite! AND it's infinite!", and "Constantly opposites united!"[12] Here we have some of the recurring features of the mystical state: ineffability, passivity, a sense of infinity, and unity (the unification of opposites, a non-dualistic state, which is felt by many as insight into the true nature of reality). In *The Varieties of Religious Experience*, James also describes unity as an essential characteristic of these transcendent experiences, a unity that can be seen as noetic (revelatory) in nature. He said his nitrous oxide experiences

all converge toward a kind of insight to which I cannot help ascribing some kind of metaphysical significance. The keynote of it is invariably a reconciliation. It is as if the opposites of the world, whose contradictoriness and conflict make all our difficulties and troubles, were melted into unity. This is a dark saying, I know, when thus expressed in terms of common logic, but I cannot wholly escape from its authority. I feel as if it must mean something, something like what the hegelian philosophy means, if one could only lay hold of it more clearly. Those who have ears to hear, let them hear; to me the living sense of its reality only comes in the artificial mystic state of mind.[13]

While nitrous oxide is not typically thought of as a psychedelic, we can see from these inhalant philosophers that it can, in fact, induce (and reliably so) noetic experiences: the feeling of direct revelation, illumination, insight, knowledge, or wisdom. Like the classic psychedelics such as psilocybin, LSD, and DMT, nitrous oxide (in sufficient doses) can make users feel they are peeking behind the curtain of consensus reality, gaining direct access to ultimate reality, which impresses one with its undeniability. One may have had an abstract notion of mystical insights, such as the collapse of duality and opposites, but it is quite another thing to *experience* this idea first-hand. Indeed, James underscores that noetic experiences do not necessarily involve new concepts or insights but learning what is already known, in a deeper and more confident way.[14]

The nitrous oxide experience is brief and fleeting. There is a sense of being confronted with a monumental truth, in all its clarity, but like James, users find this truth escapes remembrance; it seems to retreat into some enclosed domain, accessible only through mind alteration. When using nitrous oxide or DMT, one rapidly loses a grasp on the epiphany when returning to a sober state of mind, much like the forgetting of a dream upon waking. This can be frustrating or humorous (depending on your outlook), given how titanic the revelation seemed to be at the time.

Many who use psychedelics experience this sense of direct understanding, and it is often accompanied by feelings of astonishment — or *ontological shock* — due to the radical reframing of reality it forces upon people. However, depending on someone's pre-existing beliefs or attitude towards the experience after it is over, there might be no drastic change in that person's metaphysical views. The wide-eyed, slack-jawed amazement that accompanies noetic experiences can be especially pronounced if the revelation is of a cosmic nature. It is not uncommon during psychedelic mystical states to feel that one is experiencing the "ground of being"[15] or "being-itself"[16] (terms that the German theologian and philosopher Paul Tillich used to describe God). There could also be the sense of gaining cosmic insights, such as understanding the infinite or eternal nature of the universe or how the universe came into existence. These cosmic confrontations are often accompanied by feelings of awe, overwhelm, and disbelief. They are more likely to occur with the use of high doses of psychedelics or potent compounds (like DMT), and they are generally thought to be an unfathomable height (or depth) of human experience.

Whether noetic experiences are veridical is another matter. Psychedelics can heighten the meaningfulness and significance of everything that is experienced. As a result, we may be more likely to believe psychedelic-induced insights (although this says nothing about the truth value of those insights). In addition, because of the meaning-enhancing effect of psychedelics, it might be possible to experience an intense state of significance without a relevant object or idea to which it refers – a feeling of insightfulness and revelation without actual content. As the psychedelic researcher David Luke said of some people who encounter entities under the influence of DMT: "Even if there's not a specific message [from the entities] there's a sense of profundity."[17] This might be why it is so hard (or impossible) to communicate any insight because the user has only a strong *impression* of profundity, surety, and magnitude. It is not unusual, after all, for psychedelic users to say that an experience was deeply meaningful but they don't know why. The neuroscientist Michael Persinger, who is well known for studying the neural correlates of altered states, has suggested that the intense meaningfulness associated with religious and mystical experiences is elicited by activity in the temporal lobes.[18]

On the other hand, I would want to moderate this scepticism with the recognition that many philosophers and psychonauts do take away specific content from their noetic experiences. It could also be the case that some kind of understanding is possible only when the organ of understanding, the brain, is modulated in a certain way. James himself emphasised that a revelation from a mystical state can be authoritative for the individual who experienced it first-hand but not for others who have not had that experience — and other people should also not uncritically accept that revelation.[19] I would additionally want to stress that irrespective of literal truth, these experiences can remain powerful in terms of their capacity to generate personal meaning and positive changes in people's lives.

It is disputed whether these special insights or intuitions are even verifiable; disagreements about this hinge on our beliefs about how we can legitimately gain knowledge. It is also possible that mystical insights — into, say, non-duality, unity, pantheism, panpsychism, or supernaturalism — are false, albeit common. The universe could be fundamentally dualistic or pluralistic in nature (there are two or many different kinds of substances, respectively), in contrast to monistic worldviews, which postulate only one type of substance.

Undying conviction is not enough to establish veridicality. Towards this aim, the philosopher of psychedelics Peter Sjöstedt-Hughes argues that we can compare such experiences against the following criteria, which act as truth-testers: *sensibility* (what you sense with your five senses), *shared objects of experience* (experiencing something that others also experience), *coherence with other beliefs* (agreement between our sense perceptions and our prior beliefs), and *rationality* (being able to present reasons for believing in what we have experienced).[20]

Sjöstedt-Hughes gives special emphasis to the shared objects of experience criterion. This is because there are many commonly reported features of psychedelic states, such as unity or the subjective nature of space and time. He quotes the philosopher C.D. Broad, who remarked, "So far as [mystical experiences] *agree* they should be provisionally accepted as veridical unless there is some positive ground for thinking that they are not."[21] Such a view is contestable, of course. Furthermore, it is difficult to verify noetic experiences in those cases when they are ineffable — when the user feels no words or interpretation can be given to them at all. This does not necessarily mean the insights are empty; it could just mean that in our waking consensus state of consciousness, these insights are mysteriously impenetrable.

Sjöstedt-Hughes is keen to emphasise the fact that the drug-induced nature of these noetic experiences is in no way proof that they are just strange delusions. He writes that "chemically-induced correlates of mystical experience cannot per se disprove the objectivity of that which is experienced".[22] But to reiterate, we have to also be open to the possibility that one can have a feeling of insight without any actual insight. This could be like *pure significance*, as I previously alluded to. It would be interesting to find out if such an experience is possible, however, and whether any distinct brain states are correlated with it.

Studies have at least shown that the 'Aha!' moment can be elicited using false information[23] and artificially induced to make worldviews ring true.[24] Psychedelics may be especially prone to producing false insights since, as the psychedelic researcher Manoj Doss has argued, expecting to experience true insights means you're going to be more likely to attribute the feeling of revelation to any ideas you come up with.[25] He and other researchers have proposed that the acute neural plasticity associated with psychedelics increases the quantity of insights and, in turn, beliefs — including false ones. This potential of psychedelics to solicit false or maladaptive insights and beliefs can be considered a kind of *epistemic risk* and its occurrence a form of *epistemic harm*.[26]

A case of illusory insight could also be the result of psychedelics making the brain hyperconnected,[27] with the subsequent flood of information entering awareness being mistaken for genuine cosmic insights. And if the ego also drops away, this may be experienced as becoming one with 'cosmic consciousness' or the 'universal mind'. This scenario is understandable. The hyperconnected brain, after all, can provide an individual with unprecedented access to the mind, a multitude of novel thoughts and perspectives, and intricate and arresting visions centred on life and the universe.

These experiences may be truly thought-provoking but they do not necessarily mean that the altered mind has become an instrument with direct access to the cosmic and infinitesimal scales of reality. At the same time, these experiences can align with certain truths. It should not be surprising to find that a modulated, hyperconnected brain will sometimes produce insights and at other times produce creative falsehoods, the latter of which are often appealing because they can offer us novelty, narrative, meaning, purpose, certainty, and comfort.

## The Cosmic Mind in Spinoza's Metaphysics

Now I would like to connect the nature of psychedelic noetic experiences to the ideas of Baruch Spinoza, the famous Dutch philosopher who reconceived the notion of God, positing that God was identical to Nature. This pantheistic worldview, described in Spinoza's *Ethics* (1677), rejects the idea of a personal god or an individual creator, as is found in the monotheistic traditions. He was writing in opposition to "those who feign a God, like man, consisting of a body and a mind, and subject to passions".[28] On 27 July 1656, he was excommunicated from the Spanish-Portuguese Jewish community in Amsterdam (this ban, separating a person from the Jewish community, is known as *herem*). We don't know for certain what Spinoza's "monstrous deeds" and "abominable heresies" were that led to such a harsh punishment,[29] but it is reasonable to surmise that he professed beliefs he would come to detail in his works, including the rejection of a transcendent, personal, law-giving God and the immortality of the soul.

Spinoza argued instead that God or Nature is one eternal substance consisting of "infinite attributes",[30] and this single substance possesses an "infinite intellect"[31] that comprehends those attributes (we have knowledge of only two of these attributes: thought and extension). For Spinoza, there is an idea of everything in God or Nature.

Interestingly, during intense psychedelic states, it can feel as if one comes to know all the secrets of the universe; all questions are answered at once, and no mysteries remain. It is as if one has become omniscient. This can be thought of as a kind of *total noetic experience*, in which there is not only the feeling of deep understanding of some important truth but a deep understanding of everything or Ultimate Truth.

Could these kinds of noetic experiences lend credence to Spinoza's conception of God? They could, if we assume that the total noetic experience is a way of understanding the infinite intellect, coming in contact with its reality, or becoming one with it (in a state of mystical union). According to Spinoza, "the human mind is a part of the infinite intellect of God".[32] It would be quite radical to claim that such a mind, when altered by a psychedelic compound, could go from being an aspect of God to being the fullness of God. Genuinely encountering the totality that is God or Nature under the influence of a psychedelic is an extraordinary claim as well. Many people have such experiences, nonetheless, and remain convinced that they were not just subjective in nature but objective too. It is difficult to assess the supposed objectivity of these claims, but relating them to panpsychism and other theories of mind may be helpful.

Spinoza was also a panpsychist since he posited that mind (thought) is an attribute of the eternal and infinite substance that is God or Nature; and since God or Nature is everything, then everything has the aspect of mind. Every object has both a unique mode of extension and a corresponding mode of thought. As he writes,

> a circle existing in nature and the idea of the existing circle — which is also in God — are one and the same thing.... And so, whether we conceive nature under the attribute of Extension, or under the attribute of Thought ... we shall find one and the same order, or one and the same connection of causes.[33]

The panpsychist position that mind or consciousness is a fundamental and pervasive feature of the universe might sound implausible. However, it is worth underscoring that the position does not state all kinds of matter and all particles have the kind of subjectivity and complex consciousness possessed by sentient creatures like humans. Atoms, for instance, are presumed to have a very basic form of consciousness.

There is a strand of panpsychism known as cosmopsychism, which may further help link Spinoza's God to psychedelic experiences. This position states that the universe as a whole is a conscious subject, with all entities and properties, including minds like ours, being aspects of the conscious universe. Spinoza's philosophy effectively advances such a position since God or Nature has the property of mindedness: it possesses an 'infinite intellect'. Moreover, in keeping with cosmopsychism, his system of thought views matter and minds as aspects of this greater conscious entity. So now the relevant question is as follows: Can psychedelics allow one to connect to this cosmic mind (through contact or unification)?

In an attempt to answer this question, I would like to combine the cosmopsychist view with the reducing valve theory of mind. The French philosopher Henri Bergson first put forward this latter theory, which was later adopted by the English philosopher C.D. Broad, and then popularised by Aldous Huxley in *The Doors of Perception*. Huxley felt confident about this view of the mind after his first psychedelic experience (with mescaline).

Bergson believed that the human brain and nervous system served an *eliminative* function, rather than a *productive* one. By this, he meant that the purpose of the brain and nervous system is to keep certain stimuli and information out of conscious awareness. Huxley used the term 'reducing valve' to describe this function of the brain.[34] In *The Doors of Perception*, he quotes C.D. Broad, who said,

> The function of the brain and nervous system is to protect us from being overwhelmed and confused by this mass of largely useless and irrelevant knowledge, by shutting out most of what we should otherwise perceive or remember at any moment, and leaving only that very small and special selection which is likely to be practically useful.[35]

If the reducing valve of the mind did not exist, or if it allowed all information in at all times, it would, as Huxley argues, make survival impossible. Reiterating C.D. Broad's point, he states,

> To make biological survival possible, Mind at Large has to be funnelled through the reducing valve of the brain and nervous system. What comes out at the other end is a measly trickle of the kind of consciousness which will help us to stay alive on the surface of this particular planet.[36]

Under the influence of mescaline, Huxley was flooded with what he calls 'Mind at Large', the conscious mind with the filters of the brain and nervous system removed. More than 50 years after Huxley promulgated the reducing valve theory of the mind, scientific research into the effects of psychedelic drugs would come to vindicate the idea. In 2016, researchers from Imperial College London published a landmark study that showed, for the very first time, what the brain looks like on LSD.[37]

A key finding from the study was that LSD decreases activity in the default mode network (DMN): a collection of hub centres that we now know restrict the amount of sensory information that enters our conscious awareness. We can, therefore, identify the DMN as the reducing valve that Huxley had in mind; it controls communication between brain regions, creating a somewhat segregated brain in the process. Through this reduction in DMN activity, psychedelics enable freer conversations between brain regions that don't normally communicate with each other.

The anthropologist and historian of science Nicolas Langlitz refers to this materialist reinterpretation of Huxley's view as "mystic materialism".[38] Huxley argued psychedelics can induce a perennial mystical experience of Mind at Large, which we could also call universal or boundless consciousness, and his *perennial philosophy*, a rearticulation of Gottfried Leibniz's worldview, states that all religions share the same core experience and truth (Mind at Large). The modern neurobiological perspective, or that of mystic materialism, advances the idea that similar spiritual experiences exist not because there is one divine reality or truth but because human brains are alike. Mystic materialism is a worldview that emphasises the metaphysical unity of the world ('all is one'), as mysticism does, which one can grasp in the mystical experience of unity that some studies correlate with reduced DMN activity.[39] But crucially, this perspective is situated within a naturalistic framework. A naturalist might also find this meeting of metaphysics, altered states, and science to be awe-inspiring in itself.

In contrast to mystic materialism, the reducing valve theory proposed by Bergson and Huxley takes consciousness beyond the confines of the physical brain. This would be possible if we think of the brain as a receiver or modulator of the consciousness that exists outside of us, rather than an organ that produces localised consciousness. According to this hypothesis (postulated by the neurophilosopher John R. Smythies[40] and the writer Graham Hancock[41]), the brain is a modulating or tuning device, with its relationship to consciousness being like that of a TV to a TV signal. Consciousness manifests in a particular way for us, similar to how a TV signal manifests as moving pictures on a screen. If you change the tuning device — via psychedelics, for instance — then what appears on the 'TV screen' (the reality of subjective experience) will change as well. While contentious and subject to criticism, the theory that the brain is a receiver or transceiver of consciousness — rather than a generator of it — could mean that psychedelics open us up to more information than previously assumed.

Related to this idea, Huxley quotes Broad, who said, "Each person is at each moment capable of remembering all that has ever happened to him and of perceiving everything that is happening everywhere in the universe ... each one of us is potentially Mind at Large."[42] (It should be underlined that Huxley leaves out an important qualifier from the original quote: "Each person is at each moment *potentially* [emphasis added] capable...")[43] And what is the Mind at Large if not the mind of Spinoza's God (the infinite intellect)? If you were to perceive everything in the cosmos under the influence of psychedelics, which many users report, combining cosmopsychism with the reducing valve and receiver theories of consciousness could be one way to explain such a phenomenon. Under normal circumstances, we are not privy to the completeness of Mind at Large, God, or Nature — the total noetic experience — because this would be, and is, overwhelming. The experience simply does not serve the purposes of practical consciousness but rather impedes it. A DMT breakthrough does not lend itself to thinking or acting in any practical or useful way.

Cosmopsychism is not the only way to augment the reducing valve theory to illuminate noetic experiences. Bergon's ideas on memory may be relevant too. In his work *Matter and Memory* (1896), Bergson claims that there exists *pure memory*, which has a virtual nature — it does not reside in our brains or anywhere physical. It is, instead, a non-actual repository of all past events, the contents of which can be actualised at different times, depending on our present needs and concerns and what we need to make sense of the present. Pure memory, this radical idea of Bergson's, is the totality of memories existing, eternally, in a virtual state.[44] The mind as a reducing valve limits the contents of pure memory that reach our conscious awareness. But if psychedelics can weaken or disable this reducing valve, then we can be more open to the vast repository of pure memories: all past events. If one had such access, would this not fit in with the nature of the total noetic experience, with the conviction of becoming the mind of God?

This is not to say that accessing more of — or even the totality of — pure memory would correspond to Spinoza's God, but it might at least help explain why people come out of a psychedelic state convinced that they experienced or understood *everything*. The notion of 'everything' is relative and subjective. Being aware of more (but not all) of Mind at Large or pure memory could feel like the totality, in light of its immensity.

## Other Links Between Spinoza's Philosophy and Noetic States

It will also be enlightening to consider noetic experiences in relation to Spinoza's concept of the *intellectual love of God*. "[T]he highest good of the mind is the knowledge of God, and the highest virtue of the mind is to know God," says Spinoza,[45] and this highest good, he believed, could be attained by all. Since God or Nature has been conceived as an infinite substance, it is, by that very nature, the *greatest* thing that can be known. This kind of knowledge proceeds from an adequate idea of one of God's attributes to an adequate idea of God's essence, a singular thing, which is the cause of all the modes or modifications of God (i.e. every attribute in existence).

The essence of God, in Spinoza's view, is its existence, or eternity. Eternal usually means 'existing forever in time' but Spinoza redefines it to mean "existence itself, so far as it is conceived necessarily to follow from the definition alone of the eternal thing".[46] So eternity *is* existence. A thing is 'eternal' if the very definition of it includes existence, i.e. we cannot conceive of it not existing. Spinoza explains this definition as follows: "For such existence, like the essence of a thing, is conceived as an eternal truth, and on that account cannot be explained by duration or time, even if the duration is conceived to be without beginning or end."[47] This highlights how Spinoza's definition of eternity does not relate to time or duration. He calls God's eternity "an infinite enjoyment of existence, or rather (although the Latin does not lend itself to such a mode of expression) of Being (*essendi*)".[48]

Spinoza also defines God as being "absolutely infinite, that is to say, a substance consisting of infinite attributes, each one of which expresses eternal and infinite essence".[49] The eternal, singular substance that is God, he argues, "cannot be conceived unless as infinite";[50] God cannot be, as the modes of God can be, conceived as greater or smaller, divisible into parts, or limited by duration. As an eternal and infinite being, God has no boundaries or limits.

When we possess an adequate idea of God, formulated in this way, Spinoza says the mind passes to the highest state of perfection that we can possibly experience. The result is that we experience joy to the greatest degree, and because this kind of knowledge involves an understanding of God as the cause of this perfection of the mind, a love for God then arises. Spinoza calls this the "intellectual love of God"[51] (*amor dei intellectualis*). It is the knowledge of God combined with an emotional experience. For Spinoza, the intellectual love of God involves "blessedness"[52] and "the highest possible peace of mind".[53]

The German Romantic poet Novalis called Spinoza a "God-intoxicated man"[54] and we can also apply this label to the person who has a psychedelic mystical experience. Spinoza's concept of the intellectual love of God certainly has a parallel with these altered states. When one has a noetic experience related to eternity and infinity, which might involve a felt understanding of eternal existence and the infinite universe, this is often accompanied by a sense of the divine; a feeling of reverence and worship; and the highest feelings of joy, ecstasy, bliss, and peacefulness. Could we not say that such an experience is the intellectual love of God that Spinoza describes?

These mystical and noetic experiences could be interpreted in this way, but perhaps they do not always neatly align with the metaphysics and intellectual love of God that Spinoza has in mind. In some instances, the feeling of 'eternity' in the psychedelic mystical state could be unrelated to time and duration, in keeping with Spinoza's philosophy. Indeed, many people report that their psychedelic experiences took place 'outside of time', or they felt that time became meaningless. The mystical experience of so-called *pure existence* or *pure being*, occurring alongside a feeling of timelessness, might also correspond to Spinoza's notion of God's essence as existence, which is equivalent to eternity. On the other hand, many psychedelic users feel that their altered state of consciousness was eternal in the sense of it lasting forever. Other qualities of Spinoza's God may be also absent; there may be feelings of psychedelic-induced reverence and love but not be directed towards this special kind of being that Spinoza calls God.

It is difficult to establish the veracity of noetic experiences. A study published in *Scientific Reports* found that psychedelics alter metaphysical beliefs, moving people away from materialist or physicalist views and towards panpsychism.[55] These supposed metaphysical insights, gained during a psychedelic experience, might be genuine, false, or partially true. Those insights that are the most common may indicate to us where the truth lies. Yet it is also possible that these shared experiences, while profound and earth-shattering, are reflections more of the brain architecture and psychology all humans share, rather than reflections of a grand metaphysical truth. There may even be a middle ground between both views: our shared biology could, via the influence of psychedelics affecting us similarly, allow us to connect to genuine insight and wisdom.

In any case, it is fascinating that many noetic experiences induced by psychedelics resemble so closely the metaphysical ideas of certain mystics and philosophers throughout the ages. If anything, this speaks to the importance of the psychedelic state — a shift in perspective that may inform and clarify our views on the nature of reality and consciousness. To this end, psychedelics can be thought of as invaluable chemical allies, which, in certain circumstances and when used appropriately, can aid our search for truth.

## Endnotes

1.  James, W. (1902). *The Varieties of Religious Experience: A Study in Human Nature*, p. 380. New York: Longmans, Green & Co.
2.  Ibid., pp. 380–382.
3.  Stace, W.T. (1960). *Mysticism and Philosophy*, p. 61. London: Macmillan, 1973.

4.   Hood, R.W., Hill, P.C., and Spilka, B. (2018). *The Psychology of Religion: An Empirical Approach*, Fifth Edition, p. 355. New York: The Guildford Press.

5.   Streib, H., Klein, C., Keller, B., and Hood, R. (2020). Chapter 16: 'The Mysticism Scale as Measure for Subjective Spirituality' in *Assessing Spirituality in a Diverse World*, edited by Ai, A.L., Wink, P., Paloutzian, R.F., and Harris, K.A. New York: Springer Nature.

6.   Sanders, J.W. and Zijlmans, J. (2021). 'Moving Past Mysticism in Psychedelic Science'. *ACS Pharmacology & Translational Science*, 4(3), pp. 1253–1255.

7.   Davy, H. (1800). *Researches, Chemical and Philosophical; Chiefly Concerning Nitrous Oxide, or Dephlogisticated Nitrous Air, and Its Respiration*, p. 489. London: Printed for J. Johnson, St. Paul's Church-Yard, by Biggs and Cottle, Bristol.

8.   James, W. (1882). 'The Subjective Effects of Nitrous Oxide'. *Mind*, Volume 7.

9.   Blood, P.B. (1920). *Pluriverse: An Essay in the Philosophy of Pluralism*, p. vii. Boston: Marshall Jones Company.

10.  Tymoczko, D. (1996). 'The Nitrous Oxide Philosopher'. *The Atlantic*, May. https://www.theatlantic.com/magazine/archive/1996/05/the-nitrous-oxide-philosopher/376581/

11.  Ibid.

12.  Ibid.

13.  Ibid.

14.  Cole-Turner, R. (2021). 'Psychedelic Epistemology: William James and the "Noetic Quality" of Mystical Experience'. *Religions*, 12, Article: 1058.

15.  Tillich, P. (1951). *Systematic Theology*, Volume 1, p. 112. Chicago: University of Chicago Press.

16.  Ibid., p. 21.

17.  Taub, B. (2022). 'Why Do People See Elves And Other "Entities" When They Smoke DMT?', IFLScience, 14 January.

https://www.iflscience.com/why-do-people-see-elves-and-other-entities-when-they-smoke-dmt-62234

18. Persinger, M.A. (1983). 'Religious and mystical experiences as artifacts of temporal lobe function: a general hypothesis'. *Perceptual and Motor Skills*, 57(3 Pt 2), pp. 1255–1262.

19. Cole-Turner, R. (2021). 'Psychedelic Epistemology: William James and the "Noetic Quality" of Mystical Experience'. *Religions*, 12, Article: 1058.

20. Sjöstedt-Hughes, P. (2021). *Modes of Sentience: Psychedelics, Metaphysics, Panpsychism*, pp. 59–60. London: Psychedelic Press.

21. Broad, C.D. (1953). *Religion, Philosophy and Psychical Research*, p. 197. New York: Harcourt.

22. Sjöstedt-Hughes, P. (2021). *Modes of Sentience: Psychedelics, Metaphysics, Panpsychism*, p. 60. London: Psychedelic Press.

23. Grimmer, H., Laukkonen, R., Tangen, J., and Hippel, H. (2022). 'Eliciting false insights with semantic printing'. *Psychonomic Bulletin & Review*, 29, pp. 954–970.

24. Laukonnen, R., Kaveladze, B.T., Protzko, J., Tangen, J., Hippel, W., and Schooler, J.W. (2022). 'Irrelevant insights make worldviews ring true'. *Scientific Reports*, 12, Article: 2075.

25. Love, S. (2022). 'The Insights Psychedelics Give You Aren't Always True', *Vice*, 22 February. https://www.vice.com/en/article/5dgkkn/the-insights-psychedelics-give-you-arent-always-true

26. McGovern, H.T., Grimmer, H.J., Doss, M.K., Hutchinson, B.T., Timmermann, C., Lyon, A., Corlett, P.R., and Laukkonen, R.E. 'The power of insight: Psychedelics and the emergence of false beliefs'. PsyArXiv. Preprint posted online. 3 July, 2023. Updated on 11 September, 2023. https://doi.org/10.31234/osf.io/97gjw

27. Petri, G., Expert, P., Turkheimer, F., Carhart-Harris, R., Nutt, D., Hellyer, P.J., and Vaccarino, F. (2014). 'Homological

scaffolds of brain functional networks'. *Journal of the Royal Society Interface*, 11(101), Article: 20140873.

28. Smith, S.B. (2003). *Spinoza's Book of Life: Freedom and Redemption in the Ethics*, p. 41. New Haven: Yale University Press.

29. Nadler, S. (2020). *Think Least of Death: Spinoza on How to Live and How to Die*, p 7. Princeton: Princeton University Press.

30. Spinoza, B. (1677). *Ethics*, p. LXIV. Translated by White, W.H. Ware, Hertfordshire: Wordsworth Editions, 2001.

31. Ibid., p. XVIII.

32. Ibid., p. LXXXV.

33. Baird, F.E. (2010). *Philosophic Classics: From Plato to Derrida*, Sixth Edition, p. 498. Oxford: Routledge.

34. Huxley, A. (1954). *The Doors of Perception*. https://maps.org/images/pdf/books/HuxleyA1954TheDoorsOfPerception.pdf

35. Ibid.

36. Ibid.

37. Carhart-Harris, R.L., Muthukumaraswamy, S., Roseman, R., and Nutt, D.J. (2016). 'Neural correlates of the LSD experience revealed by multimodal neuroimaging'. *PNAS*, 113 (17), pp. 4853–4858.

38. Langlitz, N. (2016). 'Is There a Place for Psychedelics in Philosophy?'. *Common Knowledge*, 22(3), pp. 373–384.

39. Woollacott, M. and Shumway-Cook, A. (2020). 'The Mystical Experience and Its Neural Correlates'. *Journal of Near-Death Studies*, 38(1), pp. 3–25.

40. Smythies, J.R. (2016). 'The Role of Brain Mechanisms in the Generation of Consciousness'. https://www.imprint.co.uk/the-role-of-brain-mechanisms-in-the-generation-of-consciousness/

41. Hancock, G. (2013). 'The Consciousness Revolution'. https://grahamhancock.com/the-consciousness-revolution-hancock/

42. Huxley, A. (1954). *The Doors of Perception*. https://maps.org/ images/pdf/books/HuxleyA1954TheDoorsOfPerception.pdf
43. Broad, C.D. (1949). 'The Relevance of Psychical Research to Philosophy'. *Philosophy*, 24(91), pp. 291–309.
44. Bluemink, M. (2020). 'On Virtuality: Deleuze, Bergson, Simondon'. Epoché Magazine, Issue 36, December. https:// epochemagazine.org/36/on-virtuality-deleuze-bergson-simondon/
45. Spinoza, B. (1677). *Ethics*, p. LXXV. Translated by White, W.H. Ware, Hertfordshire: Wordsworth Editions, 2001.
46. Ibid., p. LXXXIV.
47. Ibid., p. 4.
48. Ibid., p. LXXXIV.
49. Ibid., p. 3.
50. Ibid., p. 13.
51. Ibid., p. 248.
52. Ibid., p. 93.
53. Ibid., p. 248.
54. Carlisle, C. and Melamed, Y.Y. (2020). 'God-intoxicated man', *TLS*, 15 May. https://philarchive.org/archive/ MELGMT
55. Timmermann, C., Kettner, H., Letheby, C., Roseman, L., Rosas, F.E., and Carhart-Harris, R.L. (2021). 'Psychedelics alter metaphysical beliefs'. *Scientific Reports*, 11(1), Article: 22166

## Chapter 3

# Encounters with Alien Beings: Analysing the Birth Trauma Hypothesis

Alien abduction and DMT experiences can sometimes share a very similar character, to the point where the similarity, for many people, can no longer be considered a coincidence. What can account for such phenomenological similarities? One possible explanation — which I will aim to outline, explicate, and critique — is the *birth trauma hypothesis*. The UFO researcher Alvin H. Lawson formulated this idea as the *birth memories hypothesis* with respect to UFO abduction phenomena, based on correspondences he noticed between such phenomena and the birth process, although he recognised abduction analogues in other mental phenomena, including "drug-induced hallucinations, NDEs [near-death experiences], out-of-body experiences, shamans' trances, Little People visitations, Christian visions".[1] He said an alien abduction was a rare but normal psychological delusion, and elaborated on this as follows:

A UFO abduction is an involuntary fantasy of images and events unconsciously based on the witness' own perinatal memories. During the abduction fantasy, revivified birth events symbolically become one or more abduction images or events: the womb = the UFO; the fetus = alien beings and also the witness; the dilating cervix = UFO doorways; the vaginal passage = tunnels or passageways; the comparatively bright delivery room = intensely bright UFO interiors; delivery room postnatal checkup and bath = intrusive probing by alien examiners; the parent-infant non-verbal bonding experience = the aliens' "messages," etc. Because of the abduction's peak experience intensity, sequential structure, and surreal qualities, the witness may interpret the fantasy as an actual Close Encounter with extraterrestrial creatures.[2]

The birth trauma hypothesis is somewhat interchangeable with the birth memories hypothesis, but I use the former term to highlight that I am referring not to Lawson's theory but this newer one that refers to birth memories specifically to explain the connections between UFO abduction reports and DMT experiences. This refashioned hypothesis, derived largely from the ideas of the Austrian psychoanalyst Otto Rank, sees the experience of birth, from the point of view of the person birthed, as traumatic. And this psychological trauma imprints itself on our unconscious minds.

According to the birth trauma hypothesis, the traumatic memory of birth can resurface in the form of altered states like DMT trips and alien abduction experiences, in particular, in the form of medical inspection, examination, and procedure phenomena.

## DMT and Alien Abduction Phenomena

The alien abduction experience, more often than not, features abduction by extraterrestrial beings who perform a forced medical examination or procedure on the abductee. The abductee may be lying on an operating table, with tall alien beings looming over them. The aliens are usually depicted as being featureless and having big eyes and heads.[3]

Likewise, in the DMT experience, contact is also made with entities who may be described as 'extraterrestrial', 'extradimensional', or belonging to a different species. Reports of inspection, examination, and medical procedures performed by these entities are not uncommon either. The entities may also appear to be doctors, who carry out their procedures while the subject lies on some sort of operating table.[4] In *The Ayahuasca Visions of Pablo Amaringo*, Amaringo (a painter who is well known for depicting visions induced by ayahuasca, the DMT-containing brew) recounts an ayahuasca journey he had while suffering from a serious heart condition. During the experience, he found himself in an operating room where "spirit doctors" in white coats removed his heart, fixed it, and placed it back in his chest. According to Amaringo, his heart problems ceased after this experience.[5]

Much like abduction experiences, there are usually multiple entities looking down at the subject. One experience I had with DMT somewhat matched these abduction-type phenomena. There were several doctor-type beings — caring, angelic, and made of light. They had a keen, almost medical interest in me, as if they were checking my vitals, looking after my well-being, and making sure I was safe. It was as if I was centred in one place, like on an operating table, and one being after another would come out of a doorway, zanily approach me, carry out its inspection and examination, and then exit, followed by another being that would do the same.

It is also common during alien abduction experiences to witness alien (and often baffling) technology.[6] This experience can, likewise, manifest in the DMT space.[7] During a separate experience with this compound, I felt like a baby in the cot, looking up at an alien baby mobile. There were impossible toys self-transforming above me. I felt the astonishment an ancient hominin ancestor would experience if they examined our modern technology — yet the feeling was far more intense than that. This was alien technology so advanced that it was beyond all comprehension.

Dr Rick Strassman, in *DMT: The Spirit Molecule*, postulates that the commonalities between alien abductions and DMT experiences might come down to the fact that the abduction experience involves an endogenous release of DMT in the brain.[8] This speculation was influenced by reports from his test subjects who received intravenous injections of DMT and who subsequently had abduction-like experiences.[9] Strassman notes these volunteers became the subjects of "procedures, more or less intrusive, performed by the life-forms of these nonmaterial worlds".[10] He adds, "Their [the DMT entities'] 'business' appeared to be testing, examining, probing, and even modifying the volunteer's mind and body."[11]

Despite Strassman's speculations, there is currently no conclusive evidence that shows the human brain (specifically the pineal gland) produces an endogenous supply of DMT. However, in 2013, an exciting discovery was made: the pineal gland in live rats synthesises DMT.[12] The researchers involved went on to find in a 2019 study that other parts of a live rat's brain contained the enzymes necessary to make the compound.[13] Whether the same is true for humans remains to be seen, but it is in the realm of possibility, and these discoveries regarding rats mean it may not even be that unlikely. The psychedelic researcher and chemist David E. Nichols, on the other hand, is sceptical.

In an article published in the *Journal of Psychopharmacology*, Nichols argues that there is no reason to believe that altered states of consciousness are a result of the pineal gland producing DMT. He underscores that the pineal gland weighs less than 0.2 g and produces 30 μg (micrograms) of melatonin per day.[14] To induce a psychedelic experience, it would have to produce about 25 mg of DMT. As a "rational scientist", Nichols argues that it is "simply impossible" for the organ to "accomplish such a heroic biochemical feat".[15] Furthermore, DMT is rapidly broken down by monoamine oxidase (MAO) and there is no evidence the psychedelic compound can naturally accumulate within the brain. Nichols believes we can explain out-of-body experiences and other altered states in other, more evidence-based ways.[16]

Indeed, the common features between alien abduction and DMT experiences could be more fully explained by something very fundamental about human psychology. After all, if alien abductions were caused by an endogenous release of DMT, you would expect both experiences to be extremely similar. Yet despite the features they share, these experiences are typically wildly different.

## The Birth Trauma Hypothesis

The concept of birth trauma was developed by Rank (1883–1939), who was also one of Freud's closest colleagues. In *The Trauma of Birth* (1929), he argued we are all born into trauma — in other words, we suffer trauma by virtue of being born. The trauma results from the violent and physical separation from the mother. Rank believed that prior to birth, infants live in perfect harmony and union with the mother, in a state of uterine bliss. The painful separation from the mother is the very first instance of anxiety for all human beings and, according to Rank, acts as a blueprint for all anxieties experienced in later life.[17] Freud also called birth the "first experience of anxiety, and thus the source and prototype of the affect of anxiety".[18]

The British psychoanalyst Wilfred Bion claimed that the physical event of birth is also traumatic because of its pure psychological intensity. The internal and external sensations that the infant experiences at birth are so alien, overstimulating, overwhelming, inescapable, and unbearable that the experience of birth becomes inevitably traumatic. The immature and sensitive infant brain simply cannot cope with the experience and a permanent mark of anxiety is left on its unconscious mind.[19]

We can think of birth as the first — and possibly most intense — psychedelic experience that someone will have. At the moment of birth, the infant is brought out of one reality (the bliss of the womb) into a completely different reality (one which is full of colour, lights, objects, strange and loud sounds, and other people). As such, this new reality can seem extremely chaotic and disturbing to the newborn infant. The internal and emotional responses to this new world will also be completely new to the infant.

It is no wonder then that many people who have had intense psychedelic experiences often describe a feeling of being reborn. The term *near-birth experience* is also used to denote the symbolic re-experience of being born. With DMT, a feeling of being a baby 'back in the womb' and a sense of being reunited with an archetypal mother may also be experienced. The blissful womb-like environment or experience may seem strangely familiar to the person. I did have the sense during one DMT experience, as many users do, that *I've been here before. I've come home.* I had the feeling of being back in the womb as a baby, and this was accompanied by indescribable euphoria — pure bliss and ecstasy. I felt serenely buoyant, with all of my needs and desires being met. Could this have been a manifestation of the unconscious desire to return to the blissful uterine state and union with the mother?

Stanislav Grof, a psychiatrist and one of the founders of the field of transpersonal psychology, studied LSD extensively and its relation to the human unconscious. His ideas about the human mind were detailed in his groundbreaking book *Realms of the Human Unconscious: Observations from LSD Research* (1975). Based on his patients' LSD sessions, he concluded that LSD could induce a number of distinct experiences, one type being *perinatal experiences*: experiences related to the period immediately before and after birth. Grof found that LSD could allow a subject to symbolically remember their perinatal trauma — their struggle during the clinical stages of labour and delivery.[20] The experience of travelling through a tunnel, towards a source of brilliant white light, could correspond to the journey out of the birth canal.

Symbolically experiencing long-suppressed memories of birth might also explain why birth-related and dying-type experiences are often so similar. People under the influence of high doses of LSD, psilocybin, ketamine, or DMT may use the terms 'dying' and 'rebirth' interchangeably. As Dr Karl Jansen states in his book *Ketamine: Dreams and Realities*: "Psychedelic experiences have led some people to conclude that birth and death are seen as the same process at the unconscious level."[21] The physical event of birth may also appear to the infant to be a threat to their life or as an impending catastrophe. Thus, embedded in birth trauma are the first intimations of death. This deep psychological connection between birth and death would explain why the motif of the 'dying-and-rising god' is so common in mythology: examples of gods who died and were reborn include Osiris, Tammuz, Adonis, Attis, Dionysus, and Jesus. The belief in an afterlife and reincarnation may also be attributed to this aspect of the human unconscious.

So how does the concept of birth trauma shed light on alien abduction phenomena and certain DMT experiences? What these experiences may involve is a reactivation of experiences that occurred during the birthing process. The experience of being inspected, medically examined, and operated on appears to be related to similar experiences that occurred at birth.

When born, standing over the infant will be one main doctor as well as other medical staff, which corresponds to the multiple aliens or entities observed in alien abductions and DMT experiences. The doctors and medical staff are wearing plain clothes and masks, which would explain why the aliens and DMT entities are usually featureless. The only discernible feature the infant sees may be the eyes of the doctor and staff, which could explain why the aliens in abduction experiences — and for many people, the alien entities in their DMT trips — tend to have big, imposing eyes. From the perspective of the infant, the doctor will appear to be very large and tall, with an oversized head, which corresponds to the same features of the alien.

In a sense, since the infant has never seen other humans before, they will instantly appear alien to them, perhaps imprinting the archetype of the alien on their unconscious mind. The doctors and medical staff loom over and watch the infant just as the aliens and entities do in abductions and some DMT experiences. And lastly, the operations (e.g. cutting the umbilical cord) and examinations or monitoring (e.g. checking for vital signs) would correspond to the medical theme of alien abductions and particular DMT experiences. Perhaps one reason, then, why alien abductions and DMT experiences can be so overwhelming is that they reactivate an overwhelming event from our past: the trauma of birth.

## A Critical Analysis of the Birth Trauma Hypothesis

We should bear in mind that the prevalence of 'doctor/ operation' phenomena in Strassman's studies could have been influenced by the medical setting in which they took place. DMT was administered to patients in a hospital room, which was surrounded by medical equipment and medical personnel close by. Vital signs and medical tests were also taken before the administration of the drug. Since the setting can drastically alter a psychedelic trip, it is possible that these factors could contribute to alien abduction-type phenomena. Nick Sand, a prolific underground chemist who created large batches of 'Orange Sunshine' LSD in the 1960s, argues this is the case. He writes,

> DMT is not a re-run of the X-Files. There are no aliens squiggling through psychospace to do experiments on us. That idea is just plain silly. It is fine to wonder how these perceptions occur, but it's another matter to jump to conclusions. Wouldn't it make sense to first examine the environmental design rather than look to alien origins? Over and over, Strassman's subjects describe being examined by numerous strange beings in highly technical environments during the visual phase of their DMT experience. They are

being examined, discussed, measured, probed, and observed. They are in high-tech nurseries and alien laboratories. There are 3–4 people moving around operating machinery according to some design or agenda.

Now let's look at what the physical surroundings are. These experiments are being done in a hospital room. There are a number of people in attendance, helping the one who is in charge, Dr Strassman. He has an agenda and an experimental scientific viewpoint based on intellectual assumptions. There are people from NIDA, a government agency overseeing these experiments. They are labelled "Mr. V." and "Mr. W." It seems clear to me that these individuals are the "aliens" represented in many of the experimental subjects' trips. The elements of the experimental environment seem to be cropping up in the trip world that the subjects are experiencing. Why haven't other environmental designs been considered?[22]

Nevertheless, such phenomena are not unheard of outside of a medical setting, which means that the birth trauma hypothesis is not necessarily ruled out. Still, another factor that can heavily influence a psychedelic experience is what is known as 'set' (mindset), half of 'set and setting'. Thus, if you form an idea of what a typical psychedelic experience is like, based on content you have read and watched, or people you have spoken to, you may come to expect this experience yourself, in turn encouraging that type of experience to occur. On the other hand, people may try DMT without the expectation of having a UFO/medical-type experience, who have never read Strassman's book or come across other such accounts, and yet still find themselves encountering medically themed entities and scenarios. This raises the question of whether, due to such putative cases, the birth trauma hypothesis is the most parsimonious and reasonable explanation for these experiences.

There are other possible (and perhaps tenuous) connections that can be made between alien abductions and the experience of birth. Images of doors and passageways in abduction experiences are seen to represent the opening of the cervix and the journey through it. In UFO encounters, the light beam of the spaceship is meant to correspond to the umbilical cord while the spaceship itself is interpreted to be the placenta (which has a flat and round shape). UFOs or alien spaceships have also been encountered in ayahuasca trips — they are a common motif in Amaringo's paintings. However, I am sceptical as to whether the alien spaceship motif fits into the birth trauma hypothesis. For example, it is doubtful that the infant would even see the placenta. The connection between the umbilical cord/placenta and an alien spaceship seems to be quite nebulous.

Betty Andreasson, a woman from Massachusetts, had an abduction experience in 1967 that contained several possible perinatal images, an event that Raymond Fowler documented in his book *The Andreasson Affair*. These images included being in a "cylindrical room" that was filled with grey fluid. She breathed through clear tubes fitted into her nostrils and mouth. She was also fed some sweet substance through the tube in her mouth. She floated in the fluid in a tranquil and peaceful state, until finally the fluid was drained and she was removed.[23] This experience sounds like a return to the womb and the birthing process. During Betty's examination by the humanoid aliens, which occurred in a big bright room, a long needle was inserted into her navel, which caused her a great deal of pain and discomfort.[24] Some might interpret this as related to the cutting of the umbilical cord.

This, of course, is just one abduction experience that may align with the birth trauma hypothesis; there are other experiences described by abductees that will lack the supposed perinatal features described above. Furthermore, and to re-emphasise, the connections between an experience like Andreasson's and birth — her *actual* birth — are prone to doubt. We should be wary of forcing the narrative of the birth trauma hypothesis onto abduction experiences just because it seems neatly done. Explanations like these can be susceptible to *apophenia*: the tendency to perceive patterns — meaningful connections — where none really exist. In addition, if some people who report alien encounters were born via caesarean section (C-section) or at home, outside of a medical environment, and they describe the same imagery that the birth trauma hypothesis links to a vaginal or hospital birth, this would indicate that there is no *necessary link* between such imagery and birth trauma.

Another crucial mistake that the birth trauma hypothesis could be guilty of is its presupposition that genuine perinatal experiences are possible. By this, I mean that the hypothesis can only be veridical if infants can actually retain memories of their birth experience; if they cannot, then how can there be traumatic memories that resurface during extraordinary states of consciousness?

It takes some time before human infants can begin to form their first long-term memories, although research in this area is mixed. This capacity can begin, intriguingly, at different points for people: some recollect past events from when they were just two years old,[25] whereas others might not remember anything before the age of four. However, researchers have found that people tend not to remember much of what occurred before the age of seven.[26] More recent research tells us that the average age of earliest memories is two and a half years old. This is about a year earlier than previously thought, yet this point of remembering will still differ between individuals, and it can vary depending on how you are asked to recall memories.[27] The lack of episodic memories from early childhood, known as infantile (or childhood) amnesia, may be linked to the maturation of the prefrontal cortex.[28] Memories that are created in later childhood and after are more likely because this is when the hippocampus and the frontoparietal regions undergo developments that improve our ability to bind, store, and recall details of events.[29]

There is some evidence that young children do have episodic memories of their infancy but then lose them later. For example, a 2010 study published in *Developmental Psychology* found that five-year-olds could recall events that occurred (verified by parents, where possible) when they were just one year old. By adolescence, these memories tend to be forgotten, nevertheless.[30] So, it seems that young children can form long-term memories, but these memories will fade after a certain age or stage in brain development.

As of yet, there is no convincing evidence that people can remember being born. Perinatal experiences, therefore, may not refer to the process of an individual's actual birth but they, for some other (perhaps symbolic) reason, centre on the theme of birth. We can at least point to the perennial nature of dying-and-rising gods, as well as myths and initiation rituals centred around the concept of birth, to shed light on the existence of this theme in the unconscious and its propensity to be activated and appear symbolically and dramatically in altered states like the DMT experience. This recurring theme may reflect a deep-seated desire for regeneration and transformation — to be born as a new person, in a new mode of being.

Not being able to remember events from birth and throughout early childhood makes sense biologically, based on what we know about the development of the brain. The available evidence does not mean *definitively* that infants cannot remember birth itself, but it is arguably unlikely based on our current understanding of infant development. It is generally accepted that no one can remember being born, although people will claim — and this is Rank's contention — that we do retain memories of this event. Grof, who was influenced by Rank's ideas, also claims as much when discussing types of psychedelic experiences: "there [is] a powerful record of biological birth", adding that "You can relive your birth. You can have prenatal experiences".[31] Like Rank, Grof believes our psychological ailments in adulthood stem from our hours spent in the birth canal and the anxiety and physical discomfort which that involves: "you find the whole psychopathology there, all the emotional problems, all the psychosomatic symptoms, the choking, the nausea, the headaches, the pains, the psychosomatic pains in the body."[32]

It is possible that if being born was a traumatic process, then we will be more likely to remember it. If birth is a traumatic event as Rank claims, in varying degrees for different people, then it may have an inherent *imprintability*. This could account for the human obsession with — and ability to experience at any point in life — the states of birth and rebirth. Even if the deeply traumatic nature of birth means the memory of the event becomes strongly suppressed, it should still, in theory, be stored in the mind and/or body and hence have the potential of being reactivated.

Jim Hopper, an expert in psychological trauma, has stated that a high-stress event "alters the function of the hippocampus and puts it into a super-encoding mode," and "the central details [of the event] get burned into their memory and they may never forget them".[33] However, this is in the context of a developed hippocampus. Can the same 'super-encoding' occur when this brain region has not yet fully matured in the young infant, as is the case before, during, and after its birth? Here it may be more difficult to make the case that clear memories — let alone any memories — of this event are recorded. Perhaps there are patchy memories, and the core details retained are like those described above but 'filled in' during the DMT state, creating something both familiar (relating to the birth event) but alien, owing to DMT's unique modulating power.

There might also be non-visual memories — of a somatic and emotional nature — that the infant retains; these could be the feeling of warm comfort and continual nourishment in the womb, contrasted with the tumult, confusion, separation, and fear when entering the post-birth world. And these could be the memories showing up in those alien abduction-type experiences, elicited by DMT or otherwise. The trauma of birth could be processed in a more somatic way, with traumatic memories stored in the body. Here we can refer to the ideas advanced by the psychiatrist Bessel van der Kolk and the psychotherapist Peter Levine, the latter of whom developed Somatic Experiencing (SE), a therapeutic approach that focuses on the physiological aspects of trauma. Van der Kolk, Levine, and other trauma researchers believe trauma is physically stored in the body and that to heal from it must involve working with the body, which will, in turn, help to address cognitive or emotional issues.[34]

SE, a specific approach to somatic therapy, is based on the idea that the negative effects of trauma — like anxiety, hypervigilance, aggression, and shame — result from denying the body the opportunity to fully process the traumatic event.[35] SE exercises include grounding, breathwork, self-soothing touch, and somatic mindfulness.[36] Other therapeutic techniques have been developed, in particular David Berceli's Tension and Trauma Releasing Exercises (TRE) — also known as therapeutic or neurogenic tremoring — that involve shaking the body to release tension and trauma, thus helping to regulate the nervous system.[37] Levine promotes this method of trauma resolution as well.[38] Studies show positive results for using SE to treat post-traumatic stress disorder (PTSD),[39] although the idea of trauma being literally stored in the body — in our tissues and cells — is questionable.

In any case, this outlook on trauma could be applied to psychedelic experiences since many people in these states will experience a period of spontaneous shaking that, according to the individual, is highly therapeutic. (Shaking behaviour, it is worth noting, is also considered to be a reliable effect of psychedelic drug action on serotonin receptors.)[40] But applying this outlook on trauma to DMT-induced abduction experiences might not be relevant or at least not fully explanatory. While there could be somatic aspects of these experiences that tie into trauma (how the body felt during the birthing process), the key phenomenological features that require explanation are more emotional, visual, and mystical in nature. Much remains unsolved and mysterious about these experiences, but this does not mean that theories of trauma offer us the best explanation. One could also doubt the notion that birth, even when no complications occur, is by its very nature a traumatic event.

## Scientific Accounts of Alien Abduction Experiences

To find some alternative explanations for DMT abduction-type phenomena, we can look at some of the prevailing theories of why non-psychedelic abduction phenomena occur.[41]

Firstly, sleep paralysis — when the body is paralysed while you regain awareness after waking from REM sleep — has been implicated in people's claims of being visited and experimented upon by alien beings. More specifically, this involves sleep paralysis accompanied by hypnopompic ('upon awakening') hallucinations. People who experience this will be aware of the inability to move and then experience the intrusion of dream material into waking consciousness (perceived as intruders in one's bedroom). Think of it as a waking dream. Researchers have assessed individuals who reported abduction by space alien beings, whose claims were linked to apparent episodes of sleep paralysis featuring hypnopompic hallucinations.[42] If you are already aware of what a classic alien abduction is meant to be like, then this might bolster the notion that what you experienced in that state was, in fact, a genuine visitation by inquisitive, probing aliens.

DMT does not induce sleep paralysis, however, so the above cannot offer a full explanation of what is going on in the altered state. Moreover, not all alien abduction experiences involve sleep-related phenomena, so other explanations are needed. Nonetheless, some aspects of dreaming may be relevant here. For example, Christopher Timmermann et al. stated in a paper that "DMT experiences can be said to resemble 'world-analogue' experiences (i.e. interior analogues of external worlds) — similar to the dream state".[43]

Based on electroencephalogram (EEG) tests of the electrical activity of people's brains under the influence of DMT, these researchers observed a drop in alpha waves and an increase in delta and theta waves (alpha waves are the brain's dominant electrical rhythm when awake, whereas theta waves are typically associated with dreaming). Increases in the visual quality of the participants' DMT journeys were positively correlated with increases in delta and theta waves and decreases in alpha waves.[44] Hence, the DMT state has been likened to 'dreaming while awake'.[45]

But even if DMT does induce some kind of waking dream state, this still does not tell us why alien abduction phenomena would occur or why they would be a recurring theme. This is where expectations may play a role. If awareness of alien abductions and UFO encounters in movies and books make it more likely for people to interpret sleep paralysis with hypnopompic hallucinations as visitations by alien beings, then perhaps awareness of similar DMT-related encounters — absorbed through the work of Strassman or trip reports — achieves the same result. One could be primed to either consciously or unconsciously expect the entities and one's meeting with them to have this alien character. Alternatively, the DMT experience could later be interpreted through the lens of the abduction model, as memories are certainly susceptible to all kinds of framing and embellishment.

Again, we should keep in mind the crucial factors of 'set and setting'. If Sand's analysis of Strassman's research hints at how one's environment (or 'setting') influences psychedelic experiences, then we should also highlight how one's mindset (or 'set') — including one's expectations and prior beliefs — can shape the quality of the experience.

Lucid dreaming could be another way to help clarify the matter. A 2021 study published in the *International Journal of Dream Research* suggests that some alien abduction stories may be explained by dreaming during REM sleep. Researchers recruited 152 people who claimed to have experienced a lucid dream — where you become aware that you're dreaming — and then asked them, while lucid dreaming, to "try to find or summon aliens or UFOs". They discovered that 75% of the volunteers were able to experience a dream that featured extraterrestrials or some kind of alien abduction. And of those who successfully experienced such dreams, 61% said the alien characters resembled extraterrestrials from sci-fi movies or novels (they had large and elongated heads, grey skin, large black eyes, no nose, and long arms and fingers). For others (19%), the beings looked like ordinary people, while 4% described them as invisible.[46]

According to the researchers, people might spontaneously enter dreams that *unintentionally* feature an alien abduction and then confuse this experience with reality. They note that about half of alien abduction stories occur when someone is sleeping or in a state of relaxation.[47] The point about relaxation is pertinent since daydreams or fantasies may trigger alien abduction experiences. The psychologists Leonard Newman and Roy Baumeister argue that things people have read or heard about alien abductions may be interwoven with images, dreams, and fantasies, and turned into elaborate pseudo-memories mistaken for reality, especially in a state of hypnosis.[48] It would be interesting to see if those exposed to material relating to alien abductions would then be more likely to report such phenomena in their DMT experiences.

Regarding specific brain regions implicated in the DMT experience, Timmermann et al. note,

> Although speculative, it is intriguing to consider that the emergent theta/delta rhythmicity under DMT (also observed in a non-controlled field study)[49] may have a deep (e.g. medial temporal lobe) source and reflect the recruitment of an evolutionarily ancient circuitry that has been classically associated with REM-sleep and medial temporal lobe stimulation — both of which are known to feature complex visionary phenomena.[50]

This speculative point is relevant because alien abductions have also been linked to abnormal activity in the temporal lobes. The neuroscientist Michael Persinger has long claimed that mystical experiences, out-of-body experiences, and so-called psychic experiences are connected in some way to excessive electrical activity in these particular brain regions.[51] We also know that people vary in a trait called 'temporal lobe lability', with those high in the trait having 'unstable' temporal lobes, resulting in frequent bursts of electrical activity in the region, which can be picked up by EEG. People with low lability, in contrast, rarely experience such bursts of activity and tend to be less imaginative.[52] In one paper, Persinger claims,

> Phenomenological details of visitor experiences are expected to reflect the functions of deep temporal lobe structures.... Normal people who are prone to these experiences show frequent temporal lobe signs and specific personality characteristics that include enhanced creativity, suggestibility, mild hypomania, anxiety, and emotional lability.[53]

The temporal lobe activation elicited by DMT, as well as perhaps accompanying personality traits and other aspects of 'set', may help to account for why many people report phenomena uncannily similar to alien visitation stories. There also seems to be a correspondence between the after-effects of both types of experience. As Persinger writes, "After intense [visitation] experiences, interictal-like behaviors similar to religious conversions (widening affect, sense of personal, desire to spread the word, concern about Man's destiny) emerge."[54] Indeed, many alien abduction claimants and DMT users say that these alien beings were communicating vital messages about the state of humanity and its future. As the Harvard psychiatrist John E. Mack observed, "Virtually every abductee receives information about the destruction of the earth's ecosystems and feels compelled to do something about it."[55] The environmentally attuned warnings of the aliens are intended to save us from self-destruction. It is also common for users of ayahuasca — the orally active form of DMT — to receive these kinds of messages, often from what feels like an intelligent entity.[56]

At the same time, this is not to say that DMT-induced alien encounters are exactly like those reported by self-identified abductees; the psychedelic variety has visual, emotional, and mystical features that are far removed from what an abductee will experience. But this does not mean that the scientific explanations for why alien abductions occur are not applicable to the DMT state. These neuropsychological perspectives may remain the simplest and most reasonable account of why DMT experiences — and other altered states — feature these phenomena, in contrast to the claim that when taking DMT, a user is genuinely being examined and lectured by highly advanced extraterrestrial beings. However, the complex nature of DMT-induced alien encounters lies in the fact that many psychedelic effects are involved in the overall experience. The result, then, is not only encounters with alien creatures but also broader experiences that reach an apotheosis of what *alien* truly means.

## Endnotes

1. Lawson, A.H. (1994). 'Response to the Twemlow Paper'. *Journal of Near-Death Studies*, 12(4), pp. 245–265.
2. Ibid.
3. Mack, J.E. (1994). *Abduction: Human Encounters with Aliens*, pp. 23–24. New York: Scribner.
4. Kagan, S. (2023). 'The content of complex psychedelic experiences resulting from inhalation of N,N-dimethyltryptamine'. *Journal of Psychedelic Studies*, 6(3), pp. 222–231.
5. Charing, H.G., Cloudsley, P., and Amaringo, P. (2011). *The Ayahuasca Visions of Pablo Amaringo*, p. 6. Rochester, Vermont: Inner Traditions.
6. Mack, J.E. (1994). *Abduction: Human Encounters with Aliens*, p. 223. New York: Scribner.
7. Kagan, S. (2023). 'The content of complex psychedelic experiences resulting from inhalation of N,N-dimethyltryptamine'. *Journal of Psychedelic Studies*, 6(3), pp. 222–231.
8. Strassman, R. (2001). *DMT: The Spirit Molecule: A Doctor's Revolutionary Research into the Biology of Near-Death and Mystical Experiences*, p. 55. Rochester, VT: Park Street Press.
9. Ibid., p. 219.
10. Ibid., p. 192.
11. Ibid., p. 199.
12. Barker, S.A., Borjigin, J., Lomnicka, I., and Strassman, R. (2013). 'LC/MS/MS analysis of the endogenous dimethyltryptamine hallucinogens, their precursors, and major metabolites in rat pineal gland microdialysate'. *Biomedical Chromatography*, 27(12), pp. 1690–1700.

13. Dean, J.G., Liu, T., Huff, S., Sheler, B., Barker, S.A., Strassman, R., Wang, M.M., and Borjigin, J. (2019). 'Biosynthesis and Extracellular Concentrations of N,N-dimethyltryptamine (DMT) in Mammalian Brain'. *Scientific Reports*, 9, Article: 9333.
14. Nichols, D.E. (2017). '*N,N*-dimethyltryptamine and the pineal gland: Separating fact from myth'. *Journal of Psychopharmacology*, 32(1), pp. 30–36.
15. Dolan, E.W. (2018). 'No reason to believe the pineal gland alters consciousness by secreting DMT, psychedelic researcher says', PsyPost, 18 January. https://www.psypost.org/2018/01/no-reason-believe-pineal-gland-alters-consciousness-secreting-dmt-psychedelic-researcher-says-50609
16. Ibid.
17. Rank, O. (1924). *The Trauma of Birth*, p. 11. London: Kegan Paul & Co., Ltd., 1929.
18. Freud, S. (1900). *The Interpretation of Dreams*, p. 263. Translated by Brill, A.A. Ware: Wordsworth Editions, 1997.
19. Woolverton, F. (2011). 'Are We Born Into Trauma?', *Psychology Today*, 15 September. https://www.psychologytoday.com/gb/blog/the-trauma-addiction-connection/201109/are-we-born-trauma
20. Grof, S. (1975). 'Perinatal Experiences in LSD Sessions' in *Realms of the Human Unconscious: Observations from LSD Research*, pp. 95–154. London: Souvenir Press, 1979.
21. Jansen, K. (2001). *Ketamine: Dreams and Realities*, p. 108. Sarasota: Multidisciplinary Association for Psychedelic Studies (MAPS), 2004.
22. Sand, N. (2014). 'Moving Into the Sacred World of DMT, by Nick Sand', Psychedelic Frontier, 28 April. http://psychedelicfrontier.com/moving-sacred-world-dmt-nick-sand/

23. Fowler, R.E. (1979). Chapter 5: 'Trip to an Alien Realm' in *The Andreasson Affair: The Documented Investigation of a Woman's Abduction Aboard a UFO*, pp. 65–94. Englewood Cliffs: Prentice-Hall.

24. Ibid., p. 179.

25. Usher, J.A. and Neisser, U. (1993). 'Childhood amnesia and the beginnings of memory for four early life events'. *Journal of Experimental Psychology: General*, 122(2), pp. 155–165.

26. Bauer, P.J. and Larkina, M. (2013). 'The onset of childhood amnesia in childhood: A prospective investigation of the course and determinants of forgetting of early-life events'. *Memory*, 22(8), pp. 907–924.

27. Peterson, C. (2021). 'What is your earliest memory? It depends'. *Memory*, 29(6), pp. 811–822.

28. Newcombe, N.S., Drummey, A.B., Fox, N.A., Lie, E., and Ottinger-Alberts, W. (2016). 'Remembering Early Childhood: How Much, How, and Why (or Why Not)'. *Current Directions in Psychological Science*, 9(2), pp. 55–58.

29. Amso, D. (2017). 'When Do Children Start Making Long-Term Memories?', *Scientific American*, 1 January. https://www.scientificamerican.com/article/when-do-children-start-making-long-term-memories/

30. Tustin, K. and Hayne, H. (2010). 'Defining the boundary: age-related changes in childhood amnesia'. *Developmental Psychology*, 46(5), pp. 1049–1061.

31. Ferriss T (2018). 'The Tim Ferriss Show Transcripts: Stan Grof (#347)', tim.blog, 22 November. https://tim.blog/2018/11/22/the-tim-ferriss-show-transcripts-stan-grof/

32. Ibid.

33. Chatterjee, R. (2018). 'How Trauma Affects Memory: Scientists Weigh In On The Kavanaugh Hearing, *NPR*, 28 September. https://www.npr.org/sections/health-shots/

2018/09/28/652524372/how-trauma-affects-memory-scientists-weigh-in-on-the-kavanaugh-hearing

34. Miezio, A. (2022). 'Why is Trauma Stored in the Body? +7 Answers', Psychedelic Support, 20 April. https://psychedelic.support/resources/why-trauma-stored-in-the-body-7-answers/

35. Olssen, M.C. (2013). 'Mental Health Practitioners' Views on Why Somatic Experiencing Works for Treating Trauma', Social Work Master's Clinical Research Paper, St Catherine University/University of St Thomas, Minnesota.

36. Ramirez-Duran, D. (2020). 'Somatic Experiencing Therapy: 10 Best Exercises & Examples', PositivePsychology.com, 11 November. https://positivepsychology.com/somatic-experiencing/

37. Heath, R. and Beattie, J. (2019). 'Case Report of a Former Soldier Using TRE (Tension/Trauma Releasing Exercises) For Post-Traumatic Stress Disorder Self-Care'. *Journal of Military and Veterans' Health*, 27(3), pp. 35–40.

38. Yalom, V. and Yalom, M. (2010). 'Peter Levine on Somatic Experiencing', Psychotherapy.net, April. https://www.psychotherapy.net/interview/interview-peter-levine

39. Brom, D., Stokar, Y., Lawi, C., Nuriel-Porat, V., Ziv, V., Lerner, K., and Ross, G. (2017). 'Somatic Experiencing for Posttraumatic Stress Disorder: A Randomized Controlled Outcome Study'. *Journal of Traumatic Stress*, 30(3), pp. 304–312.

40. Buchborn, T., Lyons, T., Song, C., Feilding, A., and Knöpfel, T. (2023). 'Cortical Correlates of Psychedelic-Induced Shaking Behavior Revealed by Voltage Imaging'. *International Journal of Molecular Sciences*, 24(11), Article: 9463

41. Holden, K.J. and French, C.C. (2002). 'Alien abduction experiences: Some clues from neuropsychology and neuropsychiatry'. *Cognitive Neuropsychiatry*, 7(3), pp. 163–178.

42. McNally, R.J. and Clancy, S.A. (2005). 'Sleep Paralysis, Sexual Abuse, and Space Alien Abduction'. *Transcultural Psychiatry*, 42(1), pp. 113–122.
43. Timmermann, C., Roseman, L., Schartner, M., Milliere, R., Williams, L.T.J., Erritzoe, D., Muthukumaraswamy, S., Ashton, M., Bendrioua, A., Kaur, O., Turton, S., Nour, M.M., Day, C.M., Leech, R., Nutt, D.J., and Carhart-Harris, R.L. (2019). 'Neural correlates of the DMT experience assessed with multivariate EEG'. *Scientific Reports*, 9, Article: 16324.
44. Ibid.
45. O'Hare, R. (2019). 'Ayahuasca compound changes brainwaves to vivid 'waking-dream' state, Imperial College London, 19 November. https://www.imperial.ac.uk/news/193993/ayahuasca-compound-changes-brainwaves-vivid-waking-dream/
46. Raduga, M., Shashkov, A., and Zhunusova, Z. (2021). 'Emulating alien and UFO encounters in REM sleep'. *International Journal of Dream Research*, 14(2), pp. 247–256.
47. Ibid.
48. Newman, L.S. and Baumeister, R.F. (1996). 'Toward an Explanation of the UFO Abduction Phenomenon: Hypnotic Elaboration, Extraterrestrial Sadomasochism, and Spurious Memories'. *Psychological Inquiry*, 7(2), pp. 99–126.
49. Szara, S. (1956). 'Dimethyltryptamin: its metabolism in man; the relation to its psychotic effect to the serotonin metabolism'. *Experienta*, 12(11), pp. 441–442.
50. Timmermann, C., Roseman, L., Schartner, M., Milliere, R., Williams, L.T.J., Erritzoe, D., Muthukumaraswamy, S., Ashton, M., Bendrioua, A., Kaur, O., Turton, S., Nour, M.M., Day, C.M., Leech, R., Nutt, D.J,, and Carhart-Harris, R.L. (2019). 'Neural correlates of the DMT experience assessed with multivariate EEG'. *Scientific Reports*, 9, Article number: 16324.

51. Persinger, M.A. (1983). 'Religious and mystical experiences as artifacts of temporal lobe function: a general hypothesis'. *Perceptual and Motor Skills*, 57(3 Pt 2), pp. 1255–1262.
52. Thalbourne, M.A., Crawley, S.E., and Houran, J. (2003). 'Temporal lobe lability in the highly transliminal mind'. *Personality and Individual Differences*, 35(8), pp. 1965–1974.
53. Persinger, M.A. (1989). 'Geophysical variables and behavior: LV. Predicting the details of visitor experiences and the personality of experients: the temporal lobe factor'. *Perceptual and Motor Skills*, 68(1), pp. 55–65.
54. Ibid.
55. Mack, J.E. (1994). *Abduction: Human Encounters with Aliens*, p. 401. New York: Scribner.
56. Hill, D. (2016). "Ayahuasca is changing global environmental consciousness", *The Guardian*, 30 July. https://www.theguardian.com/environment/andes-to-the-amazon/2016/jul/30/ayahuasca-changing-global-environmental-consciousness

# Chapter 4

# Psychedelics and the Experience of the Sublime

A recurring effect of psychedelics deserving of more attention is the experience of the sublime. The philosopher Peter Sjöstedt-Hughes, in his book *Noumenautics* (2015), writes that "psyphen [psychedelic phenomenology] can be an experience of inhuman aesthetic heights which embraces the sublime and the beautiful".[1] In aesthetics (the branch of philosophy that deals with the nature of beauty, taste, and art), the notion of 'the sublime' is often distinguished from the concept and experience of 'beauty'. This essay aims to underscore what this distinction consists of exactly. I will also describe — and defend the value of — the experience of the sublime occasioned by psychedelics.

## The Philosophy of the Sublime

One of the key defining features of the sublime, setting it apart from the beautiful, is the quality of greatness. In *On the Sublime*, a treatise on aesthetics thought to have been written in the first century AD, the author (unknown but referred to as Longinus) argues that "the first and most important source of sublimity [is] the power of forming great conceptions".[2] Longinus focuses on the sublime in the context of literary works — it refers to a style of writing that elevates itself "above the ordinary".[3] In the treatise, the term used to denote the sublime is *hypsos*, from the root *hypso*, which means 'aloft', 'height', or 'on high'. For Longinus, hypsos is "the sublime in one single thought"[4] and "the echo of a great soul",[5] and the root word is vital, as it emphasises the state of elevation that is central to the sublime. The author also advances five sources of sublimity: "great thoughts, strong emotions, certain figures of thought and speech, noble diction, and dignified word arrangement".[6]

In the treatise, Longinus states that hypsos produces an experience of transcendence (the idea of elevation here helps to get this across), leading to states of ecstasy, wonder, and astonishment, rather than the inferior experience of charm and pleasure that comes from the "merely persuasive and pleasant".[7] Robert Doran notes in *The Theory of the Sublime from Longinus to Kant* that this differentiation "prefigures the modern contrast between the 'mere' pleasure of the beautiful and the intense feeling produced by the sublime, which borders on pain".[8] At the heart of the experience of the sublime, for Longinus, is also the feeling of being overwhelmed, as it involves "invincible power and force" that "get the better of every hearer".[9]

British writers like John Dennis and Joseph Addison would later take an interest in the aesthetic quality of the sublime, echoing Longinus's synonymisation of the sublime with greatness but adding that the sublime was paradoxical in nature. They stressed that greatness elicited not just positive feelings; fear was also involved in the experience.[10] Dennis, in his work *Miscellanies in Prose and Verse* (1693), details his experience of journeying across the Alps. Prior to this trip, he considered the beauty of nature as a "delight that is consistent with Reason", but after traversing the imposing, majestic Alps, he remarked that his pleasurable experience of nature was "mingled with horrors, and sometimes almost with despair".[11] For contained in the greatness of the sublime is also the sense that one has become small, vulnerable, in danger, and subject to powers and forces greater than oneself. Thus, Dennis refers to the sublime as a "delightful Horror" or "terrible Joy".[12]

In a range of artistic styles — including Baroque, Romantic, Victorian, modern, and contemporary — we can see representations of this admixture of wonder and terror, often relying on natural landscapes and scenes to achieve this quality. Here it would also be helpful to note that the sublime and awe (a feeling of reverence and amazement mixed with fear) are more or less equivalent, as the philosopher Robert Clewis argues — and so both concepts can be used interchangeably.[13]

Addison made similar comments to those of Dennis in *Remarks on Several Parts of Italy*, an account of his experiences during the Grand Tour, which he began in 1699. (The Grand Tour was a customary, cultural trip through Europe that upper-class young men undertook — as an educational rite of passage — in the seventeenth and eighteenth centuries.) In his travel writing, Addison stated, paradoxically, that "[t]he Alps fill the mind with an agreeable kind of Horror".[14] For these British writers, we see that the sublime arises from the external, natural world, rather than from rhetoric, which marks a distinction between Longinus's and, for instance, Addison's views on the sublime.

In *The Spectator*, Addison uses the term "greatness" to refer to what we would call the sublime, and it is worth reiterating that this quality and related qualities — such as vastness, largeness, immensity, and unboundedness — set apart the sublime from the beautiful. In this way, an object, event, or work of art could be beautiful but not great and, therefore, not sublime. As Addison writes,

By greatness, I do not only mean the bulk of any single object, but the largeness of a whole view, considered as one entire piece. Such are the prospects of an open champaign country, a vast uncultivated desert, of huge heaps of mountains, high rocks precipices, or a wide expanse of waters, where we are not struck with the novelty or beauty of the sight, but with that rude kind of magnificence which appears in many of these stupendous works of nature. Our imagination loves to be filled with an object, or to grasp at anything that is too big for its capacity. We are flung into a pleasing astonishment at such unbounded views, and feel a delightful stillness and amazement in the soul at the apprehension of them.[15]

Another crucial figure in the philosophy of the sublime was Edmund Burke, who extolled his aesthetic views in *A Philosophical Enquiry into the Origin of Our Ideas of the Sublime and Beautiful* (1757). In his treatise, Burke would echo Dennis's position that the sublime engenders a feeling of horror. For example, in his analysis of the sublime, Burke states, "Another source of the sublime is infinity … [i]nfinity has a tendency to fill the mind with that sort of delightful horror, which is the most genuine effect and truest test of the sublime."[16]

Interestingly, though, the concept of infinity does not have to be exclusively experienced in the perception of the natural world (such as gazing into a star-filled sky) or by considering the possible limitlessness of the universe. Infinity can also delightfully horrify us in a purely conceptual way or in an artificial way, such as in videos of fractal zooming. (The relationship between infinity, the sublime, and the psychedelic experience will be developed later in this essay.)

For Burke, the sublime is more important and more valuable than the beautiful, although, unlike writers before him, his conception of the sublime was largely based on negative emotions. This is also diametrically opposed to modern-day usages of the term 'sublime': when we describe food or music as sublime, for instance, we are saying that it is sensually pleasurable. Whereas for Burke, the sublime's "strongest emotion is an emotion of distress" and "no pleasure from a positive cause belongs to it".[17] He argues,

Whatever is fitted in any sort to excite the ideas of pain, and danger, that is to say, whatever is in any sort terrible, or is conversant about terrible objects, or operates in a manner analogous to terror, is a source of the sublime; that is, it is productive of the strongest emotion which the mind is capable of feeling.[18]

The sublime may be experienced in the face of a turbulent, raging storm or some kind of natural catastrophe. Burke quotes a plethora of literary sources to underline his conception of the sublime. One example is the second book of *Paradise Lost* (1667), in which John Milton portrays the journey of the fallen angels in Hell: "through many a dark and dreary vale They passed, and many a region dolorous, O'er many a frozen, many a fiery alp, Rocks, caves, lakes, fens, bogs, dens, and shades of death; A universe of death..."[19]

Critics of Burke may claim that his views on the sublime are somewhat masochistic, given that he is placing a high value on an experience that is a great source of fear and terror. Indeed, in terms of psychedelic phenomenology, we find that the sublime can be experienced in a way that differs from Burke's conception of it (although perhaps also being consistent with it at times).

In his treatise, Burke defines the sublime as that which overwhelms us and impacts us with irresistible force. Astonishment is the concomitant feeling of the sublime, which he juxtaposes with the supposed weaker feelings of admiration, reverence, and respect. Ultimately behind all experiences of the sublime, however, is terror. Yet Burke still reiterated the paradoxicality of the sublime, emphasised by writers like Dennis and Addison. The sublime is also an experience of delight (the kind we experience when a pain or threat ceases or is removed; it is "a pleasure that retains something of the effect of the pain experienced", to quote Doran).[20] Burke regarded such delight as more intense than positive pleasure since he believed pain is more intense than pleasure.

But to experience this terror and delight simultaneously, Burke maintained, we need some distance from the source of the sublime. The sublime requires that we have "an idea of pain and danger, without actually being in such circumstances".[21] As a case in point, this could involve watching a violent storm from a safe distance. This kind of sublime experience, according to Burke, can lead to "tranquillity shadowed with horror",[22] stipulating that "[w]hen danger or pain press too nearly they are incapable of giving any delight, and are simply terrible".[23]

Immanuel Kant, in the *Critique of Judgment* (1790), calls the sublime that "which is *absolutely great*",[24] noting that beauty "is connected with the form of the object" and dependent on "boundaries", while the sublime "is to be found in a formless object" and represented by *"boundlessness"*.[25] Kant goes on to explicate his ideas on the sublime. He draws a distinction between the 'mathematical sublime' (concerned with things that have a great quantitative magnitude, in terms of size, height, or depth) and the 'dynamical sublime' (concerned with things that have a magnitude of force greater than our will, with examples given by Kant including overhanging cliffs, thunder clouds, volcanoes, and hurricanes).[26] [27]

For the purposes of this discussion, it is worth noting that, in the words of Kant, "the concept of the Sublime is not nearly so important and rich in consequences as the concept of the Beautiful" and that the "theory of the sublime [is] a mere appendix to the aesthetical judging of that purposiveness [of nature]."[28] These are views that counteract the supreme importance that Burke placed on the sublime and, I would argue, undermine the rich value to be unearthed in psychedelic sublimity.

However, aligned with Burke, Kant said that dynamically sublime objects are more attractive the more fear-inducing they are "provided only that we are in security".[29] Kant similarly points to the paradoxical essence of the sublime by describing it as an experience in which "the mind is not merely attracted by the object but is ever being alternately repelled".[30] In terms of the mathematical sublime, Kant believes that the sublime arises through "the inadequacy of the greatest effort of our Imagination to estimate the magnitude of an object".[31] We might try to imagine the size of a galaxy or the size of the universe but our senses and imagination truly cannot take in their immensity. We simply cannot comprehend such natural objects as complete in a single image in our minds. And Kant argues that pushing our senses to the limits of their powers in this way is central to the experience of the sublime.

Perhaps the best representation of the sublime in film that illustrates these ideas can be found in Danny Boyle's *Sunshine* (2007), which tells the story of a group of astronauts sent on a mission to reignite the dying Sun and save humanity from mass extinction. The spaceship is able to safely approach the Sun by reflecting the rays with a huge circular mirror. One of the most enticing aspects of the film is the ability of the crew to gaze at the Sun, in an observation room located behind the giant mirror, but only at extremely low intensities, so as not to damage their retinas.

Searle, the crew's psychiatrist, becomes obsessed with the Sun, spending hours looking at it in the observation room each day, gradually lowering the protection filter. At 3.1% of the Sun's actual intensity, the crew can look at the Sun for 30 seconds, after which irreversible damage would occur. Thus, here we have greatness beyond comprehension and physical capability — a mark of the sublime. Searle finds the brightness of the Sun overwhelming, yet as he tells his fellow crew members during dinner: "It's invigorating, like taking a shower in light. You lose yourself a little." From the safety of the observation room, the crew members can gaze at the Sun and experience this state of fascination mixed with terror, this feeling of being overwhelmed by the brilliance, size, and detail of the celestial body.

Arthur Schopenhauer, in *The World as Will and Representation* (1818), argued that there are objects or phenomena that bear "a hostile relation to the human will in general (as it presents itself in its objecthood, the human body) and oppose it, threatening it with a superior power that suppresses all resistance, or reducing it to nothing with its immense size".[32] These phenomena are so vast and potent that they can overwhelm you or reduce your existence to an insignificant speck of dust. Schopenhauer's examples of such phenomena include desert landscapes, cascades, storm clouds, and the starry night sky, among many others.[33] Yet sublime pleasure can arise in the face of these landscapes and phenomena when you calmly contemplate them in spite of their threatening nature.

For both Kant and Schopenhauer, the sublime involves the use of cognitive faculties. According to Kant, the sublime comes from the feeling that our faculty of reason makes us superior to nature as well as the recognition of our independence from nature (due to our autonomous moral agency). For Schopenhauer, the sublime likewise follows an intellectual reflection about our relationship to nature, although it does not depend on a feeling of superiority to — or independence from — nature. For both, measuring ourselves against the greatness or power of the natural world and realising our vulnerability and insignificance in the face of nature is often involved in the experience of the sublime. Burke, in contrast, posited that the sublime is based on an immediate emotional reaction. The philosopher Sandra Shapshay refers to Burke's description as the 'thin sublime' since it "is not a highly intellectual aesthetic response", whereas she describes Kant and Schopenhauer's version as the 'thick sublime', as it characterises such a response.[34]

Schopenhauer follows Kant's distinction between the mathematical and the dynamical sublime, distinguished by the threat they pose to the human will. When the threat is psychological, then the sublimity is mathematical, while if the threat is physical, then the sublimity is dynamical. Moreover, sublimity occurs in degrees for Schopenhauer, with increases in the magnitude of the threat correlating to increases in the degree of the sublime. This is encapsulated in *Sunshine*, where the crew experience increasing levels of terror the closer they approach the Sun and suffer nightmares in which they are inexorably drawn towards the surface of the brilliant star, waking up distraught at the moment of collision. In referencing a high degree of the mathematical sublime (or the felt vastness of nature), Schopenhauer writes,

> When we lose ourselves in the contemplation of the infinite extent of the world in space and time ... then we feel ourselves reduced to nothing, feel ourselves as individuals, as living bodies, as transient appearances of the will, like drops in the ocean, fading away, melting away into nothing. But at the same time ... our immediate consciousness [is] that all these worlds really exist only in our representation.... The magnitude of the world, which we used to find unsettling, is now settled securely within ourselves ... it appears only as the felt consciousness that we are, in some sense (that only philosophy makes clear), one with the world, and thus not brought down, but rather elevated, by its immensity.[35]

Shapshay points out that the experience of the sublime, for Schopenhauer, involves an oscillation between feeling insignificant relative to the spatial and temporal vastness of nature and feeling elevated by two thoughts: firstly, as thinking subjects, we create our own representation of the world, and secondly, we are unified with the vastness of the natural world. These are exalting realisations, not oppressive ones.[36]

To experience the sublime in the face of threatening, fearful, or overwhelming landscapes and natural phenomena, Schopenhauer asserts that an individual must acknowledge the fearfulness and vastness of the object in question and then consciously turn away from the object, acting against one's will.

In a state of will-less contemplation of such objects, in which you liberate both your intellect and your perception from the service of the human will (the blind, unconscious desire for self-preservation), Schopenhauer argued you would experience a "state of elevation" (the sublime).[37] Contrasting the beautiful with the sublime, Schopenhauer says the beautiful is entirely pleasurable, whereas the sublime is mixed with pain, which is in agreement with Kant's view.[38]

In *The Sublime in Schopenhauer's Philosophy*, Bart Vandenabeele takes issue with Shapshay's argument that the thick sublime is more profound than the non-cognitive, affective arousal that characterises the thin sublime simply because the former has a cognitive and scientific basis to it. Vandenabeele rebuts this position by saying it turns "the sublime into an overly intellective experience", adding that "reflection upon humanity and nature can be a valuable consequence of the experience of the sublime, and the sublime may lead to deep metaphysical insights, but these are not (necessarily) part of the aesthetic experience itself".[39]

With these preceding philosophical positions and discussions in mind, let's turn now to how these ideas on the sublime relate to the psychedelic experience. This relationship also diverges from the philosophies of Burke, Kant, and Schopenhauer, as the latter focus on the sublime as occasioned by natural phenomena and intellectual reflection. We can additionally describe the sublime in a way that is not (exclusively) based on nature or rational thought. Indeed, psychedelic phenomenology can be accompanied by the experience of the sublime in other (and perhaps more profound) ways.

## Experiencing the Sublime Through Psychedelics

Beginning with the quality of greatness intrinsic to the sublime, we can certainly see this as a repeating feature of the psychedelic experience. During the psychedelic experience, the ordinary can rapidly morph into the extraordinary, becoming great when before it was entirely absent of greatness, devoid of interest, taken for granted, and merely a backdrop in one's life. Huxley, in recounting his experience with 400 mg of mescaline in *The Doors of Perception* (1954), communicates this transformation of regular existence into psychedelic sublimity: "I was not looking now at an unusual flower arrangement. I was seeing what Adam had seen on the morning of his creation — the miracle, moment by moment, of naked existence."[40]

In an exchange of letters in 1956, Huxley and the British psychiatrist Humphry Osmond (who supervised Huxley's mescaline experience) were suggesting to each other a possible new term that would accurately classify this group of substances we now call psychedelics. Huxley's suggestion, which never took off, was 'phanerothyme',[41] based on the Greek words *phaneroin* (meaning 'visible') and *thymos* (meaning 'soul'), so the term means 'visible soul'. Osmond's preferred alternative was 'psychedelic', originating from the Greek words *psyche* (meaning 'mind' or 'soul') and *delein* (meaning 'to manifest'); thus, the word psychedelic means 'mind-manifesting'.[42] Their coinages were included in a rhyme that was meant to encapsulate the nature of psychedelics. Osmond famously said, "To fathom Hell or soar angelic, just take a pinch of psychedelic."[43]

We can, however, supplement this phrase by adding that psychedelics can allow you to experience positive and negative states of mind *at the same time*. For instance, one may feel the sublime — the mix of wonder and overwhelm — during a psychedelic-induced dissolution of the ego and subsequent feeling of unity, which is often described as merging with the universe or the totality of existence. In these non-ordinary states of consciousness, in which our perspective radically shifts, we can experience awe in a variety of other ways. We can experience it when we viscerally feel our existence in this world, when we reflect on how we exist infinitesimally in relation to the universe, or in response to fundamental concepts (such as existence and being *in and of themselves*). In addition, psychedelics can induce a feeling of pure existence and being that lends itself to the experience of awe.

Less well known is Huxley's psychedelic-inspired rhyme: "To make this trivial world sublime, take half a gram of phanerothyme."[44] While it's not clear if Huxley is using 'sublime' in the philosophical sense or the colloquial sense, we can nonetheless take it to mean the former and his rhyme still holds true. Psychedelics can lead to an experience of the sublime. More importantly, these substances can conjure up such an experience based on the everyday reality we inhabit. This contrasts with the causes of sublimity that previous philosophers had placed importance on (e.g. rhetoric and the arts for Longinus and the majesty of nature for later thinkers such as Addison, Burke, Kant, and Schopenhauer).

As Huxley discovered, the sight of a flower arrangement under the influence of psychedelics can become sublime, which rings true for many of those who venture into psychedelic states of mind. However, could you not repudiate this claim by stating that what Huxley and other explorers experience is not sublimity — for there is no essential greatness to the flower arrangement — but is instead a heightened experience of the beautiful? It is an intriguing point to consider. Just as Schopenhauer describes degrees of the sublime, can we not also invoke degrees of other aesthetic qualities, such as the ugly and the beautiful? Based on certain features of the aesthetic object in question and the quality of our perception, we can postulate that during a psychedelic experience, at least when euphorically perceiving the ordinary world, we are experiencing extreme beauty. Conversely, when dysphorically perceiving mundane objects and environments, we might be experiencing extreme ugliness.

Nonetheless, drawing on the other notable features of the sublime, we can counteract this argument by recognising that the psychedelic experience is also often overwhelming. Longinus, Burke, Kant, and Schopenhauer were keen to identify this feeling of being overwhelmed as one quality that distinguishes the sublime from the beautiful. For instance, during the psychedelic experience, normally ordinary objects — especially natural objects like plants, flowers, trees, and clouds — can become so intensely alive, energetic, and dynamic that they overwhelm the senses and the emotions.

While it is true that degrees of beauty can be amplified during the psychedelic experience, if the altered state is altered enough, then the beautiful may turn into the sublime. One's subjective feeling can shift from tranquillity, fascination, and curiosity into turbulence, amazement, and shock. In a state of psychedelic sublimity, watching the clouds move and shift across the sky can be a truly astonishing experience. This is because anything with a fractal structure (such as clouds) will have that fractality amplified by psychedelics. Clouds, then, can change from slowly billowing and slightly fractal objects of perception into intensely explosive, kaleidoscopic, fractalising patterns. Such an experience can be simultaneously wondrous and also 'too much'. Psychedelics can create a sensory overload, with one's field of perception imbued with a power that may elicit fear, uncertainty, and uneasiness. A psychedelic experience of this nature seems to fulfil another criterion of sublimity: the paradoxical marriage of wonder and fear.

The fractalisation of ordinary objects and landscapes is not the only way in which fractals feature in the psychedelic experience. One can also hallucinate such geometry, so that fractal patterns become superimposed on the walls and the ground, or they burst with aliveness and colour behind closed eyelids. In this way, ordinary objects are not suffused with fractal visuals, but rather the geometry is hallucinatory (the patterns do not depend on external stimuli). They can appear with eyes closed, in the absence of any object of perception. This

Altered Perspectives

is an intriguing and unique aspect of psychedelic sublimity, as it means you can experience the sublime based entirely on changes to your internal world.

You don't have to watch volcanic eruptions from a safe distance or survey gargantuan, snow-capped mountains to get a taste of the sublime; you can dwell in this subjective experience in the comfort of your own home. On the subject of fractal hallucinations, the psychedelic researcher Robin Carhart-Harris has suggested that these images are projections of one's very own fractal brain structure. It's "as if the brain is revealing itself to itself", he said.[45] This would mean, then, that if this psychedelic phenomenology is leading to the experience of sublimity, then it is the perception of oneself — rather than impressive external objects and landscapes — that fills one with awe.

As we have already seen, Schopenhauer maintained that we experience the sublime when we, as finite beings, come in contact with the infinite, such as in the contemplation of the infinite nature of space and time. In the psychedelic experience, we can experience a high degree of the mathematically sublime in the visions of blooming fractals that pervade the visual field or inner space (behind closed eyes). Immersed in these visions, the patterns you see have no end. They have infinite self-similarity, complexity, and depth. Witnessing this infinity in action can — as Schopenhauer argued in the case of contemplating infinity — make you feel insignificant in your limitedness. To be engulfed by such visions of infinity would, arguably, entail even greater degrees of sublimity: stronger feelings of both wonder and fear in the face of the infinite.

The continual unfolding and foreverness of fractal visions might be one reason why the psychedelic experience involves a sense of eternity. Deep in a trance of fractal visions, there is no end to the level of detail that can be revealed, which intimates a sense of infinite time, for theoretically, you can keep tumbling down the fractal patterns forever. It is one thing to contemplate infinite time, in the way Schopenhauer describes; it is quite another thing to have a visceral subjective sense of infinite time. Furthermore, it is not necessary to experience infinite geometry to feel that time is infinite. The psychedelic experience can distort time in such a way that an individual feels time to be infinite. (The terms 'eternity' and 'infinite time' are equivalent and can be used interchangeably; both mean that which 'lasts forever'.) During a psychedelic experience, an individual might feel that the journey is lasting forever or that a single moment is eternal.

In the *Critique of Pure Reason* (1781), Kant argued that time, like space, is an *a priori* sensible intuition — a mental construct existing prior to experience — that orders our experience of the phenomenal world. Time is not an inherent aspect of reality.[46] Therefore, if psychedelics can perturb this mental construct in the appropriate way, then you can lose the regular perception of the flow of time and instead be granted the felt experience of eternity. And in the presence of eternity or infinite time, you can experience the sublime, in the way that Kant and Schopenhauer claim you do when you confront the mathematically sublime.

From Kant's perspective, the sublime does not involve a sense of timelessness, of time standing still, but this can be a feature of the psychedelic experience: time can appear to stop or freeze, or it may become non-existent or meaningless. There might also be the sense that one's experiences are happening 'outside time'. Despite Kant's views, we can still apply the concept of sublimity to this psychedelic phenomenology, as this feeling of timelessness can evoke the various features of the sublime already outlined, such as paradoxical emotions and being overwhelmed.

## The Sublime Encounter with the Divine

Another way in which you can experience the sublime during a psychedelic experience is in the encounter with what many people term 'the divine'. Clewis calls this the *transcendent* sublime, the kind elicited by religious experiences, which he contrasts with what he terms the *immanent* sublime: sublimity stimulated by a vast or powerful object.[47] The German theologian and philosopher Rudolf Otto developed one of the most illuminating perspectives on the experience of the divine, which he presents in his book *The Idea of the Holy* (1917). In this seminal work, he introduces the idea of the *numinous* (derived from the Latin *numen*, meaning 'divine power').[48] This concept, while apparently etymologically similar, is distinct from Kant's *noumenon*, which stands for the unknowable reality of an object — the 'thing-in-itself' as Kant called it — that underlies our perception of that object. The numinous, according to Otto, refers to the experience of the holy, the divine, or the "wholly other" that is — so he argues — at the basis of all religions.[49]

The manner in which Otto describes the numinous is palpably close to the previous delineations of the sublime. Indeed, we could certainly ascribe sublimity to the experience of the divine that Otto is concerned with and which often manifests in the psychedelic experience. Yet while the numinous and the sublime may be closely related, they are still different and separate categories, a point that Otto himself stressed.[50] Nevertheless, I posit that the strong similarities between these two concepts, which Otto accepts, give us sufficient reason to introduce Otto's ideas in this discussion on the sublime. Furthermore, given their qualitative resemblances, the experience of the sublime can turn into the experience of the numinous, and vice versa. And based on a broad definition of the sublime and certain interpretations of the numinous, both concepts become even closer in their similarities.

Otto states that the numinous is a non-rational, non-sensory experience or feeling whose "immediate and primary reference [is] an object outside the self" and so is felt to be objective.[51] It presents itself as *ganz Andere* ('wholly other'), a mental state "perfectly *sui generis* and irreducible to any other",[52] and incomparable. *Sui generis* means the numinous is in a class by itself and thus unique. These combined features of *sui generis* and irreducibility, Otto argued, meant that the numinous cannot be defined in terms of other concepts and experiences (which makes the numinous an ineffable experience). Instead, he claimed, someone has to be "guided and led on by consideration and discussion of the matter through the ways of his own mind, until he reach the point at which 'the numinous' in him perforce begins to stir ... In other words, our X cannot, strictly speaking, be taught, it can only be evoked, awakened in the mind".[53]

Otto maintained that this conception of 'the holy' is notably different from the idea of the holy involving moral perfection. The numinous is a mysterious feeling that lies outside the spheres of rational thinking and morality. It is a characteristic of the religious experience that Otto believed to be *a priori*: "The facts of the numinous consciousness point ... therefore to a hidden substantive force, from which the religious ideas and feelings are formed, which lies in the mind independently of sense experience."[54] In clarifying this point, Otto refers to a passage from William James's *The Varieties of Religious Experience*:

It is as if there were in human consciousness *a sense of reality, a feeling of objective presence, a perception* of what we may call *'something there,'* more deep and more general than any of the special and particular 'senses' by which the current psychology supposes existent realities to be originally revealed.[55]

The divine reality, a mind-independent reality, is disclosed directly in the numinous feeling. The philosopher Mark Wynn contends that this affective response — the numinous — can present the divine reality to the individual because of its distinctive phenomenological character: the experience of the numinous is unequivocally unlike any other human experience.[56] However, you do not have to believe in divinity to experience the numinous. Otto believed that there is an innate capacity in humans to have this religious experience,[57] but it does need to be evoked or brought into consciousness in some manner (such as through the use of psychedelics). An atheist who encounters the divine may decide that the experience arises from an *internal* reality, not an *external* one; it could be an experience of *self*, not of *other*. Nonetheless, this leaves us with the question of how to explain this felt divine presence, and its qualities, in naturalistic terms.

We can put aside the questions of precisely how or why the numinous arises or what Otto means exactly when he says the object of the numinous is 'outside the self'. These topics warrant separate in-depth discussions (and they have also been explored by others, such as Henning Nörenberg).[58] For the relevance of this essay, it is worth focusing on the elements of the numinous that align it with the sublime.

Otto writes that while the numinous "may at times come sweeping like a gentle tide, pervading the mind with a tranquil mood of deepest worship", it "can sink to an almost grisly horror and shuddering" and may "become the hushed, trembling, and speechless humility of the creature in the presence of — whom or what? In the presence of that which is a *mystery* inexpressible and above all creatures".[59] Here we have a description of the numinous that bears a similarity to the sublime: the numinous involves an emotional response of being overwhelmed in the face of that which is far greater than oneself. The writer C.S. Lewis elucidated the experience of the numinous in his book *The Problem of Pain* (1940):

Suppose you were told there was a tiger in the next room: you would know that you were in danger and would probably feel fear. But if you were told "There is a ghost in the next room," and believed it, you would feel, indeed, what is often called fear, but of a different kind. It would not be based on the knowledge of danger, for no one is primarily afraid of what a ghost may do to him, but of the mere fact that it is a ghost. It is "uncanny" rather than dangerous, and the special kind of fear it excites may be called Dread. With the Uncanny one has reached the fringes of the Numinous. Now suppose that you were told simply "There is a mighty spirit in the room," and believed it. Your feelings would then be even less like the mere fear of danger: but the disturbance would be profound. You would feel wonder and a certain shrinking — a sense of inadequacy to cope with such a visitant and of prostration before it — an emotion which might be expressed in Shakespeare's words "Under it my genius is rebuked." This feeling may be described as awe, and the object which excites it as the *Numinous*.[60]

In this description, we also see parallels with the previous philosophical expositions of the sublime. We can highlight the experience of profound 'disturbance', 'wonder', 'a sense of shrinking', and 'a sense of inadequacy', all common elements of the sublime, although Lewis underscores that the feeling of awe is what is elicited by the numinous, which is the object. In any case, in Otto's threefold definition of the numinous, we find further similarities with the sublime. He argues it is *mysterium tremendum et fascinans* (a fearful and fascinating mystery), a mystery before which the individual feels both terror and fascination, or a sense of being both repelled and attracted.[61] [62] This paradoxical quality of the numinous is the same mixing of opposites that we have seen as characteristic of the sublime. The numinous is *mysterium* because it is 'wholly other', unlike anything we have ever experienced or will experience. In Otto's words, the mystery of the numinous evokes in us a "blank wonder, an astonishment that strikes us dumb, amazement absolute".[63]

The numinous is *mysterium tremendum* and *mysterium fascinosum* at the same time. It is *mysterium tremendum* (a terrifying mystery) because the wholly other fills us with dread; we shudder at the overpowering nature of the wholly other — we are terrified of its absolute unapproachability, might, and majesty. Otto spoke of the "wrath" of God and an intense sense of "energy" and "urgency" when describing this fearful aspect of the numinous.[64] [65] He thought of the *mysterium tremendum* as a "consuming fire",[66] a phrase referring to God's nature that is found in the Book of Hebrews in the New Testament.

We can see how the numinous seems to match the qualities of the Sun: unapproachable, able to consume us with fire and destroy us, and supremely majestic. It is, of course, no coincidence that the Sun was worshipped and conceptualised as a deity in myriad cultures throughout recorded history. In *The Idea of the Holy*, Otto also said that the numinous involves what he called 'creature-feeling', which is "the emotion of a creature, submerged and overwhelmed by its own nothingness in contrast to that which is supreme above all creatures".[67] Searle in *Sunshine* likewise recounts the sense of his nothingness following long periods of staring at the Sun: "Remember, Capa, we're just stardust." This ties in with Kant and Schopenhauer's account of the sublime as the measuring of our little selves against the forces of nature (or against the "apparent almightiness of nature", as Kant puts it).[68] This parallels the sense of omnipotence of the divine that Otto is referring to, which many people encounter during religious experiences, including those occasioned by psychedelics.

Otto states that the *tremendum* involves a shuddering "more than 'natural', ordinary fear. It implies that the mysterious is beginning to loom before the mind, to touch the feelings".[69] When face to face with the *mysterium tremendum*, Otto says that the soul "held speechless, trembles inwardly to the farthest fibre of its being"[70] and that there is a feeling of "horror in the real sense of the word".[71]

Coexisting with the *mysterium tremendum* is the *mysterium fascinosum* (a fascinating mystery), which has a potent charm and attractiveness, despite the fear, dread, and terror it engenders. This is because the divine also appears as merciful and loving. The numinous attracts and allures us with an irresistible force. When an individual completely contacts the divine, Otto pinpoints this as an "exuberant" level of fascination and a mystical "moment".[72]

Captain Kaneda in *Sunshine* experiences something similar in his unwavering fascination with the mystery and power of the Sun. After embarking on a spacewalk with Capa to repair damages to the craft, Kaneda realises the task will take longer than expected and so sends Capa back to the ship while he finishes the repair. He unfortunately does not have time to return to the safety of the craft before the Sun comes into view, and his obliteration becomes imminent. Accepting his fate, he turns to face the Sun coming into view, allowing him to get a glimpse of it, up close, with no protective filter. The prospect is simply too enticing to resist. As the roaring light and heat of the Sun approaches and begins to envelop Kaneda, he becomes petrified and immobile. Searle asks him from inside the ship, "Kaneda! What do you see?" There is no response. Kaneda perhaps saw what no living thing could imagine seeing. Applying Otto's thought to this deeply moving part of the film, we can say that Kaneda was stunned into silence and stupor by the majesty and annihilating power of the Sun.

## The Psychedelic Mystical Experience

Huxley was strongly influenced by Otto, especially his idea that the numinous lies at the heart of all religions. Huxley echoed this in his defence of the *perennial philosophy*, a perspective in the philosophy of religion, which states that all of the world's religions and spiritual traditions, throughout history, share a single, universal truth or origin. Huxley defined this view in his book *The Perennial Philosophy* (1945):

[T]he metaphysic that recognises a divine Reality substantial to the world of things and lives and minds; the psychology that finds in the soul something similar to, or even identical with, divine Reality; the ethic that places man's final end in the knowledge of the immanent and transcendent Ground of all being — the thing is immemorial and universal. Rudiments of the Perennial Philosophy may be found among the traditionary lore of primitive peoples in every region of the world, and in its fully developed forms it has a place in every one of the higher religions. A version of this Highest Common Factor in all preceding and subsequent theologies was first committed to writing more than twenty-five centuries ago, and since that time the inexhaustible theme has been treated again and again, from the standpoint of every religious tradition and in all the principal languages of Asia and Europe.[73]

This position of perennialism, however, has since been criticised as distorting, essentialising, and elitist. Many philosophers and scholars argue it fails to recognise the pluralism of religious and spiritual traditions as well as the ways in which cultural conditioning influences mystical experiences.[74] For example, many people's mystical experiences are not characterised by identification or unification with an ultimate divine reality but instead are dualistic in nature: they involve dyadic encounters and interactions with deities, supernatural beings, entities, or a divine presence. This presents a challenge to the dominant narrative of mystical experience, as applied in psychedelic research, which focuses on unitive experiences and neglects the spiritual significance of altered states involving duality, relation, and interaction.

In *The Doors of Perception*, Huxley also refers to Otto's notion of the *mysterium tremendum*:

The literature of religious experience abounds in references to the pains and terrors overwhelming those who have come, too suddenly, face to face with some manifestation of the *mysterium tremendum*. In theological language, this fear is due to the in-compatibility between man's egotism and the divine purity, between man's self-aggravated separateness and the infinity of God.[75]

Huxley said that he was "not so foolish as to equate what happens under the influence of mescalin or of any other drug, prepared or in the future preparable, with the realization of the end and ultimate purpose of human life: Enlightenment, the Beatific Vision".[76] (In Christian theology, the beatific vision means seeing God face to face; it is direct communication with God, which brings about ultimate happiness.) It is debatable whether a psychedelic experience can ever genuinely count as enlightenment or the beatific vision. Nonetheless, we can still certainly find personal accounts of psychedelic experiences that tie into Otto's concept of the numinous, which is a more religious or spiritual version of sublimity. Take, for example, this individual's earth-shattering experience with the potent psychedelic DMT:

> I began to weep like I never have in my life. The sobbing tears of pure, total bliss ripped themselves from me like a jet passing the speed of sound and tearing the sky to shreds. I thought I would fairly break like a twig from such light filling my being. It was more than I could have ever imagined ... the beauty, the power. It filled me and sang with every molecule of my body, every facet of my mind, every piece of my soul. All were in perfect harmony, and for a single moment I knew true, undeniable divinity.[77]

During many people's most profound psychedelic experiences, there are encounters with this unimaginably powerful divinity. Whether you want to think of psychedelics as stimulating the neural correlates of religious experience[78] or altering one's consciousness so that it can tune into an objective divine reality, or both, the quality of the experience itself is what matters. Indeed, many people's experience of the divine in the psychedelic state correlates with the phenomenology described by Otto.

One study compared 'God encounter experiences' occasioned by psilocybin, LSD, ayahuasca, and DMT with the same experiences that occurred naturally. The researchers found that most participants in both groups (three-quarters) reported that their contact with this divine other or 'ultimate reality' was among the most personally meaningful and spiritually significant experiences of their lives, and about one-third indicated it was the single-most such experience. Most respondents (two-thirds) who identified as an atheist before the experience did not identify as such after it. This could be explained by the fact that a large majority in both groups deemed the experience to be more real than everyday normal reality.

In addition, more than half of each group said that the being or reality they encountered had the attributes of consciousness, benevolence, intelligence, sacredness, eternality, and omniscience (all-knowingness). But this did not mean the experience was wholly positive or blissful. Indeed, one-third of participants in both groups rated their encounter with the divine "as among the 5 most psychologically challenging experiences of their lives, with about 15% indicating that it was the single most psychologically challenging experience of their lifetime".[79] As the researchers point out,

> That such experiences may be both attractive and extremely difficult is consistent with the classic description of the dual nature of encounters with 'the holy' both as "mysterium tremendum" (referring to its awfulness and absolute overpoweringness) and "mysterium fascinans" (referring

to its fascinating and attractive nature) by the theologian Rudolf Otto. Likewise, that psychedelic experiences can involve both positive emotion including transcendence as well as highly distressing feelings such as fear and insanity have been well-documented.[80]

Meeting divinity under the influence of psychedelics can be a truly overwhelming and astonishing experience. The titanic presence and sheer power of the divine can bring you to your knees, blind you with radiant light, and leave you utterly shaken to the core. There is an emotional quality like that associated with Kaneda's direct view of the Sun, except there is no risk of physical death. As in Otto's picture of the numinous, there can be a feeling of being insignificant and completely vulnerable.

The divine might be experienced as infinite love and knowledge or as an eternal and omnipotent (all-powerful) being. While this can, on the one hand, be an ecstatic encounter, coming in contact with the force and magnitude of the divine can also be overwhelming and somewhat distressing. Such an experience is, after all, of a qualitative nature so far beyond the normal realm of human experience. There is an extremity of qualities and traits (e.g. presence, power, knowing, and benevolence) in the divine that no concepts or words can properly convey. This kind of sublimity is, therefore, ineffable — a defining feature of the mystical experience, according to thinkers such as James and the psychiatrist Walter Pahnke.[81]

One work of fiction in which we find descriptions that match the numinous is Olaf Stapledon's sci fi novel *Star Maker* (1937). It tells the story of a nameless human narrator who leaves his body and travels through the vastness of the cosmos. The narrator visits other planets, civilisations, stars, and galaxies, with his journey culminating in a mystical encounter with the creator of the universe: the 'Star Maker'. This part of the book certainly parallels the numinous and the sublime, so it is worthwhile highlighting the author's descriptions of this "supreme moment of the cosmos".[82]

Firstly, the narrator experiences this divine presence as part of himself but also as distinctly separate from him, "as a being indeed other than my conscious self, objective to my vision, yet as in the depth of my own nature; as indeed, myself, though infinitely more than myself".[83] Both the otherness and infinite nature of the Star Maker are imposing qualities that people will similarly ascribe to the divine presence that manifests in the psychedelic experience. Just as Kant and Schopenhauer assert that the sublime follows the idea of the infinite, in either the mathematical or dynamical sublime, so too will this unique feeling arise in the context of psychedelic-induced divinity.

In expressing the exceptional power of the Star Maker, Stapledon compares this "infinite spirit" to "an overwhelmingly brilliant point, a star, a sun more powerful than all suns together".[84] Many people who take psychedelics report this kind of astonishing brightness and intensity of presence. There is this blinding, brilliant light that is perceived as divine, as radiating divine qualities. This light is also overwhelming, which is a core characteristic of both the numinous and the sublime.

In addition, Stapledon stresses the ineffability of the meeting with the Star Maker: "Barren, barren and trivial are these words. But not barren the experience."[85] The experience of the numinous and the sublime induced by psychedelics are, likewise, inexpressible in nature, although this indescribability seems even more pronounced in the case of the numinous since it has no reference point. In the case of psychedelic sublimity, one can at least refer to other instances of the sublime, such as those experienced in nature, which may go some way in illustrating the essence of the experience.

Is there, however, not some vital difference between psychedelic-induced sublimity and the non-drug-induced equivalent? This question has certainly led to some disagreements. The philosopher Walter Terence Stace and religion scholar Huston Smith, for instance, advanced the 'principle of causal indifference', which states that if two experiences are phenomenologically identical, then we cannot conclude that one of them is genuine and the other one is not, regardless of what caused these experiences to arise. They defended this principle in response to the claim that drug-occasioned experiences cannot be classed as genuine mystical experiences.[86]

Indeed, it is clear now — based on a wealth of peer-reviewed research and anecdotal reports — that psychedelic-induced mystical experiences are as authentic as those that occur spontaneously or as a result of meditation, fasting, prayer, or a near-death experience. As the researchers conducting the study on encounters with God found, the "descriptive details, interpretation, and consequences" of both naturally occurring experiences and psychedelic-induced experiences are "markedly similar".[87] Furthermore, with Stace's and Smith's principle of causal indifference in mind, I argue there is every reason to suppose that psychedelic-induced sublimity is as genuine as any other experience of sublimity.

When considering the connection between psychedelics and the sublime, we should keep in mind that psychedelics are magnifiers. They magnify whatever emotional state an individual is in, or they stimulate emotional states that are indubitably more intense than those that occur in waking consensus reality. One may experience profound bliss and ecstasy instead of happiness and joy, as well as the negative counterparts: extreme levels of despair and dread instead of mere pessimism and sadness.

Yet if psychedelics are magnifiers of mental phenomena, psychedelic sublimity could potentially be more powerful than non-psychedelic sublimity. Say that you experience the sublime in the way exemplified by Addison, Burke, Kant, and

Schopenhauer, but that you are also under the influence of a psychedelic like LSD or psilocybin. You might be watching an avalanche, hiking in the mountains, looking up at the star-filled night sky, or contemplating infinity or eternity, but in a state of mind altered by psychedelics, you could experience the sublime to a degree far beyond that imagined by these philosophers. This would be consistent with Schopenhauer's assertion that the sublime is experienced in degrees.

## Research on Awe and the Value of Psychedelic Sublimity

Evidence from a plethora of studies has demonstrated that the experience of awe — or the sublime — results in all kinds of physiological, psychological, and social effects.[88] On the physiological side of things, awe is accompanied by 'goosebumps'; the sensation of chills; and changes in heart rate, skin conductance, facial movements, and posture.

In line with philosophers such as Burke and Kant, a 2014 study by Tomohiro Ishizu and Semir Zeki showed that the sublime is not fear exactly since the brain activity observed during the experience of awe does not look the same as the activity you would see in a person experiencing fear, pain, or threat.[89] This is because, as Burke and Kant theorised, the object of the sublime is vast and powerful but we nevertheless feel safe in coming into contact with it, as we may be at a safe distance (e.g. watching a hurricane from afar). Clewis and a team of psychologists have put forward three reasons why this is (partly) a pleasurable experience. The three sources of pleasure are "the expansion of the imagination; belonging to a whole larger than us; and the rising above everyday affairs".[90]

Scientific research has, however, also contradicted some philosophising about the sublime. As a case in point, Ishizu and Zeki found that a person experiencing awe is focused on the external world, with awareness drawn away from oneself (brain regions dealing with self-awareness are deactivated). There is a felt sense of being part of something bigger, such as the vast object of the sublime or even the universe or nature as a whole. This contrasts with the Kantian perspective, which says the sublime is an experience based on recognising the superior power of one's own reason in the face of the magnitude or power of nature. For Kant, the sublime explicitly involves self-awareness, whereas what actually seems to be happening in the brain suggests otherwise. Ishizu and Zeki's fMRI brain scans of people experiencing the sublime also revealed — in line with Kant's thinking this time — that the imagination is activated. The science is thus in partial agreement with Kant's aesthetics.

The psychological effects of awe include the following:

- The 'small self' (the feeling of being small or insignificant relative to one's surroundings)
- Increased humility
- Cognitive accommodation (a concept developed by the psychologist Jean Piaget, referring to the process of new experiences changing one's worldview)
- The sense that time is plentiful
- Increased connectedness (to other people and humanity as a whole)
- Improvements in positive mood, well-being, and life satisfaction
- Decreased materialism
- Increased spiritual or religious feelings
- An embracement of scientific thinking and learning

Many psychological changes are clearly going on, then, when an individual is in a state of sublimity. What is perhaps most vital about these psychological studies, though, is they underscore that these positive changes are *lasting*. The experience of the sublime has long-term effects on the personality and well-being of the individual.

There are also pro-social effects associated with the experience of awe, such as greater levels of kindness and generosity. For example, individuals who have experienced awe are more willing to help others (which researchers hypothesise may partly come from the psychological sense of time being more plentiful and, therefore, more available for others). Awe has, moreover, been linked to increases in scores of agreeableness, perspective taking, and empathy. These pro-social effects, researchers note, could additionally be related to the 'small self' experienced in a state of awe, as this can encourage people to focus less on themselves.

Clewis says that, despite these psychological findings, he is "ambivalent about whether we should see awe as involving a kind of epiphany" and warns against the tendency to *define* awe as a life-changing and transformative experience. He argues that this "seems to raise the bar too high, rendering awe too rare, even too significant". It might be better, Clewis suggests, "to see the sublime/awe as Burke and Kant did: as a rich experience running parallel to beauty, but still aesthetic and imaginative, as beauty is".[91] We may want to resist, then, referring to sublimity as an epiphanous, monumental experience with radical implications for one's personal growth (this might more accurately characterise the numinous, which brings into focus an important difference between the immanent sublime and transcendent sublime).

To supplement Schopenhauer's idea that the sublime occurs in degrees, the ripple effects of the sublime may exist in degrees too. Psychological and pro-social benefits can be short-, medium-, or long-term, and there can also be differences in the magnitude or significance of the benefits. Contrary to Clewis's argument, however, it is clear from the available body of evidence that awe has the *capacity* to lead to life-altering, positive changes in the individual. We could say that this tendency of the emotional experience depends on certain factors, such as the type of awe and how it is experienced, interpreted, integrated, and applied to everyday life. Awe, it turns out, is a highly nuanced and complex emotion.

When looking at most of the research on awe, there is no mention of psychedelic-induced awe, so how do we know that the findings equally translate to the psychedelic experience? The first point of consideration is that there is *some* research that has examined awe in the context of psychedelics specifically.

For example, a 2018 paper suggests that the "classic psychedelic-occasioned mystical experience is characterized by profound awe".[92] Peter Hendricks, the paper's author and a clinical psychologist at the University of Alabama at Birmingham, believes awe may be a critical emotional component of the psychedelic experience, one that helps to foster compassion, empathy, and overall well-being. Furthermore, by applying Stace's and Smith's principle of causal indifference, we can say that the subjective quality of awe is what causes life-altering changes. It does not matter what causes the experience. Whether you have the experience in the Himalayas or in a room while on LSD, the lasting positive effects may be the same or similar.

A final point to make, or at least reiterate in a more research-based context, is that there is a dark side to the sublime. In a 2017 paper, a team of researchers explored the negative aspect of awe, which they say had rarely been emphasised by previous research, even though philosophers have long pointed to the fear, terror, and dread that are central to this emotional experience. These researchers found that there is a negative variation of awe that arises when an individual is confronted with vast, threatening stimuli (e.g. tornadoes, a terrorist attack, or a wrathful god). They state that "people experience this type of awe with regularity".[93]

Another important result from this study was that this "threat-based variant of awe" differed from other, more positive types of awe in terms of "underlying appraisals, subjective experience, physiological correlates, and consequences for well-being".[94] Threat-based awe experiences feature a greater degree of fear and increased sympathetic autonomic arousal (which contributes to the fight-or-flight response to a perceived danger or threat). Positive awe, in contrast, is associated with increased parasympathetic arousal (the part of the autonomic nervous system that helps to calm the body down). Positive awe leads to enhanced feelings of well-being, whereas negative awe does not. The researchers discovered that this latter outcome is partly explained by increases in the individual's feeling of powerlessness.[95]

This distinction between positive awe and negative awe may complicate the definition of the sublime that various philosophers have worked on. Nevertheless, the burgeoning research on awe is just further proof that we should be wary about narrowly defining the sublime. It is, after all, a multifarious emotion, often varying in its quality and intensity. To further illustrate this, we can point to psychedelic experiences that involve negative awe rather than positive awe.

You will recall that the numinous features the *mysterium tremendum*, as a result of the will, power, and presence of a wrathful God — and this inspires trembling, shuddering, and a feeling of being overpowered and overwhelmed. Such terror is also mixed with wonder and positive feelings. Yet, based on the sublime's multifaceted nature, we should grant that the different qualities of the numinous or the sublime do not always appear in equal measure. In psychedelic-induced sublimity or divinity, for instance, fear and fascination do not necessarily exist in equal parts. There can be varying degrees of each. Hence, in a state of psychedelic sublimity, there can be a preponderance of the negative aspects of awe: fear, terror, dread, anxiety, and powerlessness. In the numinous occasioned by psychedelics, the divine may be perceived as predominantly terrifying — appearing as a malignant or evil presence.

Many people who have negative DMT experiences will often report encounters with evil or demonic entities,[96] rather than the loving — yet still overwhelming — entities encountered during positive experiences. It is certainly possible to come face-to-face with a 'wholly other' that is wholly malevolent, and during and after such a psychedelic experience, there may be no improvements in well-being. Instead, there could be a worsening of well-being. Such experiences can entail terror and panic of the sort that, if not dealt with appropriately, may lead to short- or long-term negative effects.

Moreover, psychedelic-induced negative awe does not have to concern itself with a being or presence greater than oneself. The negative awe may relate to the visual or visionary aspect of the experience (e.g. being in a chaotic space or floating helplessly in a cosmic void) as well as the cognitive aspect (e.g. contemplating infinity or eternity), with either inspiring more terror than elation. Such psychedelic phenomenology may rightly be classified as awe, in the negative sense. But unlike the way in which awe is usually framed by psychologists (in a positive sense), these distressing psychedelic journeys can lead to negative short-term effects on well-being. In some instances, these negative effects can persist for a longer period of time, although any disturbances in well-being, personality, and functioning are subject to remedy, through integration, guidance, and support.

There is great value to be gained from psychedelic-induced sublimity. But given how much this phenomenon can vary, any individual using a psychedelic would be wise to have the experience in the optimal setting and with the right kind of mindset. This might include, if possible, having a psychedelic experience while under the supervision of a guide. In this scenario, even if one did quickly get into a panic-ridden state of negative awe, a guide (or even just someone you trust) could help you to steer the experience in the other direction, allowing you to swing towards a more balanced kind of awe or positive awe.

When used sensibly and in thoughtful contexts, psychedelics may reliably lead to the experience of the sublime that is most conducive to overall well-being and enduring positive changes. Of course, given the illicit status of most psychedelics in most of the world, the vast majority of people cannot have their psychedelic experience supervised by a trained therapist (unless they enrol in a clinical trial or seek out an underground guide). Many other people will simply be put off psychedelics due to their illegal or stigmatised status. This is a disappointing fact we have to contend with, for as we know, the experience of the sublime or the numinous under the influence of psychedelics can be one of the most profound and life-changing experiences available to us.

But the tide is slowly turning. We are in the midst of a psychedelic renaissance, with renewed scientific and public interest in the therapeutic potential of psychedelics. Indeed, these compounds are increasingly gaining mainstream acceptance. When legal — as a treatment; as regulated, commercially sold products; to cultivate at home; or to pick in the wild — psychedelics will give more people the opportunity to experience the sublime and reap the benefits that this entails.

## Endnotes

1.  Sjöstedt-Hughes, P. (2015). *Noumenautics*, p. 33. Falmouth: Psychedelic Press UK.
2.  Brody, J. (1958). *Boileau and Longinus*, p. 54. Geneva: Droz.
3.  Leitch, V.B. (2001). 'Longinus, first century C.E.' in *The Norton Anthology of Theory and Criticism*, p. 135. New York: Norton & Co.
4.  Morris D.B. (1972). *The Religious Sublime: Christian Poetry and Critical Tradition in 18th-Century England*, p. 37. Lexington, KY: University Press of Kentucky.
5.  Longinus (c. 100 CE). *On the Sublime*, Poetry Foundation website, 13 October, 2009. https://www.poetryfoundation. org/articles/69397/from-on-the-sublime

6. Leitch, V.B. (2001). 'Longinus, first century C.E.' in *The Norton Anthology of Theory and Criticism*, p. 136. New York: Norton & Co.

7. Doran, R. (2015). *The Theory of the Sublime from Longinus to Kant*, pp. 9–10. Cambridge: Cambridge University Press.

8. Ibid., p. 41.

9. Ibid., p. 10.

10. Ibid., p. 125.

11. Dennis, J. (1688). *The Critical Works of John Dennis*, Vol. 1 p. 381. Edited by Hooker, E.N. Baltimore: Johns Hopkins University Press, 1943.

12. Ibid., p. 380.

13. Clewis, R. (2019). 'Awe and Sublimity'. *Philosophy Now*, 132, June/July, pp. 20–21.

14. Addison, J. (1753). *Remarks on Several Parts of Italy: In the Years 1701, 1702, 1703*, p. 261. London: J. and R. Tonson and S. Draper.

15. Addison, J. (1712). 'The Pleasures of the Imagination', *The Spectator*, 412, 23 June. http://sublime.nancyholt.com/Addison/index.html

16. Burke, E. (1757). *A Philosophical Inquiry into the Origin of Our Ideas of the Sublime and Beautiful*, p. 99. London: Thomas McLean, 1823.

17. Ibid., pp. 122–123.

18. Ibid., p. 45.

19. Milton, J. (1667). *Paradise Lost*, Book II, p. 62. Oxford: Oxford University Press, 2005.

20. Doran, R. (2015). *The Theory of the Sublime from Longinus to Kant*, p. 148. Cambridge: Cambridge University Press.

21. Burke, E. (1757). *A Philosophical Inquiry into the Origin of Our Ideas of the Sublime and Beautiful*, p. 65. London: Thomas McLean, 1823.

22. Ibid., p. 37.

23. Ibid., p. 46.

24. Kant, I. (1790). *Critique of Judgment*, p. 64. Translated by Bernard, J.H. New York: Cosimo, 2007.

25. Ibid., p. 61.

26. Ibid., p. 81

27. Ibid., p. 75.

28. Ibid., p. 63.

29. Ibid., p. 75.

30. Ibid., p. 62.

31. Ibid., p. 70.

32. Schopenhauer, A. (1818). *The World as Will and Representation*, Vol. 1, p. 225. Translated and edited by Norman, J., Welchman, A., and Janaway, C. Cambridge: Cambridge University Press, 2010.

33. Ibid., pp. 228–229.

34. Shapshay, S. (2018). 'At once tiny and huge: what is this feeling we call the 'sublime'?', *Aeon*, 4 December. https://aeon.co/ideas/at-once-tiny-and-huge-what-is-this-feeling-we-call-sublime

35. Schopenhauer, A. (1818). *The World as Will and Representation*, Vol. 1, p. 230. Translated and edited by Norman, J., Welchman, A., and Janaway, C. Cambridge: Cambridge University Press, 2010.

36. Shapshay, S. (2018). 'At once tiny and huge: what is this feeling we call the 'sublime'?', *Aeon*, 4 December. https://aeon.co/ideas/at-once-tiny-and-huge-what-is-this-feeling-we-call-sublime

37. Schopenhauer, A. (1818). *The World as Will and Representation*, Vol. 1, p. 226. Translated and edited by Norman, J., Welchman, A., and Janaway, C. Cambridge: Cambridge University Press, 2010.

38. Shapshay, S. (2012). 'Schopenhauer's Transformation of the Kantian Sublime'. *Kantian Review*, 17(3), pp. 478–511.

39. Vandenabeele, B. (2015). *The Sublime in Schopenhauer's Philosophy*, p. 124. London: Palgrave Macmillan.

40. Huxley, A. (1954). *The Doors of Perception*. https://maps.org/images/pdf/books/HuxleyA1954TheDoorsOfPerception.pdf

41. Bisbee, C.C., Bisbee, P., Dyck, E., Farrell, P., Sexton, J., and Spisak, J.W. (2018). *Psychedelic Prophets: The Letters of Aldous Huxley and Humphry Osmond*, pp. 265–266. Montreal: McGill-Queen's University Press.

42. Rucker, J.H.J., Iliff, J., and Nutt, D.J. (2018). 'Psychiatry & the psychedelic drugs. Past, present & future'. *Neuropharmacology*, 142, pp. 200–218.

43. Bisbee, C.C., Bisbee, P., Dyck, E., Farrell, P., Sexton, J., and Spisak, J.W. (2018). *Psychedelic Prophets: The Letters of Aldous Huxley and Humphry Osmond*, p. 267. Montreal: McGill-Queen's University Press.

44. Ibid., p. 266.

45. Szalavitz, M. (2012). 'Magic Mushrooms Expand the Mind By Dampening Brain Activity', *Time*, 24 January. https://healthland.time.com/2012/01/24/magic-mushrooms-expand-the-mind-by-dampening-brain-activity/

46. Kant, I. (1781). *Critique of Pure Reason*, p. 426. Translated and edited by Guyer, P. and Wood, A.W. Cambridge: Cambridge University Press, 1998.

47. Clewis, R. (2019). 'Awe and Sublimity'. *Philosophy Now*, 132, June/July, pp. 20–21.

48. Otto, R. (1917). *The Idea of the Holy*, p. 7. Translated by Harvey, J.W. London: Oxford University Press, 1923.

49. Ibid., p. 26.

50. Ibid., pp. 41–42.

51. Ibid., pp. 10–11.

52. Ibid., p. 7.

53. Ibid.

54. Ibid., pp. 113–114.

55. Ibid., p. 10, quoting James, W. (1902). *The Varieties of Religious Experience: A Study in Human Nature*, p. 58. New York: Longmans, Green & Co.

56. Wynn, M. (2022). 'Phenomenology of Religion', Stanford Encyclopedia of Philosophy', 2 November. https://plato.stanford.edu/entries/phenomenology-religion/

57. Otto, R. (1917). *The Idea of the Holy*, p. 61. Translated by Harvey, J.W. London: Oxford University Press, 1923.

58. Nörenberg, H. (2017). 'The Numinous, the Ethical, and the Body. Rudolf Otto's "The Idea of the Holy" Revisited'. *Open Theology*, 3(1), pp. 546–564.

59. Otto, R. (1917). *The Idea of the Holy*, pp. 12–13. Translated by Harvey, J.W. London: Oxford University Press, 1923.

60. Lewis, C.S. (1940). *The Problem of Pain*, pp. 4–5. New York: The Macmillan Company, 1947.

61. Otto, R. (1917). *The Idea of the Holy*, pp. 12–13. Translated by Harvey, J.W. London: Oxford University Press, 1923.

62. Ibid., pp. 31–36.

63. Ibid., p. 26.

64. Ibid., p. 18.

65. Ibid., p. 23.

66. Ibid., p. 24.

67. Ibid., p. 10.

68. Kant, I. (1790). *Critique of Judgment*, p. 75. Translated by Bernard, J.H. New York: Cosimo, 2007.

69. Otto, R. (1917). *The Idea of the Holy*, p. 15. Translated by Harvey, J.W. London: Oxford University Press, 1923.

70. Ibid., p. 17.

71. Ibid., p. 15.

72. Ibid., p. 36.

73. Huxley, A. (1945). *The Perennial Philosophy*, p. 1. London: Chatto & Windus, 1947.

74. Evans, J. (2020). 'What can we learn from the perennial philosophy of Aldous Huxley?', *Aeon*, 19 February. https://aeon.co/essays/what-can-we-learn-from-the-perennial-philosophy-of-aldous-huxley

75. Huxley, A. (1954). *The Doors of Perception*. https://maps.org/images/pdf/books/HuxleyA1954TheDoorsOfPerception.pdf

76. Ibid.

77. Anonymous (2014). DMT Nexus, 31 December. https://www.dmt-nexus.me/forum/default.aspx?g=posts&m=584325

78. Azari, N.P., Nickel, J., Wunderlich, G., Niedeggen, M., Hefter, H., Tellmann, L., Herzog, H., Stoerig, P., Birnbacher, D., and Seitz, R.J. (2001). 'Neural correlates of religious experience'. *European Journal of Neuroscience*, 13(8), pp. 1649–1652.

79. Griffiths, R.R., Hurwitz, E.S., Davis, A.K., Johnson, M.W., and Jesse, R. (2019). 'Survey of subjective "God encounter experiences": Comparisons among naturally occurring experiences and those occasioned by the classic psychedelics psilocybin, LSD, ayahuasca, or DMT'. *PLoS One*, 14(4), Article: e0214377.

80. Ibid.

81. Greyson, B. (2014). 'Congruence Between Near-Death and Mystical Experience'. *International Journal for the Psychology of Religion*, 24(4), pp. 298–310.

82. Stapledon, O. (1937). *Star Maker*. https://www.astro.sunysb.edu/fwalter/AST389/TEXTS/StarMaker.pdf

83. Ibid.

84. Ibid.

85. Ibid.

86. Cole-Turner, R. (2021). 'Psychedelic Epistemology: William James and the "Noetic Quality" of Mystical Experience'. *Religions*, 12, Article: 1058.

87. Griffiths, R.R., Hurwitz, E.S., Davis, A.K., Johnson, M.W., and Jesse, R. (2019). 'Survey of subjective "God encounter experiences": Comparisons among naturally occurring experiences and those occasioned by the classic

psychedelics psilocybin, LSD, ayahuasca, or DMT'. *PLoS One*, 14(4), Article: e0214377.

88. Allen, S. (2018). 'The Science of Awe', Greater Good Science Center, September. https://ggsc.berkeley.edu/images/uploads/GGSC-JTF_White_Paper-Awe_FINAL.pdf

89. Ishizu, T. and Zeki, S. (2014). 'A neurobiological inquiry into the origins of our experience of the sublime and beautiful'. *Frontiers in Human Neuroscience*, 8, Article: 891.

90. Clewis, R. (2019). 'Awe and Sublimity'. *Philosophy Now*, 132, June/July, pp. 20–21.

91. Ibid.

92. Hendricks, P.S. (2018). 'Awe: a putative mechanism underlying the effects of classic psychedelic-assisted psychotherapy'. *International Review of Psychiatry*, 30(4), pp. 331–342.

93. Gordon, A.M., Stellar, J.E., Anderson, C.L., McNeil, G.D., Loew, D., and Keltner, D. (2017). 'The dark side of the sublime: Distinguishing a threat-based variant of awe'. *Journal of Personality and Social Psychology*, 113(2), pp. 310–328.

94. Ibid.

95. Ibid.

96. Davis, A.K., Clifton, J.M., Weaver, E.G., Hurwitz, E.S., Johnson, M.W., and Griffiths, R.R. (2020). 'Survey of entity encounter experiences occasioned by inhaled *N,N*-dimethyltryptamine: Phenomenology, interpretation, and enduring effects'. *Journal of Psychopharmacology*, 34(9), pp. 1008–1020.

## Chapter 5

# Altered States, Asemic Writing, and Alien Symbols

*Asemic* means 'having no specific semantic content'. Asemic writing, then, refers to writing, letters, alphabets, symbols, and glyphs that are without semantic meaning but which are artistic in nature, and so they may have a meaning that derives from the intention and mindset of the artist or the interpretation and reaction of the viewer. Asemic writing, however, may be inspired by real, natural languages.

I have found myself drawn to the asemic, purely artistic dimension of imaginary languages. Language clearly has an aesthetic value independent of whether it is meaningful or not (I can find Arabic, Hebrew, and Sanskrit writing beautiful, even though I don't understand it). So it makes sense that people might have an impulse to construct imaginary languages, alphabets, glyphs, sigils, and runes that are non-functional. These artistic creations can, moreover, be incorporated into works of art — into drawings and paintings that feature this imaginary writing for aesthetic reasons. I would like to explore the drive to create asemic writing in more depth, including its more psychedelic and visionary varieties — these are the alien alphabets, runes, and glyphs that often appear in the psychedelic experience, which several artists have recreated.

## Asemic Writing and the Drive to Create Imaginary Languages

In 1997, the visual poets Tim Gaze and Jim Leftwich applied the term asemic to their quasi-calligraphic works, which they were sending to various poetry magazines at the time.[1] Although they coined asemic writing as a mode of expression to describe their own work, the term inspired a new generation of artists; and through the circulation of this art form on blogs in the late 1990s, it soon grew to become a global movement. Leftwich wrote the following in a letter to Gaze in 1997:

A seme is a unit of meaning, or the smallest unit of meaning (also known as a sememe, analogous with phoneme). An asemic text, then, might be involved with units of language for reasons other than that of producing meaning. As such, the asemic text would seem to be an ideal, an impossibility, but possibly worth pursuing for just that reason.[2]

In an interview for *Asymptote*, the writer and artist Michael Jacobson defines asemic writing as follows:

Personally, I think asemic writing is a wordless, open semantic form of writing that is international in its mission. How can writing be wordless, someone may ask. The secret is that asemic writing is a shadow, impression, and abstraction of conventional writing. It uses the constraints of writerly gestures and the full developments of abstract art to divulge its main purpose: total freedom beyond literary expression. The subcultural movement surrounding asemic writing is international because the creators of asemic works live all over the world. It's a global style of writing we are creating, with the creators of asemic works meeting up on the Internet to share our works and exchange ideas.[3]

Asemic writing can take on a variety of forms, but what defines an artistic creation as asemic is its resemblance to traditional writing and its abandonment of specific semantics and syntax. To Jacobson, "not all emotions can be expressed with words, and so asemic writing attempts to fill in the void,"[4] and the artist Christopher Skinner has described asemic writing and visual poetry as "different sides of the same coin".[5] On the other hand, not all asemic writing necessarily comes from the motive to express something meaningful. It can be done merely to create language-esque patterns that are aesthetically pleasing, which may take the form of abstract calligraphy or strange hieroglyphs, for example. Asemic writing can resemble — and be inspired by — a multitude of actual languages, including Asian, African, and Middle Eastern alphabets as well as ancient writing systems like Egyptian and Mayan hieroglyphics and the runes of Germanic peoples.

Some asemic writing, however, appears much more alien, otherworldly, and futuristic. It is intriguing that some writing stands out as *alien*, as if there is something that characterises it as *not of this world*. For example, some sci-fi comics and TV shows depict writing systems that we can imagine would be used by an intelligent species on another planet. Perhaps, then, there are certain artistic deviations from natural language that deviate to such a degree that they take on a distinct quality of alienness — these are forms that, for one reason or another, impress us with a fantastical notion of another world.

One of my favourite examples of asemic writing can be found in Luigi Serafini's *Codex Seraphinianus* (1981), an illustrated encyclopaedia of an imaginary world, replete with surreal flora, fauna, machines, clothing, customs, and architecture. The book is also full of the invented Serafinian script, written in a way that gives the appearance of annotations and descriptions. Members of the University of Oxford's Society of Bibliophiles previously tried to decrypt Serafinian; that was until Serafini delivered a talk at the society in 2009 and confirmed that the text is meaningless.[6] His talk was not published or recorded, but one of the attendees, Enrico Prodi, made some notes throughout the talk. Based on these notes, Serafini has the following to say about his invented script:

The book creates a feeling of illiteracy which, in turn, encourages imagination, like children seeing a book: they cannot yet read it, but they realise that it must make sense (and that it does in fact make sense to grown-ups) and imagine what its meaning must be…. The writing of the Codex is a writing, not a language, although it conveys the impression of being one. It looks like it means something, but it does not; it is free from the cage of a language and a syntax. It involves a visual process, not a linguistic process.[7]

To me, the writing system looks like a mixture of illegible English cursive and Arabic. The Codex was most likely inspired by the mysterious Voynich Manuscript, a fifteenth-century illustrated codex that is also written in an indecipherable language. (The Voynich Manuscript's text is widely considered to be asemic; both amateur and professional cryptographers have tried — and failed — to decipher it, so it could be untranslatable and meaningless.[8]) This script, known as 'Voynichese', is reminiscent of Sinhala and early Persian alphabets like Avestan and Pahlavi.

Another notable example of asemic writing comes from Hélène Smith (whose real name was Catherine-Elise Müller), a famous late nineteenth-century Swiss medium. She claimed to be able to communicate with Martians during séances and write out such communications in the Martian language, which she would then translate into French. The psychologist Théodore Flournoy took an interest in Smith, grew closely acquainted with her, and was present at many of her séances so that he could carry out research into her mediumship. Flournoy described one of these séances in his book *From India to the Planet Mars: A Study of a Case of Somnambulism with Glossolalia* (1900):

After various characteristic symptoms of the departure for Mars … Hélène went in a deep sleep…. [Léopold] informs us that she is en route towards Mars; that once arrived up there she understands the Martian spoken around her, although she has never learned it; that it is not he, Léopold, who will translate the Martian for us — not because he does not wish to do so, but because he cannot; that this translation is the performance of Esenale, who is actually disincarnate in space, but who has recently lived upon Mars, and also upon the earth, which permits him to act as interpreter.[9]

The historian Daniel Rosenberg clarifies who these other people are:

"Léopold" is a reincarnation of Joseph Balsamo, physician and lover to Marie Antoinette and Hélène Smith's primary spirit-guide. "Esenale" is a reincarnation of Alexis Mirbel, deceased son of one of the sitters in Smith's circle and primary interpreter of the Martian language.[10]

The scene described above is what Flournoy refers to as "the Martian cycle"[11]: these are séances where Smith would enter a trance state and journey to Mars. The trances were somnambulistic in nature, in that Smith appeared to enter a state of sleep combined with wakefulness. Flournoy believed that her automatic writing was a mere "romance of the subliminal imagination",[12] derived mainly from forgotten sources (for example, books she read as a child). He coined the term *cryptomnesia* to describe this phenomenon: when a forgotten memory returns without a subject recognising it as such, and instead he or she thinks of it as an original creation.[13]

The Surrealists dubbed Smith "the Muse of Automatic Writing",[14] in light of her practice of *automatic writing* (also called *psychography*), which refers to producing words in a trance-like state, involuntarily and unconsciously. Mediums like Smith believe such writing comes from psychic abilities, that the writing comes from a source outside of themselves.

The Surrealists took particular interest in automatism, which involves suppressing conscious control of the creative process, allowing material from the unconscious to spontaneously arise; and for this reason, they saw great value in automatic drawing and writing. In his *Manifesto of Surrealism* (1924), the French writer André Breton defined surrealism as

> Psychic automatism in its pure state, by which one proposes to express — verbally, by means of the written word, or in any other manner — the actual functioning of thought. Dictated by thought, in the absence of any control exercised by reason, exempt from any aesthetic or moral concern.[15]

The Surrealists thus saw automatic writing as revelatory. Scientists and sceptics have attempted to explain automatic writing — as well as how Ouija boards work — in terms of the ideomotor effect, which is an example of unconscious, involuntary movement. It refers to the process whereby a thought or mental image leads to a reflexive, automatic response from the body, which occurs without you consciously 'telling' your body to act in that way.[16] In any case, Smith seemed to have produced her asemic script while in this state of automatic writing.

Interestingly, Serafini stated during his talk at Oxford that the experience of writing his fabricated language was similar to automatic writing.[17] This makes sense, given the task of producing the Codex (it took Serafini two and a half years to complete it). It would have simply been too time-consuming to create over 300 pages of purely artistic text that appeared to encode a language, writing that looks so language-like that amateur cryptographers would try to decipher it and expend great effort in their attempts. In a 2007 phone interview for *El País*, Serafini described the Codex as water that gushed out of him, and in relation to his language, he said it was artistic but added, "I realized that it was coming out of the pencil on its own.... I made it up suddenly. It is a vision, a dream language. The mystery, for me, simply consists in the artistic act."[18] We may suppose, therefore, that he was able to compose his work in the aforementioned timeframe because the writing for him was like an automated act, requiring little to no conscious effort.

Automatic writing — whether you believe it is inspired by aliens, divine beings, spirits, or human creativity — is like the written form of glossolalia ('speaking in tongues'). The latter refers to unintelligible speech uttered in a trance state, which usually takes place in the context of religious worship, especially among Pentecostal and charismatic Christians. The creation of fake writing in an automatic state, like glossolalia, often has mystical connotations attached to it. In addition, it is comparable to other creative acts involving no or minimal conscious effort, such as musical improvisation, doodling, scribbling, and dreaming.

Asemic writing may arise from a spontaneous and organic artistic impulse, something you feel inclined to do without much forethought or plan. Putting pen to paper, movement occurs, in an experimental fashion, and then novel writing appears; yet the process is unguided — or guided by some unconscious force. Asemic writing is distinct from automatic writing (since asemic writing can be a highly conscious activity); although, I believe the two often go hand in hand. And in these instances, I think we need a new term to refer to the creative act. The term I propose is *pseudographia* (which literally means 'fake writing'). Pseudographia is asemic writing that is produced in an automatic way. It also seems to involve the unconscious drive to engage in such writing. I derive the term from *hypergraphia*, a behavioural condition — associated with temporal lobe epilepsy and certain mental health conditions — that is characterised by the intense desire to write and draw. (Pseudographia is not pathological, of course.)

## Gestures and the Origins of Writing

With the aim of connecting asemic writing to psychedelic altered states, I now want to explore the gestural nature of the former: how meaningless, language-like letters are scribbled unconsciously — issuing from the unconscious — as a form of *gesture*.

Related to this notion is the belief that asemic writing may shed light on the origins of writing. I will consider this hypothesis and the idea that psychedelic variations of this art form support it. I will then address the more radical hypothesis that it is not only spoken language that may find its origin in the psychedelic experience (as argued by the psychonaut Terence McKenna)[19] but written language as well, via the runes, glyphs, and symbols seen in psychedelic visions.

It will be helpful, first, to examine the ideas expressed in the essay *'The Gesture of Writing'* by the Brazilian Czech-born philosopher Vilém Flusser. It features in his collection of essays titled *Gestures* (1991), which examines the meaning of gestures in various human activities (e.g. speaking, destroying, painting, photographing, filming, listening to music, smoking, and telephoning). Flusser defines a gesture as "a movement of the body or of a tool attached to the body for which there is no satisfactory causal explanation".[20] In his essay on writing, he states,

To write means, of course, to perform an action by which a material (for instance chalk, or ink) is put on a surface (for instance a blackboard or a sheet of paper), to form a specific pattern (for instance letters). And the tools used during this action (for instance brushes and typewriters), are instruments that add something to something. Thus one would suppose that the gesture of writing is a constructive action, if by 'construction' we mean the bringing together of various objects to form a new structure ('con-struction'). But this is misleading. If we want to grasp what the gesture of writing is really about, we have to consider its original form. If we may trust archaeology, writing, at least as far as the Occident is concerned, was originally an act of engraving. The Greek verb '*graphein*' still connotates this. Some place, some time in Mesopotamia, people began to scratch soft clay bricks with sticks, and then to burn them to harden the scratched surfaces. And although we no longer do such a thing very often, it is this half-forgotten gesture of scratching which is the essence ('*eidos*') of writing. It has nothing to do with constructing. It is, on the contrary, a taking away, a de-structing. It is, both structurally and historically, closer to sculpture than to architecture. It is a gesture of making holes, of digging, of perforating. A penetrating gesture. To write is to in-scribe, to penetrate a surface, and a written text is an *in*scription, although as a matter of fact it is in the vast majority of cases an *on*scription. Therefore to write is not to form, but to in-form, and a text is not a formation, but an in-formation. I believe that we have to start from this fact, if we want to understand the gesture of writing: it is a penetrating gesture that informs a surface.[21]

Elsewhere, Flusser states that "the gesture of writing is the answer to the question 'What am I trying to express?'"[22] In a blog post for the Institute of Network Cultures, Matt Beros links Flusser's ideas to asemic writing in the following way:

Vilém Flusser develops the concept of the 'gesture of writing', to describe the characteristic patterns of movement for producing writing. Like Friedrich Kittler in his discussion of Nietzsche in 'Gramophone, Film, Typewriter', Flusser makes a phenomenological distinction between the act of handwriting, inscribing a surface with a pen or stylus, from the more pianistic gesture of typing. To grasp the essence of writing, Flusser suggests, we must consider writing in its earliest forms, the half-forgotten gestures that form the primal basis of writing.

Asemic writing, being empty of formal semantic content is a purely visual form of writing occasionally resembling primitive writing systems and preliterate forms of proto-writing.... If, as Flusser notes, writing is a phenomena [sic] obscured by habit, then the practice of asemic writing is a method of rendering the writing act unfamiliar in a way that engages viewers with the gestural origins of writing.[23]

In their book *The Gestural Origin of Language* (2007), David Armstrong and Sherman Wilcox present their case for how spoken language emerged from manual gestures, rather than primate calls.[24] This is not a new idea; it dates back at least to the eighteenth century[25] and was revived by the anthropologist Gordon W. Hewes in 1974,[26] whose claims were later corroborated by a number of other researchers.[27] Nevertheless, Armstrong and Wilcox highlight a variety of more recent evidence that supports the notion, including evidence from sign language and the fossil record. Other evidence that appears to bolster the gestural theory includes the fact that gestural language and vocal language depend on similar neural systems[28] as well as the fact that non-human primates use many of the same gestures for communication as human infants.[29] Furthermore, human infants can gesture before they can speak — later on, these gestures then supplement and predict speech,[30] which parallels the idea that gestures evolved first and then spoken language was built upon them (this is also known as the 'gesture-first' hypothesis).[31]

Similarly, written language could have begun as gestures long forgotten. Might asemic writing be a way to re-engage these basic gestures, to place us in the mindset of our ancestors who were the inventors of proto-writing and writing? If so, then this art form could point to the gestural origins of writing. However, part of me is sceptical about this potential, given that asemic artists are influenced by real languages, either consciously or unconsciously. Much of asemic writing resembles well-developed writing systems (e.g. calligraphy, Mayan, and Hanzi). Yet, on the other hand, some asemic writing can resemble much older writing systems (such as Sumerian cuneiform) or proto-writing (like Rongorongo, a system of glyphs from Easter Island that may be one of the few independent inventions of writing in human history).[32] Beros also underlines this point about the similarities between asemic and ancient writing.[33]

To better explore the relationship between gestures and writing, it will be useful to turn our attention to the Belgian-born poet and artist Henri Michaux (1889–1984), whose asemic writing represents some fascinating examples of pseudographia. He was influenced by Asian calligraphy, Surrealism, and automatic writing. He was also a pioneering asemic artist — you can see such writing in his early works like *Alphabet* (1925) and *Narration* (1927).

In a poem accompanying the drawings from his *Mouvements* project (1950–1951), drawings that look like a cross between moving figures and traditional Chinese calligraphy, Michaux introduces the concept of "pre-gestures".[34] He believed sufficiently articulating these pre-gestures within the physical, tangible realm was impossible. In a later prose poem titled 'Signs', Michaux reflected on *Mouvements* and described the figures he drew as "interior gestures for which we have no limbs, but only a desire for limbs".[35] These interior gestures (or pre-gestures) precede and are "much larger" than the visible gesture, Michaux says. Only partial meaning of these interior, subjective movements can be expressed. They are characterised by a "SPEED!" that contrasts with the timid strokes displayed on the canvas; they are, according to Michaux, "movements of dislocation and inner exasperation more than marching movements … inward foldings … in place of other movements which cannot be shown but inhabit the mind".[36]

Referring to the figures in *Saisir* (*Grasp*, 1979), which are reminiscent of the markings in *Alphabet* and *Mouvements*, Michaux remarked that

line is not an abbreviation of volume or surface, but an abbreviation of hundreds of gestures and attitudes and impressions and emotions…. A dynamic abbreviation made up of spears, not forms.

What I wanted to represent was the gesture *within* the human, taking off from the inside, releasing, ripping free; the eruption of this intense, sudden, ardent concentration from which the stroke will proceed, rather than the stroke's arrival at its destination.[37]

The artist also experimented with mescaline later in life and produced several writing-esque drawings while under the influence of the drug, published in *Miserable Miracle* (1956) and *Thousand Times Broken: Three Books* (1956–1959). His aim was to bring out his unconscious gestures. The works he produced in his altered state consist of frenetic and repetitive squiggles, scrawls, and zig-zags. Pre-gestures, Jay Hetrick informs us, are "the vibratory kinesthetic inner movements that he tried to record, like a seismograph, in his mescaline drawings".[38]

Gesture, as expressed in asemic writing, was central to Michaux's work. According to Michaux, prehistoric cave markings — like the abstract signs found in the cave of Lascaux — show us the kinetic basis of writing. In *Agency and Embodiment* (2009), Carrie Noland underscores that *Mouvements* was Michaux's attempt to mimic the gestural movements that created these ancient markings. By imitating Palaeolithic humans, the artist hoped to generate a sign-based language — a kinetic vocabulary — that would be universally understood. We should all be able to understand the meaning of these corporeal movements. These traces of gesture are meant to be a form of language that connects humankind to its primitive form.[39]

Despite the influence of Asian calligraphy, perhaps Michaux was able to discover — and illustrate to us — the gestural origins of writing. I say 'despite the influence' here, but I recognise too that calligraphy may *itself* point to these origins. It is, after all, highly gestural. (It is easy to see why Michaux had a penchant for this art form, given his deep interest in the gestural and physical dimension of writing.)

In 1925, Michaux penned a critique of Breton's Surrealist manifesto, levelling two main criticisms, which the American poet Gillian Conoley summarises in an interview for the Poetry Foundation:

One was that he didn't believe the human hand could move fast enough to capture human thought, and in particular, the speed or accelerations of whatever might be going on in the unconscious. The other was that he didn't think language as a construct or system was quick enough to access thought either. For Michaux, it seems that automatic writing would look like something closer to what he was doing with "Alphabet," marks which could move faster since they didn't concern themselves with either language or straightforward representational gesture.[40]

This is an interesting point. If the aim of automatic writing is to represent the unconscious as fully as possible, then relying on a real, meaningful language may not be the best route towards such a representation. We can question just how unconscious automatic writing is since it uses real words, phrases, sentences, and syntax. Does this not involve elements of conscious thought? Morton Prince, an American neurologist who focused on abnormal psychology, believed this to be the case. He stated in his paper 'Some of the Revelations of Hypnotism' (1890) that automatic writing "is not a purely unconscious reflex act, but, the product of a conscious individuality".[41]

Conoley — who published the first English translation of Michaux's *Thousand Times Broken*, a volume of poetry, prose, and art — writes that Michaux "seems most interested in thought *before* it finds expression, its origin".[42] And so he sought to liberate himself from language — from filtered thoughts — through the medium of asemic writing. While asemic writing can end up appearing similar to real languages (such as in Michaux's *Mouvements* project), one is not relying on constructing semantic meaning, so one can instead make gestural movements with the hand purely based on unconscious feeling. Michaux regarded written language as somehow disfiguring, an act that compromised the original creative impulse. Through his works of asemic writing, like *Alphabet*, *Narration*, and *Mouvements*, Michaux instead relied on gesturally drawn characters. These are attempts to spontaneously match form with feeling.

Rather than use the straightforward representational gesture one would use when writing meaningful words in automatic writing, Michaux experimented with unconstrained gestures, emanating from whatever 'interior gestures' he was experiencing. Again, these interior gestures or 'pre-gestures' are the internal movements and impulses we have. In a poem accompanying his *Mouvements* project, he describes these pre-gestures as movements of "explosions", "inner shields", "refusal", "impossible desires", "stretching every which way", as movements which "one cannot display but which dwell on the mind". He goes on to say these are gestures of "the ignored life", "the impulsive life", "defiance", "retort", "excess".[43]

In much of his work, Michaux attempted to bring these movements to the surface via the gestural movements of the hand. It is curious, then, to see results like *Mouvements*, which features drawings that not only resemble Chinese characters but also human figures that are highly expressive, moving, and dancing. In some figures, there is a sense of flailing, reaching, contracting, opening up. The Canadian choreographer Marie Chouinard translated Michaux's figures into dance, bringing these gestures to life.[44]

However, if the hand cannot move fast enough to capture thought, as Michaux concedes, then no form of writing or drawing can ever truly communicate thought. So what we see in Michaux's work, therefore, is the attempt to *closely represent* thought. Even though Michaux regarded automatic writing as impossible, since he believed it is unable to translate the unconscious, he still practised some version of it. This seems to speak to the human predicament of existential isolation: wanting to truly communicate one's inner world to another — so as to be heard, seen, and understood — and yet never being able to achieve this.

In *Thousand Times Broken*, "Michaux continues to explore his lifelong fascination and tormented investigation of whether the self can be accessed, whether words or drawings best capture meaning, and whether communication is possible at all," writes Caite Dolan-Leach in a piece for *Music & Literature*.[45] Michaux was trying to access his unconscious through the mescaline experience and to "illustrate it in as unfettered a way as possible," as Dolan-Leach further points out.[46] But even if Michaux's mescaline-influenced drawings are the pinnacle of his translation of the unconscious mind, Dolan-Leach stresses that

> Michaux seems to be devoted to something for which failure is inevitable: translating the within of the inner self to the without of a medium, be it language or drawing. And ineluctably feeling frustration and discontent with the results. All three texts in this volume return to Michaux's sense of inadequacy, of falling short.[47]

Indeed, Michaux took issue with drawing as well, asserting that, like writing, it was a conscious construct with — as Conoley says — "conventions and agendas of [its] own, and therefore problematic in accessing or representing anything, much less deeper levels of consciousness".[48] So Michaux, throughout his artistic career, decided to focus on asemic writing. To reiterate, Michaux sought to find a universal language — based on gestures — that was "somewhere between writing and drawing", remarks Conoley.[49] And in the spirit of surrealism, pseudographia — or automatic asemic writing — could still reveal the unconscious, through spontaneous gestures, in ways that cannot be achieved through the automatic writing that Breton had in mind.

Michaux's work does raise some important questions. Could there really be some pseudographic writing (automatic asemic writing) that is largely free from the influences of other writing systems? And is it possible to enter a preliterate, automatic state, and produce quasi-glyphs and quasi-words, in a way that unearths some primordial relationship between gestures and writing? These are difficult questions to answer. Beros, nevertheless, thinks asemic writing can be illuminating in these respects. We can at least entertain the idea that automatic writing, psychedelic experiences, and other altered states may allow us to return to a primordial way of writing.

Additionally, it is conceivable that the mock or pseudo writing that children engage in before they begin to write actual words could reveal something about primitive writing, about the meaning conveyed by the gestural act of writing. We could then think of pseudographia in a similar way, as a state of child-like writing. Peter Schwenger, the author of *Asemic: The Art of Writing*, for example, associates asemic writing with "a preliterate experience from childhood".[50] (It would be interesting to see brain scans of individuals thinking about — or engaging in — asemic writing, and to then compare the results with brain scans of people carrying out actual writing. This experiment may not necessarily resolve the thorny, aforementioned questions, but it could still help to highlight the similarities and differences between these two forms of writing. Would creating asemic writing activate all of the same brain regions involved in the writing of meaningful words?[51])

The widely accepted and well-evidenced explanation for the origin of writing is that the practice began with clay tokens in Mesopotamia (dating back to the eighth millennium BC). The French-American archaeologist Denise Schmandt-Besserat notes, "[t]he development from tokens to script reveals that writing emerged from counting and accounting." These differently shaped tokens and the carvings on them represented units of goods. Schmandt-Besserat then traces the evolution of writing as follows: three-dimensional tokens were turned into two-dimensional pictographic signs (still used exclusively for accounting), which took place around 3,500–3,000 BC; and then phonetic signs — introduced to transcribe the names of individuals — marked the point at which writing started to emulate spoken language (3,000–1,500 BC). After this, alphabets were developed.[52]

The symbols found in 30,000-year-old Palaeolithic cave paintings — which may show some attempt at written language[53] — appear to represent concepts (e.g. animals) symbolically. The same seems to apply to the case of the possibly independent writing system of Rongorongo. It is debatable whether the gestural and expressive nature of asemic writing — displayed in Michaux's work, for example — correlates in any meaningful way with those ancient or independent writing systems that indicate how writing actually emerged.

Based on this agreed-upon theory of the origins of writing, asemic writing — either seen in psychedelic visions or produced in a psychedelic state — seems unrelated. However, with the gestural theory of the origins of writing in mind, then the spontaneous language-like scribbles created in an altered state, whether psychedelic-induced or not, could be a return to a primitive mode of expression. If psychedelics (owing to how they are literally defined) are mind-manifesting — including unconscious-manifesting — then these substances may aid in bringing interior gestures to the surface, as Michaux tried to display in his mescaline-inspired work.

Furthermore, in the visions of asemic symbols elicited by psychedelics, what we may be seeing, with eyes open or closed, is the visualisation of interior gestures.. Could written gestures or symbols specifically inspired by psychedelics, therefore, point to the origins of writing? To explore this question, we can refer to McKenna's 'Stoned Ape Theory' of human consciousness. There are controversial aspects of this hypothesis, which seeks to explain the evolution of distinct human traits through the consumption of psilocybin mushrooms, but for the sake of this discussion, the trait of language shall be the focus.

In support of this hypothesis, Dennis McKenna (Terence's brother) has proposed that psilocybin could have caused synaesthesia in our ancestors. Synaesthesia refers to a condition or experience in which one sensory modality is translated into another. Examples of a synaesthetic experience would be 'seeing sounds' or 'hearing colours'. Dennis argues that meaning, symbol, and metaphor (all central to language) depend on this cross-wiring of different sensory systems. Language is inherently synaesthetic because it involves attributing meaning to mouth noises. He maintains that the synaesthetic experience of a magic mushroom trip could have made the synaesthetic experience of language possible and that, once the benefits of language were discovered, this ability would be naturally selected from then on.[54]

While meaning is not a sensory modality per se, it is a kind of modality or perception, and one which is cross-wired with sound in both the generation and reception of language. Moreover, the meaning attached to mouth noises tends to paint visual images in our minds (as conveyed by the common phrase 'I see what you mean'), so there is, in a sense, the cross-wiring of sound and vision, thus making language synaesthetic in nature.

Similarly, psychedelic consumption among our ancestors may have caused synaesthesia in the sense of attributing meaning to the strange symbols they perceived or those created during or after their altered states. But this does not necessarily mean that this origin of writing is gestural in nature. It could be that the symbols are unrelated to specific gestures bursting forth from the unconscious and instead are simply visions with a kind of visual or geometric character that people felt compelled to tack meaning onto. Other psychedelic geometry can feel imbued with meaning and significance, which could apply to these strange symbols as well. As with spoken language, once the synaesthetic experience of written language became possible, it could be repurposed, with symbols and their meaning evolving over time, eventually giving us the writing systems that we are familiar with.

This kind of explanation is highly speculative, and by describing it, I am not endorsing it as the most plausible or strongest hypothesis available. In terms of McKenna's belief that our ancient ancestors consumed psilocybin mushrooms and this made our brain size, art, religion, and spoken language possible, we do not have concrete evidence that these ancestors consumed psychedelics during the period when these traits emerged. Besides, even if they did, it is not clear that this would have been the sole or major factor involved in making us human, or even a relevant factor. There are, moreover, non-psychedelic explanations for the emergence of our distinctly human traits.

## Psychedelic Visions of Alien Symbols

The relationship between psychedelics and asemic writing is a topic that is rarely discussed. However, there is a curious connection between the two, as revealed by the many visionary and psychedelic artists who have created alien alphabets, either as the focus of their work or as one of many features of the psychedelic state they are trying to reify. Allyson Grey — wife to fellow visionary artist Alex Grey — is one artist who has attempted to represent the visions of asemic writing seen during a psychedelic experience. She has stated,

Intending to create spiritual art, I feel naturally attracted to abstraction and to a written sacred language. Every known religion reveres its holy writing. Sacred writing of all faiths, however, come into conflict through human interpretation as the written word defines the differences of philosophy and traditions, when truly the basis of all religion is unity and infinite love. In 1975 I began writing automatically in an invented or transmitted language. I do not give meaning to the symbols in my art as it is meaning that separates experience from expression. The alphabet that I use points to the notion of a sacred language beyond meaning. Some of the works call to mind the experience of seeing an illuminated text in a foreign language and religion.

In recent work, I combine the icons of perfection (the Jewel Net) with the secret language, and images of chaos. Chaos in my art is the entropy of the units of spectrally arranged squares. Using a system of 'planned randomness,' allows each spectral system to fall apart in a unique way. The three elements used in my work, Chaos, Order and Secret Writing, are symbols of the sacred, non-literal representations of a cosmology.[55]

As we can see, Grey engages in pseudographia, just like Serafini, Smith, and Michaux. However, the inspiration for her untranslatable alphabet came from an LSD journey in the early 1970s in which secret writing appeared to her. We can say, then, that Grey is one artist engaged in *psychedelic pseudographia*: automatic asemic writing influenced by the psychedelic experience. (Michaux could also be considered a psychedelic pseudographic artist but, unlike Grey, he produced writing-esque works while under the influence of a psychedelic. Nevertheless, much of his post-mescaline work has the out-of-control, vibratory, seismographic quality that we see in his mescaline drawings.)

After practising automatic writing for a while, Grey eventually decided on 20 letters to use in her asemic, geometric, and intricate artwork. Other visionary artists who use asemic writing include Hakan Hisim, INCEDIGRIS, and SalviaDroid (Kyle Sawyer). You can see this type of writing in the latter's piece *Death by Astonishment*, the title of which comes from Terence McKenna, who quipped: "People say, 'is there risk, to DMT? It sounds so intense. Is it dangerous?' The answer is yes, it's tremendously dangerous. The danger is the possibility of death by astonishment."[56]

I have also created psychedelic-inspired asemic writing.[57] Ever since trying DMT, I have felt an impulse to create alien-looking letters and runes. I never had an intention to recreate writing that I have witnessed during a DMT experience since I have no clear memories of seeing such writing. Nonetheless, I am inclined to believe these altered states featured it since my natural inclination to create asemic writing, in an automatic way, only emerged after such experiences. Much of the content of the DMT experience has always seemed meaningful and symbolic, and if this aspect had the characteristic of a quasi-language, then it is possible that asemic writing has become a way to recreate these patterns. In addition, a number of people have told me the asemic runes I have drawn are the same, or similar, to ones they have seen during their own experiences with this compound. (Results from the first brain scans of participants under the influence of DMT were published in 2019,[58] but nothing was revealed about the common hallucinations of writing, letters, and glyphs. It would be intriguing to see what brain activity might be correlated with these types of experiences.)

McKenna, well known for his elucidations of DMT's effects, once described an experience in which he smoked DMT at the peak of an LSD trip. A woman named Rosemary shared the house he was living in at the time, but she was away, so he used the opportunity to embark on a solo psychedelic journey. But much to his surprise, "Right in the middle of this trip, this woman came back to the house ... and started beating on my door furiously."[59] He was on his bed while experiencing his DMT flash, heightened by LSD, and when he heard the racket, he jumped up, landed on his feet, and found himself half in reality and half in the DMT realm. He recounts,

And something about moving so suddenly had shattered the distinction between the two continuums and I carried it all with me so that the room was then filled with elves. They were hanging off my arms and spinning me around and there was this geometric object in the room that was spinning and clicking. And every time it would click, it would hurl a plastic chip across the room that had a letter in an alien language written on it. And these elves were screaming and bouncing off the walls. This machine was spinning in the air. The chips are ricocheting off the walls, and I was trying to deal with Rosemary in the middle of this.[60]

Another psychonaut, Diana Reed Slattery, who is the author of *Xenolinguistics: Psychedelics, Language, and the Evolution of Consciousness* (2015), also discovered an alien script in a psychedelic-induced altered state. Slattery describes this event, which took place in 1999, as a "download". Based on this experience — and hundreds of subsequent trips involving several types of psychedelics — she developed Glide, a visual, gestural language comprised of 27 glyphs.[61] This psychedelic language contrasts with Grey's in that the glyphs and their combinations have assigned meanings, but it is questionable whether the alien script witnessed in the experiences themselves was meaningful. In this way, we can suppose that Slattery saw psychedelic asemic writing and then constructed a meaningful language out of it.

In any case, accounts of seeing alien letters during psychedelic experiences are common. Many people report that they have seen the same writing depicted by Grey during their own LSD journeys, or at least alien symbols of some sort. Visions of alien symbols also seem to be a particularly persistent feature of the DMT experience. Users of the compound — much like McKenna — will find alien letters and hieroglyphs painted on surfaces and objects in the DMT world.

It is hard to know *why* people perceive (with eyes open or closed) such strange writing or why this feature of the experience might recur for some users but not others. Similarly, a phenomenon like face pareidolia — seeing faces in objects, such as clouds — seems to regularly crop up for certain individuals when they take psychedelics, an experience which may entail seeing faces everywhere (or just on particular surfaces or objects). These faces can have a clear character and expression to them, and they may be morphing, patterned, or integrated into geometric hallucinations. But not everyone tends to see these peculiar faces. Do individual differences in brain structure or personality account for varying instances of psychedelic phenomena like face pareidolia and alien alphabets?

Studies have indicated that those who score higher in neuroticism, and those in negative moods, are more likely to experience pareidolia.[62] The reason for this is likely evolutionary: feeling more tense and nervous puts you in a state of high alert; in other words, you are on the lookout for potential threats. This can lead you to perceive danger where none exists. In the case of a psychedelic experience, this effect can be heightened, with the 'danger' taking the form of clearly defined faces, which reflect a neurotic personality type or an anxious emotional state that is present before or during the experience. However, many users of psychedelics report commonly seeing faces without being neurotic or in a negative state of mind. So it could be that the fusiform face area (FFA), a brain region specialised for facial recognition, is, for some reason, affected differently by psychedelics in some individuals compared with others. But I am not sure what could explain the occurrence of — or variations in — the perception of alien writing, symbols, hieroglyphs, runes, and sigils.

While it remains a mystery as to why alien symbols frequently appear in the psychedelic state, perhaps areas of the brain related to language are implicated. For example, there is a universal reading network, known as the visual word form area (VWFA), which is specialised to see words before we are exposed to them.[63] One study showed that when Japanese subjects were asked to imagine writing complex Kanji ideograms, the VWFA was activated.[64] Perhaps this brain region is activated under the influence of psychedelics, thereby leading to the visualisation of word-like images. Other regions related to language might also be involved in the perception of strange writing.

After examining a patient who reported hallucinations of text, a team of psychiatrists revealed that the hallucinations matched the known specialisations of the VWFA. However, they ultimately rejected the idea that the VWFA was responsible for this effect, given that these patients had alexia: an inability to recognise or read written words or letters, resulting from damage to the VWFA. Instead, they suggested that the experience is related to the cortical network involved in the auditory hallucinations of schizophrenia.[65] Yet regardless of the correct explanation, these are still hallucinations of correct, meaningful written sentences or phrases. How are we to explain hallucinations of asemic alien writing? Patients with damage to the temporoparietal cortex, which serves the function of language, have experienced hallucinations of written words, but again, these words were meaningful.[66]

Andrew Gallimore, a computational neurobiologist, has suggested in his book *Alien Information Theory* (2019) that DMT can give us genuine access to a hyperdimensional realm, inhabited by hyperdimensional entities.[67] Based on this speculative idea, we might want to ask the following question: Could visions of alien writing in the DMT experience, which users commonly experience, be a *truly* alien language? Is it the writing system of these hyperdimensional, hyperintelligent entities?

Alien languages (or xenolanguages) — the languages of extraterrestrial or extradimensional beings — may very well exist in the universe. Xenolinguistics — research into what these languages might be like — is a legitimate area of study that attracts a diverse array of scientists.[68] However, it is hard to imagine how you would go about verifying that the writing seen in the DMT experience — or any altered state — is, in fact, an authentic xenolanguage. You could use linguistic methods to ascertain whether the writing has the characteristics of a language, but this would not prove that it came from alien beings. Moreover, if this alien writing is so radically different from human language that we could not even recognise it as a language, then there would be no way to distinguish it from gibberish.

A more conservative position would be that we do not need to invoke the notion of contact with actual aliens or an alien dimension in order to account for how psychedelics could generate images of quasi-writing that looks 'alien', given how easy it is to conjure up imaginary symbols. The brain, especially under the influence of psychedelics, is a highly creative organ.

Again, brain scans of people perceiving alien symbols in a psychedelic state could shed light on exactly what brain regions are implicated. It may be that the cross wiring of different systems in the brain[69] (visual, language, and meaning) could be leading to the perception of asemic alien symbols that appear meaningful. Hallucinated geometric shapes might combine with memories of existing writing to create a sense of an alien language, which visionary artists (such as Grey) then recreate in their artwork. Furthermore, since hallucinations of real (but meaningless) text can occur, it is not difficult to imagine that psychedelic visions of an alien language could arise from the reconfigurations of the basic symbolic patterns of letters and numbers. As a text- and number-oriented species, psychedelics may trigger our innate capacity for symbolic representation, but do so in a novel and creative way — trading recognisable symbols for unrecognisable ones.

Indeed, alien letters could be influenced by an individual's memories of other writing. If so, a psychedelic might reshape this material in a unique way, making it appear 'alien'. Or perhaps people simply attach connotations (e.g. Egyptian-like) to these psychedelic hieroglyphs but the symbols are nonetheless original and free from influence. This does raise the question, nevertheless, of whether someone who had never been exposed to any writing would be able to perceive alien symbols during a psychedelic experience.

To reiterate, the perception of alien symbols during psychedelic experiences is not universal; it can occur in some experiences but not in others. Yet when it does occur, it can present an opportunity for creative or inspired individuals to bring these symbols — or some semblance of them — back to the real world in the form of drawings, paintings, or digital art.

The mind's tendency to generate images of alien letters during psychedelic experiences is mysterious, as is the potential of psychedelics to inspire the impulse to produce such writing. Whatever the explanation behind these phenomena may be, we are still left with an apparent paradox of asemic writing:

the symbols themselves are meaningless but the creation or interpretation of them is not.

## Endnotes

1.  Leftwich, J. (2016). 'Asemic Writing: Definitions & Contexts: 1998 - 2016', Internet Archive, January/March. https://archive.org/details/AsemicWritingDefinitionsAnd Contexts19982016

2.  Leftwich, J. (2018). 'The Nearness of Asemic Writing', Galatea Resurrects 2018, 8 February. http://galatearesurrects2018. blogspot.com/2018/02/featured-essay-by-jim-leftwich.html

3.  Jacobson, M. (n.d.). 'On Asemic Writing', Asymptote. https:// www.asymptotejournal.com/visual/michael-jacobson-on-asemic-writing/

4.  Ibid.

5.  Giovenale, M. (2015). 'Four questions about asemic writing, #10: Christopher Skinner', SCRIPTjr.nl, 8 October. https://scriptjr.nl/four-questions-about-asemic-writing-10-christopher-skinner#.Y7LKkuzP0Wo

6.  Babinka, K. (2015). 'Luigi Serafini On How and Why He Created an Encyclopedia of an Imaginary World', Bird in Flight, 1 June. https://birdinflight.com/en/media/luigi-serafini-on-how-and-why-he-created-an-encyclopedia-of-an-imaginary-world.html

7.  Stanley, J.C. (2010). 'To Read Images Not Words: Computer-Aided Analysis of the Handwriting in the Codex Seraphinianus', Masters Degree, North Carolina State University.

8.  Ouellette, J. (2019). 'No, someone hasn't cracked the code of the mysterious Voynich manuscrupt', Ars Technica, 15 May. https://arstechnica.com/science/2019/05/no-someone-hasnt-cracked-the-code-of-the-mysterious-voynich-manuscript/

9.  Flournoy, T. (1900). From India to the Planet Mars: A Case of Multiple Personality with Imaginary Languages, p. 107. Princeton: Princeton University Press, 1994.

10. Rosenberg, D. (2000). 'Speaking Martian', *Cabinet Magazine*, Issue 1. https://www.cabinetmagazine.org/issues/1/rosenberg.php

11. Flournoy, T. (1900). *From India to the Planet Mars: A Case of Multiple Personality with Imaginary Languages*, p. 87. Princeton: Princeton University Press, 1994.

12. Ibid., p. 13.

13. Ibid., p. 8.

14. Parrish, A. (2020). 'The Umbrage of an Imago: Writing Under Control of Machine Learning', Serpentine Galleries, 14 August. https://www.serpentinegalleries.org/art-and-ideas/the-umbra-of-an-imago-writing-under-control-of-machine-learning/

15. Breton, A. (1924). *Manifestoes of Surrealism*, p. 26. Translated by Seaver, R. and Lane, H.R. Ann Arbor, MI: University of Michigan Press, 1969.

16. Romano, A. (2018). 'How Ouija boards work. (Hint: It's not ghosts.)', *Vox*, 6 September. https://www.vox.com/2016/10/29/13301590/how-ouija-boards-work-debunked-ideomotor-effect

17. Stanley, J.C. (2010). 'To Read Images Not Words: Computer-Aided Analysis of the Handwriting in the *Codex Seraphinianus*', Masters Degree, North Carolina State University.

18. Manetto, F. (2007). 'Historia de un libro raro'. *El País*, 8 November. https://elpais.com/diario/2007/11/11/eps/1194765358_850215.html.

19. Lopez, N. (2020). 'An Exploration of Linguistic Relativity for Consideration of Terence McKenna's "Stoned Ape Theory" on the Origins of Consciousness and Language: Implications for Language Pedagogy'. *Journal of Conscious Evolution*, 16(1), Article: 6.

20. Flusser, V. (1991). *Gestures*, p. 2. Translated by Roth, N.A. Minneapolis: University of Minnesota Press, 2014.

21. Roth, N.A. (2012). 'A Note on 'The Gesture of Writing' by Vilém Flusser and The Gesture of Writing'. *New Writing: The International Journal for the Practice and Theory of Creative Writing,* 9(1), pp. 24–41.

22. Flusser, V. (1991). *Gestures*, p. 22. Translated by Roth, N.A. Minneapolis: University of Minnesota Press, 2014.

23. Beros, M. (2015). 'Asemia and the Gesture of Writing', Institute of Network Cultures, 18 March. https://networkcultures. org/blog/2015/03/18/asemia-and-the-gesture-of-writing/

24. Armstrong, D.F. and Wilcox, S.E. (2007). *The Gestural Origin of Language,* p. 30. Oxford: Oxford University Press.

25. Corballis, M.C. (2010). 'The gestural origins of language'. *Wiley Interdisciplinary Reviews: Cognitive Science,* 1(1), pp. 2–7.

26. Hewes, G.W. (1973). 'Primate Communication and the Gestural Origin of Language'. *Current Anthropology,* 14(1-2), pp. 65–84.

27. Gillespie-Lynch, K. (2017). 'Gestural Theory' in *Encyclopedia of Evolutionary Psychological Science,* pp. 1–5. Edited by Shackleford, T. and Weekes-Shackleford, V. New York: Springer.

28. Aussems, S. (2018). 'What hand gestures tell us about the evolution of language', iCog, 31 January. https://icog. group.shef.ac.uk/what-hand-gestures-tell-us-about-the-evolution-of-language/

29. Daley, J. (2018). 'Chimps and Toddlers Use Same Gestures to Get Attention', *Smithsonian,* 12 September. https://www. smithsonianmag.com/smart-news/chimps-and-toddlers-share-same-gesture-language-180970272/

30. Rowe, M.L. and Goldin-Meadow, S. (2009). 'Early gesture *selectively* predicts later language learning'. *Developmental Science,* 12(1), pp. 182–187.

31. Aussems, S. (2018). 'What hand gestures tell us about the evolution of language', iCog, 31 January. https://icog. group.shef.ac.uk/what-hand-gestures-tell-us-about-the-evolution-of-language/

32. Wieczorek, R.M., Frankiewicz, K.E., Oskolski, A.A., and Horley, P. (2021). 'The *rongorongo* tablet from Berlin and the time-depth of Easter Island's writing system'. *Journal of Island and Coastal Archaeology*, 18(2), pp. 309–328.

33. Beros, M. (2015). 'Asemia and the Gesture of Writing', Institute of Network Cultures, 18 March. https:// networkcultures.org/blog/2015/03/18/asemia-and-the-gesture-of-writing/

34. Michaux, H. (2001). *Oeuvres Complètes II*, p. 439. Edited by Bellour, P. Paris: Gallimard.

35. Ibid., p. 431.

36. Ibid., p. 438.

37. Michaux, H. (2006). *Saisir* (*Grasp*) in *Stroke by Stroke*, n.p. Translated by Sieburth, R. New York: Archipelago Books.

38. Hetrick, J. (2017). 'Cinematic Gestures between Henri Michaux and Joachim Koester' in *Gestures of Seeing in Film, Video and Drawing*, p. 56. Edited by Grønstad, A., Gustafsson, H., and Vågnes, Ø. New York: Routledge.

39. Noland, C. (2009). *Agency and Embodiment: Performing Gestures/Producing Culture*, p. 130. Cambridge, Massachusetts: Harvard University Press.

40. Joron, A. (2014). '*Thousand Times Broken*: Gillian Conoley on the Works of Henri Michaux', Poetry Foundation, 18 November. https://www.poetryfoundation.org/harriet-books/2014/11/thousand-times-broken-gillian-conoley-on-the-works-of-henri-michaux

41. Prince, M. (1890). 'Some of the Revelations of Hypnotism'. *Boston Medical and Surgical Journal*, 122(20), pp. 463–467.

42. Joron, A. (2014). '*Thousand Times Broken*: Gillian Conoley on the Works of Henri Michaux', Poetry Foundation,

18 November. https://www.poetryfoundation.org/harriet-books/2014/11/thousand-times-broken-gillian-conoley-on-the-works-of-henri-michaux

43. Michaux, H. (1951). *Mouvements*, n.p. Paris: NRF/Le Point de jur.

44. Chouinard, M. (2011). *Henri Michaux: Mouvements*, ImPulsTanz, Vienna International Dance Festival, Vienna, Austria, 2 August.

45. Dolan-Leach, C. (2015). 'Henri Michaux's *Thousand Times Broken*', *Music & Literature*, 27 January. https://www.musicandliterature.org/reviews/2015/1/25/henri-michauxs-thousand-times-broken

46. Ibid.

47. Ibid.

48. Joron, A. (2014). '*Thousand Times Broken*: Gillian Conoley on the Works of Henri Michaux', Poetry Foundation, 18 November. https://www.poetryfoundation.org/harriet-books/2014/11/thousand-times-broken-gillian-conoley-on-the-works-of-henri-michaux

49. Ibid.

50. Schwenger, P. (2019). *Asemic: The Art of Writing*, p. 83. Minneapolis: University of Minnesota Press.

51. Planton, S., Longcamp, M., Péran, P., Démonet, J., and Jucla, M. (2017). 'How specialized are *writing-specific* brain regions? An fMRI study of writing, drawing and oral spelling'. *Cortex*, 88, pp. 66–80.

52. Schmandt-Besserat, D. (2015). 'Writing, Evolution of' in *International Encyclopedia of Social and Behavioral Sciences*, pp. 761–766. Edited by Wright, J.D. New York: Elsevier.

53. McKie, R. (2012). 'Did Stone Age cavemen talk to each other in symbols?', *The Guardian*, 11 March. https://www.theguardian.com/science/2012/mar/11/cave-painting-symbols-language-evolution

54. Paulson, S. (2019). 'Did Magic Mushrooms Shape Human Consciousness?', To The Best Of Our Knowledge, 6 June.

https://www.ttbook.org/interview/did-magic-mushrooms-shape-human-consciousness

55. Grey, A. (2006). *CoSM Journal 4: Entheo Art*. Edited by Grey A and Grey A, pp. 21–22. Wappinger Falls: CoSM Press.

56. Lin, T. (2014). 'Death and the Imagination', *Vice*, 29 July. https://www.vice.com/en/article/jmbbm4/death-and-the-imagination

57. Timmermann, C., Roseman, L., Schartner, M., Milliere, R., Williams, L.T.J., Erritzoe, D., Muthukumaraswamy, S., Ashton, M., Bendrioua, A., Kaur, O., Turton, S., Nour, M.M., Day, C.M., Leech, R., Nutt, D.J., and Carhart-Harris, R.L. (2019). 'Neural correlates of the DMT experience assessed with multivariate EEG'. *Scientific Reports*, 9, Article: 16324.

58. 'Terence on DMT: An Entheological Analysis of McKenna's Experiences in the Tryptamine Mirror of the Self' (2010). Reality Sandwich, 28 June. https://realitysandwich.com/terence_dmt/

59. Ibid.

60. 'Asemic glyphs/runes' (2023). Imgur, 26 August. https://imgur.com/a/dwPEWJj

61. Slattery, D.R. (2008). 'How I Became a Xenolinguist', MAPS Bulletin, Volume XVIII, Number 1, Spring. https://maps.org/news-letters/v18n1/v18n1-MAPS_11-12.pdf

62. Dahl, M. (2015). 'Neurotic People See Faces in Things', *Slate*, 20 July. https://slate.com/culture/2015/07/study-neurotic-people-see-faces-in-things-it-s-called-pareidolia.html

63. Li, J., Osher, D.E., Hansen, H.A., and Saygin, Z.M. (2020). 'Innate connectivity patterns drive the development of the visual word form area'. *Scientific Reports*, 10, Article: 18039.

64. Cohen, L., Lehéricy, S., Chochon, F., Lemer, C., Rivaud, S., and Dehaene, S. (2002). 'Language-specific tuning of visual cortex? Functional properties of the Visual Word Form Area'. *Brain*, 125(5), pp. 1054–1069.

65. Ffytche, D.H., Lappin, J.M., and Philpot, M. (2004). 'Visual command hallucinations in a patient with pure alexia'. *Journal of Neurology, Neurosurgery & Psychiatry*, 75(1), pp. 80–86.

66. Rousseaux, M., Debrock, D., Cabaret, M., and Steinling, M. (1994). 'Visual hallucinations with written words in a case of left parietotemporal lesion'. *Journal of Neurology, Neurosurgery & Psychiatry*, 57(10), pp. 1268–1271.

67. Sjöstedt-Hughes, P. (2019). 'Book Review — Alien Information Theory: Psychedelic Drug Technologies and the Cosmic Game', Psychedelic Press, 13 June. https://www.academia.edu/39562839/Book_Review_Alien_Information_Theory_Psychedelic_Drug_Technologies_and_the_Cosmic_Game

68. Gomes, M. (2018). 'From xenolinguistics to cephalopods', Diaphanes, 10 April. https://www.diaphanes.net/titel/xenolinguistics-5623

69. Keim, B. (2014). 'Science Graphic of the Week: How Magic Mushrooms Rearrange Your Brain', *Wired*, 30 October. https://www.wired.com/2014/10/magic-mushroom-brain/

## Chapter 6

# On the Jester and Trickster Entities in the DMT Realm

A jester is an entertainer that a monarch or nobleman would employ to entertain him and his guests. These court jesters thrived in the medieval and Renaissance eras. These jovial entertainers wore hats featuring floppy, pointed protrusions, with a bell hanging from the tip of each protrusion. They also donned motley clothing (the traditional costume of the jester and Harlequin — a patchwork made up of a variety of bright colours, iconically arranged in a chequered pattern). Jesters were often adept at many forms of entertainment, including singing, music, storytelling, acrobatics, juggling, comedy, and magic. The jester is also depicted as the Fool, one of the 78 cards in a Tarot deck, which itself is similar in appearance to the Joker playing card.

Strangely, jester-type entities commonly appear in the DMT experience. In Rick Strassman's research on the effects of this compound, detailed in his book *DMT: The Spirit Molecule,* many participants reported encountering "clowns", "jesters", "jokers", and "imps" during their experiences.[1] Many users also describe these types of entities as 'tricksters'. These entities are often engaged in elaborate and mind-boggling performances and tricks. Moreover, the environment they inhabit can reflect their entertaining nature, with many users finding themselves in strange dimensions that resemble a circus, carnival, or casino. In fact, the psychonaut Terence McKenna said that

> when you put a whole bunch of DMT trips together, certain things seem to emerge. My notion — coming at it from a

sort of a Jungian attitude — is: if we had to say what is the archetype of DMT, the archetype is the circus. It's the circus. And let me say why. First of all, a circus is a place of wild exotic activity. And clowns. You don't have a circus without clowns. Clowns are wonderful for children. A circus is a wonderful place for a child. DMT — there is something very, very weirdly child-like about it in a very un-childish way.[2]

The prevalence of jesters and tricksters in the DMT experience is quite curious. Why do so many people come to meet them? I believe that the ideas of the Swiss psychologist Carl Gustav Jung (1875–1961) can shed some light on this phenomenon, which McKenna alludes to in the quote above. I propose that the jester-type DMT entities are archetypal: manifestations of the collective unconscious. However, a Jungian perspective on the DMT experience may be able to (partly) explain *why* these entities exist, but it may not resolve the mystery of why DMT — as a specific substance — has a propensity to bring these entities to the surface, and in such a peculiar, idiosyncratic fashion. Of course, other archetypes may appear in the DMT experience, but when jesters make their showy entrance, there must be a reason they do so.

The ultimate explanation for the appearance of jesters in the DMT experience is unclear to me. Nonetheless, I posit that — since they are archetypal in some sense — we can learn from these jesters. We can understand the trickster aspect of ourselves and find immense value in that if we dig deep enough. In this essay, I aim to explore the meaning of the trickster from a mythological, cultural, psychological, and philosophical perspective, and apply insights from these disciplines to encounters with these specific entities in the psychedelic state. To begin with, we need to illuminate Jung's ideas on archetypes so we can better understand the nature of the trickster.

## The Jungian Archetypes

An archetype is a universal symbol, which other more specific symbols are based on. The word *archetype* has its root in ancient Greek and roughly means 'original pattern'. Archetypes are interpreted differently, depending on the discipline in question. In psychology, archetypes are understood to be models contained in the human psyche, whereas, in philosophy, archetypes are the ideal forms of more specific objects. The ancient Greek philosopher Plato expounded the notion that there is a pure, perfect form (Form) — or archetype — that is common to many objects in reality.[3]

The study of archetypes in psychology was set in motion by Jung. Due to the work of Jung and those who followed in his footsteps, such as the famous mythologist Joseph Campbell (1904–1987), it is clear that archetypes are essential elements of folklore, myths, stories, and the world's most perennial examples of literature.

Jung sits firmly in the ranks of Sigmund Freud as one of the most famous thinkers of the twentieth century. He is well known for developing the concepts of *extroversion* and *introversion* and, as a psychologist, he had some unique interests, particularly related to religion, myth, mysticism, and alchemy. For Jung, archetypes originate from the *collective unconscious*. The collective unconscious is distinct from the *personal unconscious*, which is each individual's own collection of experiences that they are unaware of. In contrast, the collective unconscious contains the archetypes shared by all people. Furthermore, the collective unconscious does not develop but is something that is inherited. So when each of us is born, we are infused with these universal images, which we are not immediately aware of.[4]

Freud, in some sense, supported the idea of archetypes, as he said that within each person's mind there are *archaic remnants* — or mental forms — whose existence cannot be explained by that particular individual's life experiences. The forms are innate, inherited, and shared by everyone.[5] According to Jung, the archetypes represent important motifs of our evolutionary history. That is why they evoke a strong emotional response in us and why they repeat in myths found all over the world.

There is a plethora of *Jungian archetypes*, as they are called. Jung identified some main archetypes, which he describes in his various works. These include the *Self*, which each individual might think is simply their personality. However, for Jung, the Self is the unification of the conscious and unconscious life of the individual. The Self is created through a process called *individuation*, in which all the aspects of the personality are integrated into a unified whole. For Jung, the Self as an archetype is best represented by the mandala.[6] The word mandala in Sanskrit means 'circle' and it is a highly significant symbol in Hindu and Buddhist rituals and spiritual practices, such as certain forms of meditation. The transpersonal psychologist David Fontana remarks in his book *Meditating with Mandalas* that the mandala's symbolic nature can help an individual "to access progressively deeper levels of the unconscious, ultimately assisting the meditator to experience a mystical sense of oneness with the ultimate unity from which the cosmos in all its manifold forms arises".[7]

Another of Jung's famous archetypes is the *Shadow*. The Shadow represents our most basic, primitive instincts, and the life and sex drives. If the Shadow were to reside anywhere in the brain, it would be in our *limbic system,* which plays a central role in the processing of emotions. The limbic system is associated with emotions such as anger, lust, jealousy, and fear. The Shadow is comprised of repressed ideas, weaknesses, desires, and instincts. It is the dark, hidden aspect of our minds. As such, it can be dangerous — if we deny parts of our shadow, such as weaknesses we have, Jung said we might project these weaknesses onto others, thereby distorting our view of ourselves and other people.[8] According to Jung's analysis of dreams, the

Shadow is usually symbolised by monstrous characters, such as demons.

There is the *Anima*, which is a feminine image in the male mind, and the *Animus*, which is a masculine image in the female mind. In Jung's view, being able to combine our feminine and masculine natures, rather than letting one dominate, leads to wholeness.[9] The last of Jung's main archetypes is the *Persona*, a term which is derived from the Latin word for 'mask'. The Persona represents all of the different social masks that we put on. This means that each individual's persona may contain a work mask, a family mask, a friend mask, a romantic mask, etc.[10]

There are, of course, various other archetypes, some of which are more recognisable and feature heavily in stories around the world. In his book *Man and His Symbols*, Jung examines some of them and what they stand for: the Father (authority), the Mother (comfort), the Child (innocence), the Wise Old Man or Woman (guidance), the Hero (champion), the Maiden (desire), and the Trickster (trouble-maker), the last of which will be elucidated further in this discussion. One can immediately think of some characters in books and films that represent these archetypes: Yoda from *Star Wars* as the Wise Old Man, Satan in the Book of Genesis as the Trickster, Rapunzel as the Maiden, Zeus as the Father, and so on and so forth.

Campbell, following in the tradition of Jung, would become well known for examining the different myths, folklore, stories, and religions from around the world and picking out the fundamental, universal elements of them. In his highly influential book *The Hero with a Thousand Faces*, Campbell discusses the journey of the archetypal hero. According to Campbell, all the iconic stories involving heroes — such as the labours of Hercules or the life of the Buddha — share a basic structure. Campbell called this structure the *monomyth* and in short, it involves *a call to adventure, a road of trials, the boon* (or discovery), *a return to the ordinary world,* and, finally, *the application of the boon.*[11] This structure is clever because Campbell is able to apply it to history's most famous stories, such as *The Odyssey* and the life of Christ as depicted in the gospels. The trickster also appears in the hero's journey, exemplified by characters such as the Cheshire Cat from *Alice in Wonderland,* Dobby from *Harry Potter,* and Merry and Pippin from *The Lord of the Rings.*

Campbell seems to vindicate Jung's assertion that archetypes are something that we can easily identify with and which evoke a strong emotional response from us because they symbolise our evolutionary experiences. The hero's journey represents the primitive struggle of our ancestors in entering an unknown world of danger but overcoming the danger and bringing back to the tribe or group some discovery or treasure that will benefit everyone.

Campbell's idea of the monomyth has been highly influential in the world of cinema — George Lucas credited Campbell with providing inspiration for his *Star Wars* films, and the template of the hero's journey also helped to structure the plot of *The Matrix* and Disney films such as *Aladdin, The Lion King,* and *Beauty and the Beast.* The most successful books and films do appear to commit to many of Jung's archetypes and Campbell's monomyth (*The Lord of the Rings* trilogy comes to mind), which attests to the very real existence and power of these universal symbols.[12] [13] [14] [15]

## Jesters and Tricksters in Mythology, Culture, and Psychology

James Hollis, a Jungian analyst, claims that the trickster is "the personification of the autonomy of nature".[16] He adds,

> We gain a provisional recognition of trickster energy when we personify it as coyote, fox, hare, imp, devil, Kokopelli,

"Murphy's Law," and the like. If we can image it, we can then begin to establish some conscious relationship to it. It is most autonomous, most likely disruptive to the expected order of things, when it operates unconsciously in our lives.[17]

These tricksters are archetypal because they appear in different parts of the world, yet they are uniquely expressed due to cultural differences. For example, in the Native American tradition, the coyote features as a trickster figure in various myths, whereas Loki — the trickster god of Norse mythology — is depicted in a more anthropomorphic way. In English folklore, Puck, who plays a pivotal role in Shakespeare's *A Midsummer Night's Dream,* is a trickster that takes the form of a fairy. And then we have the jester, who is commonly characterised as a trickster figure. While the two do share much in common, they are, nevertheless, different in several respects.

If we take the standard definitions of each, a jester was a person wearing colourful garb and a fool's hat who amused people at a royal court through jesting, mockery, and jokes. In medieval times, there were also itinerant jesters who entertained common folk at fairs and markets. The trickster, in contrast, is a mythological figure who is impish and playful; they perform tricks and are responsible for teaching others through guile. In her book *Fools Are Everywhere: The Court Jester Around the World*, Beatrice K. Otto notes,

> The distinction between jester and trickster lies in the fact that the trickster is a completely free entity, not affiliated with any particular person in authority. In addition — and this may be the most significant difference — he is generally less discerning than the jester in choosing the victims of his pranks and wit. Jesters are often guided in their mockery by a certain kindliness that prevents their treating a friendly old farmer in the same way as an avaricious cardinal or a venal

magistrate, and their mockery is often intended to show up a vice of some sort. The trickster, on the other hand, rarely has scruples about cheating anybody for fun or gain. The jester is usually aware of the effect he can have and frequently uses his talents to help others, cause merriment, give advice, or defuse a perilous situation. It is perhaps this more ethical input, together with his close relationship to the king, that distinguishes him from the boundless trickster.[18]

In marketing, archetypes are used in branding because it anchors the brand against a universal symbol that is embedded within the collective unconscious of humanity. We can, therefore, easily identify and find resonance with the archetype in question. This is one key reason why marketing gets your attention. Based on Jungian psychology, marketers have designated 12 archetypes, one of which is the jester, usually synonymised with the trickster.

Clowns, tricksters, comedians, practical jokers, and the fool seem to share a certain kind of playful energy in common. The jester is at home in the world of paradoxes. They embody humour and masterfully use it with powerful effect, to teach certain lessons and important truths. Comedy is the medium by which the ridiculousness and hypocrisy of the world can be illuminated. Jesters infectiously project joy and fun and want to invite others into their world of silliness and carefree living. By doing so, they lighten up tense situations and brighten the mood of others who are sullen.

Jung argued that the trickster is "an archetypal psychic structure of extreme antiquity".[19] In his essay 'On the Psychology of the Trickster Figure', Jung provides some insight into, as well as analysis of, the trickster archetype. He notes that the trickster figure is found throughout the world's myths, although they do also differ widely in their characteristics and presentation. In the storytelling traditions of Africa — and later, African

American literature — the trickster takes the form of a rabbit, while the fox plays the role of the trickster in Dogon, Scottish, Bulgarian, Russian, French, and Finnish folklore. In this text, Jung also states,

> A curious combination of typical trickster motifs can be found in the alchemical figure of Mercurius; for instance, his fondness for sly jokes and malicious pranks, his powers as a shape-shifter, his dual nature, half animal, half divine.[20]

Franchot Ballinger, who taught English at the University of Cincinnati for nearly 40 years, wrote extensively on the subject of Native American tricksters. He underlines that "we can see in the Native American trickster an openness to life's multiplicity and paradoxes largely missing in the modern Euro-American moral tradition".[21] In the European and American tradition of the picaresque novel, stories often depict a roguish but likeable trickster figure (known as a *picaro*, which is Spanish for 'rascal') who uses his wit, cunning, and carefree attitude to pursue a life of adventure. The picaro is a jester-like anti-hero.

Since the trickster lives in the world of paradoxes and is a shape-shifter, we can find contrasting qualities in the Native American trickster when we compare different stories. The trickster may be a beacon of wisdom in one tale and terribly foolish in another. He may exemplify heroism in one story but stand out as a villainous character in the next. In his book *Trickster Makes This World*, the scholar Lewis Hyde brings to light the universal playful and disruptive side of the human mind. We all have a trickster aspect. Hyde points out that the Coyote spirit and Raven spirit of Native American mythologies — who both stole fire from the gods (like Prometheus of the ancient Greek legend) — are viewed as jokesters and pranksters. He also emphasises the pivotal and wise role of Coyote — in Native

American creation myths, this trickster taught humans how to catch fish.[22]

Coyote as the trickster in the Native American tradition holds great power. According to the tradition of the Crow people (an indigenous tribe in Montana), Old Man Coyote mimics the Creator, making people out of the mud. The Chelan people tell a similar story: Coyote has abilities like those of the Creator. In a letter to the comedian George Carlin, the American historian Byrd Gibbens wrote about the significance of the trickster in indigenous myths:

> Many native traditions held clowns and tricksters as essential to any contact with the sacred. People could not pray until they had laughed, because laughter opens and frees from rigid preconception. Humans had to have tricksters within the most sacred ceremonies lest they forget the sacred comes through upset, reversal, surprise. The trickster in most native traditions is essential to creation, to birth.[23]

The trickster-as-creator is exemplified by Raven in Inuit mythology. For the Inuit people of Alaska and the western Arctic region, Raven is the creator of the world, light, man, and the animals, but he is also a trickster god, hero, and shape-shifter (in Inuit tales, he can assume the shape of a bird or human).

In many cultures, clowns — as comic performers — are typical tricksters and closely related to the jester. Like jesters, they serve a similar and important function. A Hopi Indian explains that "clowns represent us in our misdeeds ... the clowns show life as it should not be ... the clowns show, mimic the 'hidden immoralities' and bring them into the open so we can see where we have gone wrong ... the clowns show what is the essence of morality".[24] Otto says this points to an "age-old, deep-rooted human need for clowns".[25]

Jesters are ubiquitous, as are clowns — they are found in tribes and indigenous cultures all over the world. Clowns often play a key role in rituals, adopting the same license that the jester has to engage in comic criticism and social satire. Interestingly, there can be a correspondence between the attire of the jester and clown, despite these characters being found in different cultures (although whether the appearance of these tricksters has been influenced by other cultures, in some cases at least, is up for debate). There may be a curious human proclivity to 'paint' the trickster in a certain way. For instance, in India, the Tamil village clown (*komali*) dons a conical cap and wears small bells on his legs, which is reminiscent of the court jester of medieval Europe. The komali skips, dances, laughs, sings songs, and taunts.

Pueblo clowns, also known as sacred clowns, are the tricksters of the New Mexico Pueblo Indians. Known as the *Koshare* (or 'Delight Makers') in tribal traditions, the main duty of these clowns is to make people merry. Clowns heal people through laughter, according to the Pueblo tradition. They are witty and make efforts to point out the ludicrous nature of various situations. As well as evoking feelings of mirth during festive occasions, the sacred clown also has a sinister side, much like many other tricksters. After all, ridicule can make us laugh or recoil in discomfort if it is directed at our shortcomings. The Koshare have their bodies painted in stripes and wear pointed hats, as medieval court jesters do.

The *heyoka* is another sacred clown, belonging to the culture of the Sioux, a group of Native American tribes, which includes the Lakota and Dakota people. Certain tribe members adopt the role of heyoka (the well-known Lakota medicine man Black Elk identified as one). In *Fools and Jesters in Literature, Art, and History*, Vicki K. Janik notes, "The heyoka dress, act, and speak in contrary ways."[26] The heyoka's unconventional actions — like mounting ponies backwards, wearing boots backwards, shivering in the heat, walking naked in the winter (and complaining how hot it is), or saying the opposite of what is expected — all have the effect of producing laughter. Their antics also cause tribe members to laugh at medicine men or holy men — but this does not cause friction in the community; instead, it helps to revitalise people. This is achieved in two ways: through laughter (which acts as a tonic, opening people up to immediate experience and elevated mood) and through the revelation of higher truths.

Modern society has somewhat forgotten that jesters, clowns, and buffoons are not just there to amuse us. In traditional stories and fables, they act as spiritual mentors and guides for the young, they console those who are mourning, and they comfort the downtrodden. Their advice is sought and is taken as sacrosanct. Among the Wolof people of Senegal and Gambia, these jesters and buffoons are often more powerful than the master, despite being lower than the poorest servant — a strange dichotomy, indeed.

On the other hand, modern society also continually honours the role of the trickster. The importance of jesters and tricksters cannot be understated. This is why we cannot help but repeatedly express them. They crop up in modern films, as Helena Bassil-Morozow details in her book *The Trickster in Contemporary Film*, with trickster actors including people like Jim Carrey (e.g. his role in *The Mask*) and Sacha Baron Cohen (who plays the gonzo trickster Borat).

Bassil-Morozow insists that we should not underestimate the serious role played by tricksters in films. We cannot simply laugh at them, be outraged at them, and then move on. What they do is invite contemporary audiences to question the order of things in society and present a picture of what change might look like. The author writes that the trickster's crossing of boundaries "in narrative terms, is the trigger, the beginning of the conflict".[27] The trickster shows us what we can achieve if we too are willing to step outside the social, cultural, and personal edifices that act as boundaries — obstacles to individuation. Bassil-Morozow points out that

> raising your voice ... against "higher powers" is bound to be dangerous ... the learning path is fraught with errors. Only fools are prepared to leave the safety of the womb/mother/nature/the village/paradise, and "go and seek their fortune".[28]

## Encounters with Jester and Trickster Entities in the DMT Realm

Before providing an analysis of the DMT jesters and tricksters, I would like to briefly describe some of my personal encounters with these entities. Doing so, I hope, will hint at the utter strangeness of their nature and behaviour as well as connect them to the aforementioned jesters and tricksters found in various cultures. The following descriptions (compiled from different experiences) should be taken with a pinch of salt: I have tried my best to recall memories or a vague sense of what these beings were like and then characterise them to the best of my ability.

Unfortunately, however, memories of the experience are often difficult to recall. I am always alert to the possibility that post-experience, 'definite details' can be subject to creative embellishment and fabrication, based on the natural tendency to tell riveting stories and 'fill in the gaps' as well as the impulse to give form and sense to the ineffable. This applies to memories more generally, but in the case of the DMT experience, this is especially true, given how prone the experience is to forgetfulness and ambiguity.

***

At times these entities have been sort of gliding around, in an angelic and inviting fashion. They would do somersaults and spin my consciousness with them, landing me in a different place. One realm they have resided in has been something like an alien circus (one of the repeating themes that McKenna mentioned in his trips) or a playground, with odd, complex entertainments going on. There was intricate geometry seemingly pouring out of the walls in this space. The entities would come out of these walls as well, do some mind-bending, cheeky acrobatics move, and then take my consciousness with them to a different room or scene. It was like a programme was being run, or a ceremony was being conducted, in which these entities had to show me everything they possibly could. They were in control, as gods, in this alien circus. There was also the sense that I had shown up unannounced, but that I was a very close friend, so although the entities looked surprised to see me, they were also celebrating my arrival.

There is infinitely unfolding geometry and zany patterns (alive, hyper-complex, and self-transforming), which are one and the same with the entities. These beings are the silly, loving, entertaining, giving, and unfolding essence of this dimension. The realm they inhabit bears a striking similarity to some of Ilene Meyer's paintings, such as *Spheres of Enchantment*, *Bagatelle*, and *It's All in the Wrist*. These paintings of fantasy worlds featuring circus performers and jesters make me wonder if Meyer herself was inspired by the DMT experience.

There are alien workshops where these merry creatures are making celestial toys; and they are constructing these toys in a jolly, comic, and frenzied manner. It's like being inside an alien cuckoo clock world, a wacky factory that pumps out endless fun, play, and beauty. These beings appear to be turning the engines of creation. I would also liken the experience to travelling through a giant pinball machine with a carnival atmosphere. Entertainers appear out of cuckoo clock doorways — like cosmic, magic portals — and they make their entrance with a sweet, smooth, and graceful motion. These entities are constantly opening and closing these portals to other dimensions. They cheekily and seductively edge out, make an appearance, do something profoundly bizarre, and then make their leave to give a fellow trickster the chance to outdo the performance.

There are circus-themed spinning tops, which the entities will draw my attention to. They then open the lids of these spinning tops — like the opening of a treasure chest — to reveal what's inside. These beings also wear hats like these tops, similar to those multi-coloured propeller hats. Both the hat and the propeller are spinning at an incredible speed. An entity will go to lift it off its head in a very intentional way, as if to say, "Okay, now pay attention to what I'm about to show you." And what is revealed is astounding. This peculiar action will turn into hallways, which contain another entity doing another 'revealing' action, and this process repeats *ad infinitum* — exponentially increasing in complexity and novelty.

The entertainer entities delicately spring apart, in a jack-in-the-box-style motion. They're made up of playing card patterns and have cosmically black, deep eyes that sparkle with lively excitement. The manner of their communication is like a performance, which is characterised by an unveiling, spiralling quality — they are sacred comedians delivering holy punchlines. There is this quick, seductive glossolalia ('speaking in tongues') emanating from the entities. They're whispering sweet nothings and secrets into my ears. Their glossolalia is high pitched, glitchy, vibratory, and visual, and is spoken like some sort of puerile, elfin gobbledygook.

The entities are giggling, grinning, sticking out their tongues, pulling faces, tilting their heads, capering, twirling, performing magic tricks, outstretching their arms in a *ta-da* kind of way, and doing all kinds of weird poses. Like many trickster figures, these beings are nimble and unpredictable. And they seem to make gestures that are typical of jesters and entertainers, which we could call *jestures* or *jesticulations*.

They are caressing and tickling me, patting me on the head, pinching my cheeks, blowing on my face, telling me to *shh* (not in a reprimanding way like a parent, but with a playful, secretive attitude). These magician-, performer-type entities are twisting their moustaches fast and excitedly. These jovial characters love to make twizzling motions. They will turn or spin around and look surprised and joyous with such intense (almost manic) energy — shimmering and alert.

The entities also sometimes display a distinctive sense of humour. One time they recognised when my foot touched something in the room, creating a kind of *oops* moment, as I accidentally added this external interruption to the experience. In response, these cheeky little entities started their own creative interruptions, rushing around me and bumping into me. Then they would turn around to apologise and say something like "Oh sorry, excuse me, pardon me" — in a sarcastic, innocent, and childish kind of tone. They wanted to poke fun at my frustration with the outside world briefly interrupting the experience. And they would let out a squeaky *tee-hee* while doing this.

Owsley Stanley, a countercultural chemist in the 1960s (who, by his own account, produced 10 million doses of LSD between 1965 and 1967), describes these entities as "Tinkertoy men".[29] And I can see what he means. Their 'bodies' and movements are very much like those Tinkertoys — mechanical, colourful, and cartoon-like. Because of their jocular nature, the entities will play games like peekaboo and poke their head around a corner to take a sneaky and caring glance at me. They insistently compete for my attention, elbowing each other aside to get to me; then they will point at something important for me to look at. I have to see as much as possible during my short and hurried stay here.

When the experience starts to fade and wind down, the entities — before completely disappearing, along with the space they inhabit — give a last cheer and say 'goodbye' in a mischievous, paradoxical manner, because it also feels like they are saying 'hello'. When they retreat, another message they express at this point is "Voila, now you know, please come again soon". They grin and laugh as the Cosmic Joke is revealed. I am left filled with disbelief, wonder, contentment, bliss, gratitude, and humility.

## An Analysis of DMT Jesters and Tricksters

Based on varied experiences (not just my own), a DMT entity can be your typical trickster: a clown, imp, fairy, joker, jester, Harlequin, and so on, but they can take multifarious forms too: an alien, child, animal, angel, god, or goddess but manifesting strangely, idiosyncratically, and in an incomprehensible fashion, as is DMT's nature. They can be combinations of forms or appear as mythical entities, abstract concepts (e.g. love and understanding), or pure fractal geometry. Yet, all these other types of entities can still typify, be imbued with, and exude the trickster archetype.

Hyde describes the trickster archetype as a "boundary-crosser".[30] They break both societal and physical rules. The writer Paul Mattick reiterates this point, noting that tricksters "violate principles of social and natural order, playfully disrupting normal life and then re-establishing it on a new basis".[31] And this is exactly what the jesters and trickster entities in the DMT realm like to do. They break the rules, in an absolutely confounding manner. The way they manifest themselves, move and perform tricks, and deconstruct and construct reality bends all notions of causality, normality, and sense. These entities will casually throw all of your reference points and preconceptions out the window. Breaking the laws of physics and playing games with reality is what they do best.

The clown or 'dance manager' of the Tübatulabal people of Southern California was a participant in ceremonies who would dance backwards and talk in a nonsensical way. Here we find another parallel with the strange language and surprising movements of the DMT trickster entities. In some parts of the world, the trickster has superhuman capacities, employs magic and shape-shifting powers, and appears as a godlike figure. Similarly, the DMT trickster entities are often shape-shifting and carrying out alluring magic tricks, in a perplexing fashion. They too may take on the appearance of deities (e.g. Egyptian, Mayan, and Hindu gods) yet retain their essential trickster nature.

Relevant to this discussion is the trickster Mercurius (or Mercury), the god of commerce, messages, communication, and trickery. His name is related to the Latin word *merx*, from which we get the English words merchandise, merchant, and commerce. It may also correspond to the Latin word *mercari* ('to trade'). It is interesting to note that the tricksters of the DMT realm can act like enthusiastic traders, pushing their strange and astounding products and gifts onto you, like a hyperactive vendor at a busy market in Morocco or India.

In a word, McKenna described the DMT entities as "zany",[32] which means amusingly unconventional and idiosyncratic. The word zany is derived from Zanni, a character in the *commedia dell'arte*, an early form of professional theatre that originated in Italy in the fourteenth century. These types of theatrical performances featured masked characters and were popular forms of entertainment in the sixteenth to eighteenth centuries. Zanni, a clever servant and trickster, is one of the character types. Arlecchino, or Harlequin, is the best known of the Zanni or comic servant characters in the *commedia dell'arte*.

One of the most impressive and emphatic traits of Harlequin is his physical agility and nimbleness. He would perform all sorts of acrobatics, such as somersaults, cartwheels, and flips. Harlequin was always on the move. And here we find another curious parallel with the trickster entities in the DMT experience since they behave in a similar way, except their level of acrobatics and Harlequin-like gesticulations are intensified beyond comprehension. Harlequin is one of the masked characters you will come across at the Carnival of Venice, which is said to have originated in 1162. In this centuries-old Italian tradition, we can find many other masks and costumes that bear an eerie resemblance to the jester and trickster entities in the DMT experience and the patterns that adorn them.

Carnivals themselves have been around since the Middle Ages and are present throughout the world. They traditionally precede Lent in the Christian calendar, providing time for debauchery, indulgence, feasting, and celebration, before the period of fasting and spiritual rigour that characterises Lent. The carnival epitomises a party atmosphere, featuring various kinds of entertainment and parades while combining elements of the circus. As with the Carnival of Venice, people wear elaborate costumes and masks.

The Russian philosopher and literary critic Mikhail Bakhtin has argued that a carnival involves a general reversal of everyday norms and rules — and this quality, as we have seen, is central to the spirit of the trickster. The jester-like aspect of ourselves, or the trickster archetype that resides deep within us, finds its home in the expression of the carnival. Bakhtin additionally claimed that the carnival is deep-rooted in the human psyche, as clowns and jesters seem to be. Indeed, we find many parallels between the traditional conception of the jester and the *carnivalesque*, a concept coined by Bakhtin and spelled out in his book *Rabelais and His World* (1965). The carnivalesque is the spirit of the carnival, which Bakhtin refers to as the subversion of hierarchies and social norms. "[O]ne might say that carnival celebrated temporary liberation from the prevailing truth and from the established order; it marked the suspension of all hierarchical rank, privileges, norms, and prohibitions," says Bakhtin.[33] And this spirit is connected to laughter. He writes,

Clowns and fools ... are characteristic of the medieval culture of humor. They were the constant, accredited representatives of the carnival spirit in everyday life out of carnival season ... carnival is the people's second life, organized on the basis of laughter. It is a festive life. Festivity is a peculiar quality of all comic rituals and spectacles of the Middle Ages.[34]

The Feast of Fools, a feast day celebrated by clergy in Europe in the Middle Ages, typified the carnivalesque. The celebration involved an inversion of power, in which fools became kings and popes for the day. The Feast of Fools inside the church may have been much tamer than rumours at the time made it out to be,[35] yet the celebrations and parades outside the church doors featured drinking, merry-making, cross-dressing, singing, and other mischievous behaviour that would not normally be tolerated. In representations of the event, such as in Pieter Bruegel the Elder's engraving *The Festival of Fools* (circa 1570), we see that the celebration is depicted as chaotic, playful, and disruptive, just like the trickster. Perhaps the natural motif associated with the inversion of order is the circus or carnival (both are closely related). If the DMT experience is an expression of the inversion of order (the trickster archetype and the carnivalesque), then it makes sense that a circus or parade-type environment would be the visual corollary of the experience. McKenna might have been correct after all when he stated that the archetype of DMT is the circus.

In *Problems of Dostoevsky's Poetics* (1963), Bakhtin discusses the 'carnival sense of the world', an attitude that "is opposed to that one-sided and gloomy official seriousness which is dogmatic and hostile to evolution and change, which seeks to absolutize a given condition of existence or a given social order".[36] The carnival tradition stems from a "culture of folk humor" (subverting norms), according to Bakhtin.[37] This is a culture that has developed over thousands of years. The jester is likewise born out of such a culture. Bakhtin also includes the "popular sphere of the marketplace" in his account of the carnivalesque since the marketplace was a site of transgressive discourse and laughter,[38] a counterpoint to the serious church and feudal culture of the Middle Ages.[39] This aspect of the carnivalesque is relevant to this discussion because the DMT realm, also known as 'hyperspace', can have the appearance of a market, or at least have the atmosphere of one.

The proliferation and ubiquity of the carnival seem to point to an intrinsic part of human nature: our jovial, wild, and celebratory side. However, while our natural proclivities may help to explain why the themes of carnival, circus, jester, and trickster are commonly reported in the DMT experience, it is still somewhat mysterious that these themes are so deeply ingrained in human psychology. We also do not know *why* DMT, as a substance, is so efficacious in bringing these themes to the surface, particularly in the bizarre manner it does so. While a Jungian analysis of the DMT experience offers some fascinating insights, it can only take us so far.

Many psychonauts have also reported negative DMT experiences involving jesters and tricksters, and this might have to do with the darker or shadowy aspects of the user. If the jester is a partial reflection or representation of who we are, then a negative DMT experience — where sinister jesters mock you and mess with you — may point to something uncomfortable about yourself that needs to be addressed. For example, the uncomfortable truth may be about a lack of self-control in your life, which has led to negative consequences. Similarly, the jester itself has a darker, shadow form, making him prone to constant inebriation, drug abuse, or perversion — essentially, any negative attribute that is caused by a loss of impulse control. The jester's desire (so, our desire) for present-minded joy can be beneficial or harmful, depending on how it is harnessed. In the words of Jung: "The trickster is a collective shadow figure, an epitome of all the inferior traits of character in individuals."[40]

The message conveyed during these challenging experiences is often not at first palpable but, after a period of introspection, meaning can be unearthed and integrated. You should pay close attention to the evil jesters and clowns in the DMT realm, rather than cower in fear at them. They may be making an appearance because you have been hiding from certain negative aspects of yourself. The jester, however, leaves no stone unturned and may poke fun at you in quite a disturbing way in order to teach you an important lesson.

Even when these beings do not appear blatantly unfriendly, mocking, or malevolent, there can be a sense that they have that potential. One of the participants in Strassman's studies on DMT recounted the following from her high-dose experience:

I started flying through an intense circus-like environment. I've never been that out-of-body before.... We went through a maze at an incredibly fast pace. I say "we" because it seemed like I was accompanied.... There was a crazy circus sideshow. It was extravagant. It's hard to describe. They looked like Jokers. They were almost performing for me. They were funny looking, bells on their hats, big noses. However, I had the feeling they could turn on me, a little less than completely friendly.[41]

There is an argument to be made that the expectation of seeing jesters and clowns, which have become associated with DMT for many users, leads to people encountering them in that state. This role of the user's mindset (or 'set') is plausible. Nevertheless, clearly there are many users who do not have such an expectation, like the participants in Strassman's research, so this explanation may apply only in some cases. One could argue that Strassman's research subjects — or other DMT users — saw jester entities due to the influence of McKenna's talks; however, we can find descriptions of elf-like entities seen in the DMT space that precede those of McKenna.

In an article from 1966, titled 'Programmed Communication During Experiences with DMT', the psychedelic guru Timothy Leary describes encountering "a band of radar-antennae, elf-like insects merrily working away".[42] But could Leary himself have been influenced by earlier trip reports? In his article, he mentions the work of the Hungarian chemist Stephen Szára, who was the first person to scientifically study the psychoactive effects of DMT. Szára recounts in a 1958 paper how one participant under the influence of the drug "saw strange creatures, dwarfs or something, they were black and moved about".[43]

Thus, it appears that elf-like entities have long been encountered in the DMT realm, independent of reports that could have had the potential to influence people's experiences. Now you may be thinking, *but elves and dwarfs are not jesters*. That is true, but there are similarities between these entities. Firstly, they share a mischievous nature. Secondly, elves, dwarves, and gnomes are often imagined or depicted wearing pointy and/ or floppy hats, not unlike the jester hat. 'Elf', 'dwarf', 'gnome', 'clown', or 'jester' may all be different ways to describe the *type* of entity one may meet in the DMT space; in other words, there are many forms, or approximate descriptions, unified by the same underlying character. In the artwork of Harry Pack, for instance, there are depictions of cheeky DMT creatures that look both elf-like and clown-like.

Graham Hancock, in his book *Supernatural: Meetings with the Ancient Teachers of Mankind* (2005), suggests that altered states could be the origin of clowns, rather than clowns appearing on the cultural landscape first and then making their way into people's altered states. He writes,

[W]here did the idea for clowns come from in the first place? Were the visions of carnival-type figures seen by Strassman's subjects, Maria Sabina, Michael Harner, and others influenced by strictly modern and culturally contingent television and circus spectaculars? Or is it possible that the direction of influence really flows the other way, and that the inspiration for the earliest clowns came from visions and hallucinations seen in altered states of consciousness — whether entered spontaneously or under the influence of DMT-linked hallucinogens? We know that at least as far back as ancient Greece, a land rich in psychoactive plants, stage plays, farces, and mimes frequently featured performances by dwarves and children dressed up in ways quite similar to modern circus buffoons. Before that, the history of such theatrical figures is obscure — as well it might be if they had emerged from occult realms that were originally accessible only in visions.[44]

In a 2018 paper, Michael Winkelman — an anthropologist and researcher of altered states — analyses psychedelic entities from an evolutionary perspective. He found that ayahuasca and DMT entities were similar to conceptions of gnomes, dwarves, elves, angels, and extraterrestrials. Psychedelic entities, he states, "exemplify the properties of anthropomorphism, exhibiting qualities of humans".[45]

Winkelman argues the features of these entities reflect certain innate aspects of human psychology, which confer a biological advantage. These capacities also help explain why people experience spirits and believe in them. These human tendencies include *agency detection*: perceiving agents with intentions in one's surroundings, *anthropomorphism*: attributing human characteristics to non-human things or events, and *Theory of Mind* (ToM) or *mindreading*: inferring the mental states of others. These faculties, if activated by DMT, could account for the anthropomorphic appearances and behaviours of the DMT entities.

The entities may be the end result of the brain trying to predict patterns in ambiguous stimuli, combined with agency detection and the complex fractal imagery that is characteristic of DMT. Indeed, many users report that these beings are highly geometric in nature. Certain fractal or geometric shapes may also lend an 'elfin' quality to the beings or, as other users may report, a 'jester' quality.

Dennis McKenna, a psychedelic researcher and the brother of Terence McKenna, was once asked whether he thought DMT entities were archetypes in the mind or autonomous beings. He responded,

That's the $64 million dollar question right there — is it another dimension? [Terence and I] were convinced that it was a portal into another dimension. But now, I think it's impossible to say. I think these are archetypes, but the crux of the question is, is it another place? It certainly has that feeling about it.[46]

## An Evaluation of Jungian Archetypes

There are some conceptual difficulties related to the Jungian archetypes. These need to be discussed if we want to properly assess the archetypal explanation of DMT jesters and tricksters. Strictly speaking, Jung stressed that archetypal figures, such as the trickster, are not *archetypes-as-such* but archetypal images that have crystallised out of archetypes-as-such, or underlying patterns or forms shared by many images.[47] In *Man and His Symbols*, Jung writes that "definite mythological images of motifs ... are nothing more than conscious representations; it would be absurd to assume that such variable representations could be inherited".[48] These representations originate from deep, instinctual sources or 'archaic remnants' — residues of the long history and evolution of the human species — which Jung called 'archetypes' or 'primordial images'. "The archetype is a tendency to form such representations of a motif — representations that can vary a great deal in detail without losing their basic pattern," says Jung.[49] One problem is that Jung did not define the exact relationship between an image and its archetype.

In order to help resolve this issue, the Jungian analyst Anthony Stevens explains that the *archetype-as-such* is both an innate predisposition to create an image (e.g. the trickster) and something deep in us that prepares us for — and allows us to appropriately respond to — that image. Essentially, we know a trickster when we see one. The common fear of snakes, which is felt by urban dwellers who are not exposed to these creatures, seems to provide supporting evidence for the existence of inherited mental contents.[50] We can also offer an evolutionary explanation for these types of fears. Vestigial snake and spider phobias make sense since our ancient ancestors would have been more likely to survive by having such fears, thereby passing them on to their progeny. But what, we may ask, is the evolutionary advantage of an archetype that fosters the trickster, or any other archetypal figure for that matter?

To offer one perspective, various researchers have suggested that humour and laughter evolved, not as an accidental by-product of something else advantageous but as a distinct feature of human psychology that aids our survival. When Pueblo Indians maintain that humour and laughter heal, there is a strong scientific basis for this claim. For example, Dr Lee Berk and his colleagues in the 1980s discovered that laughter helps the brain to regulate the stress hormones cortisol and epinephrine. They also discovered a link between laughter and the production of antibodies and endorphins (the latter are the body's natural pain and stress relievers).[51] We also know that laughter is associated with a range of positive psychological outcomes: reductions in anxiety, tension, and depression as well as improvements in mood, self-esteem, hope, energy, vigour, creativity, friendliness, helpfulness, interpersonal interaction, and quality of life.[52]

Studies also indicate that humour engages brain regions involved in reward responses.[53] Evolutionary scientists posit that humour and laughter are rewards for being able to spot a pattern. This pattern can take various forms: 'it's so true' humour, the similarity between the comedian's storytelling and the mental image in the listener's mind, the contrast between expectation and reality, or some form of reversal (as achieved with sarcasm). The British science writer Alastair Clarke proposed an evolutionary theory of laughter in his book *The Faculty of Adaptability*, known as Pattern Recognition Theory. Speaking on the theory, Clarke states,

Effectively it explains that humour occurs when the brain recognizes a pattern that surprises it, and that recognition of this sort is rewarded with the experience of the humorous response, an element of which is broadcast as laughter.[54]

He adds,

An ability to recognize patterns instantly and unconsciously has proved a fundamental weapon in the cognitive arsenal of human beings. The humorous reward has encouraged the development of such faculties, leading to the unique perceptual and intellectual abilities of our species.[55]

These evolutionary ideas, at the very least, provide some food for thought as to what substantial benefits tricksters can offer us. Yet despite the advantages of having, expressing, and encountering a trickster side to humanity, there are still other criticisms of Jung's conception of archetypes that need to be addressed. Firstly, many critics have argued that Jung, in formulating and expounding his archetypes, is guilty of essentialism.[56] This is the idea that things have an essence, a set of attributes that are necessary to their identity, and these attributes can be shared among many things that demarcate them as belonging to a certain category (e.g. a table, tree, person, and so on). At face value, essentialism may seem uncontroversial. However, in the discussion of archetypes, it results in various difficulties.

While we may think we can discern the essential nature of the trickster, for example, this archetypal motif — and archetypal motifs in general — is vaguely defined. As the above discussion highlights, portrayals of the trickster are noticeably diverse. The very fact that we use the term 'trickster' is not itself supportive of essentialism — it could simply be a sign that helps us to group together similar archetypal images, rather than denote one essential characteristic they have in common. But if archetypes cannot be adequately generalised or specified, then they may elude rigorous study and systematic analysis. How can you tell one archetype from another? As the philosopher Walter A. Shelburne puts it, "archetypal motifs are not easily divided into unambiguous, discrete types."[57]

Furthermore, if the archetypes are interpreted as residing in a kind of metaphysical or supernatural realm, how do you go about proving their existence?[58] By what scientific methods can we locate the trickster? Jungian analysts and mythologists can point to the plethora of tricksters found in cultures around the world. However, this cultural analysis does not shed light on the evolutionary reason that archetypes exist — we might need to speculate further, as I did previously, that tricksters are in some way connected to the evolution of humour and laughter.

Perhaps neuroscience could help us better understand the archetypes. As Jung stated, "The universal similarity of human brains leads to the universal possibility of a uniform mental functioning. This functioning is the collective psyche."[59] If we were to take on board at least some version of the physicalist or materialist conception of the human mind, then it might be possible to identify certain brain regions or processes that relate to the trickster archetype. Nonetheless, some critics of archetypal theory believe that it is a non-falsifiable theory, meaning it is not capable of being proven false.[60] The philosopher Karl Popper argued that falsifiability is a basic scientific principle. As he maintained, "In so far as a scientific statement speaks about reality, it must be falsifiable; and in so far as it is not falsifiable, it does not speak about reality."[61] If a claim or idea cannot be proven false, then it cannot lead to progress in human knowledge.

This may mean that archetypes are not a suitable subject for scientific inquiry. But perhaps this is not so problematic. After all, experiences can still be valuable, meaningful, profound, and life-changing, even if they cannot be neatly categorised and solidified. Moreover, Jung emphasised that archetypal theory is best suited to descriptive psychological study.[62] This is a non-experimental approach that is chiefly concerned with comprehensive phenomenological descriptions (reports of what is experienced from the first-person point of view). The lack of experimentation does not mean that this approach is pseudoscientific, only that its methods of theorising, research, and application are different in nature from the scientific method.

Jung argued that archetypal theory did not belong in the camp of experimental psychology, which is the application of the scientific method to how individuals respond to controlled experiments. Instead, Jung believed that analysts could precisely reveal certain things about human psychology based on clinical case studies: what patients display in psychotherapy sessions. (Cross-cultural instantiations of archetypes are viewed as evidence too; the available methods for discovering the existence of archetypes, then, are not *only* introspective in nature.)[63] Nevertheless, we can still take issue with Jung's prioritisation of inner experience over empirical data, which makes it difficult for archetypes to shed their quasi-mystical status and become something a bit more clear, grounded, and verifiable. In addition, as Shelburne writes,

> The archetypal theory is postulated to be the end result of the interaction between the innate archetype per se [the archetype-as-such] and the environment. But ... the archetypal theory does not attempt to specify precisely how these two factors interrelate to produce the archetypal image. Thus, in the absence of any archetypal laws specifying how these two factors interact to produce the archetypal images, the question arises as to how the innateness of the archetype per se is to be established. For if we are not in fact able to separate these two factors through some sort of isolation experiment, it might well seem that the claim that the archetypes are innate, rather than acquired as a result of experiences in individual development, would be on very weak ground. Moreover, if we cannot substantiate the innate nature of the archetype per se, then the theory as a whole will lack a credible basis.[64]

Leaving aside these criticisms of Jung's theory of archetypes, let us return to the relevant archetype in question. In his reflections on the trickster, Jung drew attention to the omnipresent, perennial nature of this character as well as its ancient origins. He said,

> In picaresque tales, in carnivals and revels, in magic rites of healing, in man's religious fears and exaltations, this phantom of the trickster haunts the mythology of all ages, sometimes in quite unmistakable form, sometimes in strangely modulated guise. He is obviously a "psychologem," an archetypal psychic structure of extreme antiquity. In his clearest manifestations he is a faithful reflection of an absolutely undifferentiated human consciousness, corresponding to a psyche that has hardly left the animal level.[65]

He adds that the trickster

> is a forerunner of the savior, and, like him, God, man, and animal at once. He is both subhuman and superhuman, a bestial and divine being, whose chief and most alarming characteristic is his unconsciousness.[66]

Here again, we see how the trickster is the embodiment of paradoxicality. The trickster has, at once, superhuman abilities yet an animal level of consciousness. However, does this correspond to people's experiences of the trickster during their DMT journeys? Of those experiences featuring jesters and tricksters, descriptions and interpretations will inevitably vary — even wildly so. But it is hard for me to say whether the tricksters I have encountered were unconscious in the Jungian sense of being driven by instincts (making them animal-like), resulting in a lack of inhibition. In some sense, they did possess that wild, unrestrained energy, yet they also seemed to have an awareness, intelligence, and wisdom of their own. It is possible, of course, that the tricksters springing out of hyperspace are intermingled with other, more 'conscious' archetypes (such as the Wise Old Man, the Mother, or the Goddess). This could help explain their other features, such as the exuberant giving of wisdom and knowledge, or tender loving care.

But the intermingling of Jungian archetypes cannot exhaust all of the characteristics of DMT entities, especially since their nature may completely defy language itself. Nonetheless, it is endlessly fascinating to note the prevalence of jesters. What is even more interesting is that when DMT is ingested in the form of ayahuasca, which includes the addition of the MAOI-containing *Banisteriopsis caapi* vine, the jesters lose their predominance. Instead, we find the archetype of the Mother becomes more prominent (users commonly refer to this entity or presence as 'Mother Ayahuasca').

People can, undoubtedly, have archetypal experiences of the Mother or motherly energy in the DMT experience and can come across jesters under the influence of ayahuasca. However, for some strange reason, the type of archetype that will arise appears to be closely related to how the DMT is taken (whether it is smoked in crystalline form or ingested along with an MAOI). Nevertheless, we should not lose sight of the possibility that *expecting* certain entities or presences to appear (jesters with DMT and the Mother with ayahuasca) — in other words, your *set* — may influence the predominance of those entities. Furthermore, let's not forget that users of other psychedelic compounds can meet jesters during their experiences.

It is not clear whether the experience of different archetypes corresponds to markedly different levels of activation in certain areas of the brain. Brain scans of people under the influence of DMT have already been carried out. It would be illuminating to see in further studies if reports of jesters and tricksters are associated with different brain activity than what is seen during encounters with other archetypal entities. Jungian archetypes have been criticised for their lack of scientific credibility, but could modern brain imaging technology help to improve our understanding of them?

## Jester Therapy

We should not underestimate the healing, therapeutic potential of tricksters. In contemporary society, we see real-life percolations of our trickster side in the form of stand-up comics. Comedians point out and probe taboos and controversial subjects, meddle with our expectations, and elicit shock and surprise. To sit in a comedy show and laugh as a collective at the jokes of these modern-day jesters can be curative in a number of ways. Laughing at the dark and forbidden elements of human nature and society is an unburdening of sorts. It makes the darkness lighter. Moreover, when a comedian's jokes strike a chord — or hit a nerve — this can help us examine the beliefs and attitudes that we deeply cling to.

But I believe that comedians are expressing an innate trickster quality that we all have, by virtue of the trickster's archetypal nature. In the DMT experience, we can witness the projection of the trickster in manifold ways. It can be expressed in recognisable trickster barb — appearing as, say, a jester or clown — or it may be expressed through the intent and actions of the DMT entities, even if they do not appear as jesters. What matters is the message the entities are trying to convey. Personally, when encountering trickster-type entities, I have attempted to see if I can apply their manifestation and behaviour to my own life. What meaningful message can I take from these strange entities?

In light of the Jungian concept of individuation, that is, integrating the conscious and the unconscious, I think it is important to recognise the DMT tricksters as being part of myself, representing me in the experience. And so it seems that wholeness and harmony must come from integrating this trickster nature, as well as the other archetypes. Much can be gained from the trickster aspect of human psychology; after all, the trickster is often a wellspring of wisdom and joy. I believe this is showcased in the DMT experience in the form of *jester therapy*.

The DMT trickster entities radiate silliness and play, perhaps communicating the message that we should be more like them. I believe that if we assimilate the trickster archetype, we will notice various improvements in our life. This is something that is hinted at in the DMT experience, in the way that it offers us a fresh perspective. For example, the DMT jesters help to make things lighter by quickly lifting the burden of seriousness and heaviness that we have become so accustomed to feeling in our everyday lives. They show us an alternative, more joyful mode of being. We can also think of these entities as the court jesters of the mind, appearing because the inner king or ruler (i.e. the ego) needs to be mocked and kept in check, thereby helping to achieve a greater degree of psychological balance.

These psychedelic jesters reveal to us that the extent to which we take life seriously is ridiculous — a hilarious joke. This can be an extremely therapeutic experience and realisation, so long as the wisdom is deeply integrated. Indeed, one common takeaway message from the DMT experience is that we would be psychologically healthier if we could view the world as an absurd game deserving of playfulness and laughter. In everyday situations, we can practise jester therapy. By mocking and laughing at the world and ourselves, we can approach life much more cheerfully.

## Endnotes

1.  Strassman, R. (2001). *DMT: The Spirit Molecule: A Doctor's Revolutionary Research into the Biology of Near-Death and Mystical Experiences*, p. 192. Rochester, VT: Park Street Press.

2.  McKenna, T. (1994). 'Rap Dancing into the Third Millennium', organism.earth. https://www.organism.earth/library/document/rap-dancing-into-the-third-millennium

3.  Plato (c. 360 BC). *Timaeus*, p. 41. Translated by Zeyl, D.J. Indianapolis: Hackett Publishing Company, 2000.

4.  Jung, C.G. (1959). Part 1: *Archetypes and the Collective Unconscious* in *The Collected Works of C.G. Jung, Volume 9*, pp. 4–5. Edited and translated by Adler, G. and Hull, R.F.C. 2nd ed. Princeton: Princeton University Press, 2014.

5.  Jung, C.G. (1964). *Man and His Symbols*, p. 57. New York: Dell Publishing.

6.  Jung, C.G. (1963). *Memories, Dreams, Reflections*, pp. 195–196. Edited by Jaffé, A. and translated by Winston, R. and Winston, C.B. New York: Vintage Books, 1989.

7.  Fontana, D. (2006). *Meditating with Mandalas: 52 New Mandalas to Help You Grow in Peace and Awareness*, p. 10. London: Duncan Baird.

8.  Storr, A. (1998). *The Essential Jung*, pp. 91–94. Glasgow: Fontana.

9.  Ibid., pp. 109–118.

10. Ibid., pp. 93–96.

11. Campbell, J. (1949). *The Hero with a Thousand Faces*, pp. 23–31. Novato, CA: New World Library, 2012.

12. Vogler, C. (1985). 'A Practical Guide to The Hero with a Thousand Faces'. https://www.mccc.edu/~voorhees/dma135/Vogler_Practical_Guide.pdf

13. Seastrom, L. (2015). 'Mythic Discovery Within the Inner Reaches of Outer Space: Joseph Campbell Meets George Lucas - Part I', Star Wars website, 22 October. https://www.starwars.com/news/mythic-discovery-within-the-inner-reaches-of-outer-space-joseph-campbell-meets-george-lucas-part-i

14. Vogler, C. (2019). 'How The Lion King Got the Hero's Journey Treatment: Thanks to Synchronicity and Some Help from a Plagiarist', Chris Vogler's Writer's Journey Blog, 7 August. https://chrisvogler.wordpress.com/2019/08/07/how-the-lion-king-got-the-heros-journey-treatment/

15. Mann, D. (2011). 'Joseph Campbell and the Hero with a Thousand Faces' in *Understanding Society*, pp. 224–230. Oxford: Oxford University Press.

16. Hollis, J. (2017). 'Trickster', Jung Society of Washington website, 15 October. https://www.jung.org/blog/5332703

17. Ibid.

18. Otto, B.K. (2001). *Fools Are Everywhere: The Court Jester Around the World*, p. 41. Chicago: University of Chicago Press.

19. Jung, C.G. (1956). 'On the Psychology of the Trickster Figure' in *The Trickster: A Study in American Indian Mythology*, p. 200. Edited by Radin, P. New York: Greenwood Press.

20. Ibid., p. 195.

21. Ballinger, F. (1991-1992). '*Ambigere*: The Euro-American Picaro and the Native American Trickster'. *MELIUS*, 17(1), pp. 21–38.

22. Hyde, L. (1998). *Trickster Makes This World: How Disruptive Imagination Creates Culture*, pp. 17–39. Edinburgh: Canongate Books, 2008.

23. Carlin, G. (2001). *Napalm and Silly Putty*, dedication page. New York: Hyperion Books.

24. Otto, B.K. (2001). *Fools Are Everywhere: The Court Jester Around the World*, pp. 41–42. Chicago: University of Chicago Press.

25. Ibid., p. 42.

26. Janik, V.K. (1998). *Fools and Jesters in Literature, Art, and History: A Bio-Bibliographical Sourcebook*, p. 247. Westport, CT: Greenwood Press.

27. Bassil-Morozow, H. (2011). *The Trickster in Contemporary Film*, p. 20. London: Routledge.

28. Ibid., p. 23.

29. Entheogenesis Australia - Entheo TV. 'Bear Stanley: Reflections on Life, LSD and DMT'. 20 January, 2014. YouTube video, 28:06. https://www.youtube.com/watch?v=geRXSVuPRhU

30. Hyde, L. (1998). *Trickster Makes This World: How Disruptive Imagination Creates Culture*, p. 7. Edinburgh: Canongate Books, 2008.

31. Mattick, P. (1998). 'Hotfoots of the Gods', *The New York Times*, 15 February. https://archive.nytimes.com/www.nytimes.com/books/98/02/15/reviews/980215.15mattict.html

32. McKenna, T. (1990). 'Time and Mind', Erowid, 26/27 May. https://erowid.org/culture/characters/mckenna_terence/mckenna_terence_time_mind.shtml

33. Bakhtin, M. (1965). *Rabelais and His World*, p. 10. Translated by Iswolsky, H. Bloomington, IN: Indiana University Press, 1984.

34. Ibid., p. 8.

35. Laskow, S. (2017). 'The New Year's Feast That Transformed Fools Into Popes and Kings', *Atlas Obscura*, 29 December. https://www.atlasobscura.com/articles/feast-of-fools-medieval-tradition

36. Bakhtin, M. (1963). *Problems of Dostoevsky's Poetics*, p. 160. Minneapolis: University of Minnesota Press, 1984.

37. Bakhtin, M. (1965). *Rabelais and His World*, p. 4. Translated by Iswolsky, H. Bloomington, IN: Indiana University Press, 1984.

38. Ibid., p. 9.

39. Ibid., p. 4.

40. Jung, C.G. (1956). 'On the Psychology of the Trickster Figure' in *The Trickster: A Study in American Indian Mythology*, p. 209. Edited by Radin, P. New York: Greenwood Press.

41. Strassman, R. (2001). *DMT: The Spirit Molecule: A Doctor's Revolutionary Research into the Biology of Near-Death and Mystical Experiences*, p. 169. Rochester, VT: Park Street Press.

42. Leary, T. (1966). 'Programmed Communication During Experiences with DMT'. *Psychedelic Review*, 8. https://erowid.org/chemicals/dmt/dmt_journal5.shtml

43. Böszörményi, Z. and Szára, S. (1958). 'Dimethyltryptamine Experiments with Psychotics'. *Journal of Mental Science*, 104(435), pp. 445–453.

44. Hancock, G. (2005). *Supernatural: Meetings with the Ancient Teachers of Mankind*, pp. 526–527. London: Arrow Books.

45. Winkelman, M.J. (2018). 'An ontology of psychedelic entity experiences in evolutionary psychology and neurophenomenology'. *Journal of Psychedelic Studies*, 2(1), pp. 5–23.

46. O'Neill, L. (2015). 'What are the machine elves?', *Monster Children*, 4 June. https://www.monsterchildren.com/articles/what-are-the-machine-elves

47. Anthony, S. (2006). 'The archetypes' in *The Handbook of Jungian Psychology: Theory, Practice and Applications*, pp. 74–90. Edited by Papadopolous, R.K. London: Routledge.

48. Jung, C.G. (1964). *Man and His Symbols*, p. 57. New York: Dell Publishing.

49. Ibid., p. 58.

50. Anthony, S. (2006). 'The archetypes' in *The Handbook of Jungian Psychology: Theory, Practice and Applications*, pp. 84–85. Edited by Papadopolous, R.K. London: Routledge.

51. Berk, L.S., Tan, S.A., Fry, W.F., Napier, B.J., Lee, J.W., Hubbard, R.W., Lewis, J.E., and Eby, W.C. (1989). 'Neuroendocrine and Stress Hormone Changes During Mirthful Laughter'. *The American Journal of the Medical Sciences*, 298(6), pp. 390–396.

52. Yim, J. (2016). 'Therapeutic Benefits of Laughter in Mental Health: A Theoretical Review'. *Tohoku Journal of Experimental Medicine*, 239(3), pp. 243–249.

53. Franklin, R.G., Jr. and Adams, R.B., Jr. (2011). 'The reward of a good joke: neural correlates of viewing dynamic displays of stand-up comedy'. *Cognitive, Affective, & Behavioral Neuroscience*, 11(4), pp. 508–515.

54. 'Mechanism and function of humor identified by new evolutionary theory' (2008), *EurekAlert!*, 27 June. https://www.eurekalert.org/news-releases/580536

55. Ibid.

56. Colman, W. (2018). 'Are Archetypes Essential?'. *Journal of Analytical Psychology*, 63(3), pp. 336–346.

57. Shelburne, W.A. (1988). *Mythos and Logos in the Thought of Carl Jung: The Theory of the Collective Unconscious in Scientific Perspective*, p. 136. Albany, NY: State University of New York Press.

58. Mills, J. (2014). 'Jung as philosopher: archetypes, the psychoid factor, and the question of the supernatural'. *International Journal of Jungian Studies*, 6(3), pp. 227–242.

59. Jung, C.G. (1976). *The Portable Jung*, p. 94. Edited by Campbell, J. and translated by Hull, R.F.C. London: Penguin Books.

60. Mills, J. (2014). 'Jung as philosopher: archetypes, the psychoid factor, and the question of the supernatural'. *International Journal of Jungian Studies*, 6(3), pp. 227–242.

61. Popper, K. (1935/1959). *The Logic of Scientific Discovery*, p. 316. London: Routledge, 2002.

62. Shelburne, W.A. (1988). *Mythos and Logos in the Thought of Carl Jung: The Theory of the Collective Unconscious in Scientific Perspective*, p. 136. Albany, NY: State University of New York Press.

63. Ibid., p. 123.

64. Ibid., p. 133.

65. Jung, C.G. (1956). 'On the Psychology of the Trickster Figure' in *The Trickster: A Study in American Indian Mythology*, p. 200. Edited by Radin, P. New York: Greenwood Press.

66. Ibid., p. 203.

## Chapter 7

# On Plant Spirits and Psychedelic Teleology, Part I

There are many different ways to conceptualise psychedelics (how we define what they are and what they do). A common definition of these compounds is teleological in nature. This is the belief that psychedelic plants and mushrooms have a purpose, goal, or end. More specifically, those who subscribe to this belief may view natural psychedelics as 'plant spirits' or 'plant teachers' that have a purpose *with us in mind*. These compounds supposedly exist as wise emissaries of the planet (the organismic Earth commonly referred to as Gaia),[1] and by ingesting them, we can become cognisant of wisdom that will serve to benefit life, the natural environment, delicate ecosystems, and the planet as a whole.

There are often ecological messages contained in the psychedelic experience. According to the teleological view, this tells us that psychedelic plants and mushrooms are teachers, and they produce psychoactive compounds to deliver important lessons to us. In his article 'Another Green World: Psychedelics and Ecology', the author Daniel Pinchbeck writes,

I tend to view the naturally occurring psychedelics as emissaries from the larger community of life, bearing elder-species wisdom. As the herbalist Morgan Brent has proposed, it is almost as if the vegetal world assigned certain plants to be the diplomats and teachers to our young and confused species, to help put us on a different path than the one we have chosen, racing to ecological decimation and self-extinction.[2]

For Pinchbeck, there appears to be no other way to explain the "consistent messages" conveyed in the psychedelic experience "of a world out of balance, of the need to take responsibility" and the need to regain a harmonious relationship with the natural world.[3]

I believe there are some issues with this teleological view of psychedelics and Pinchbeck's designation of certain plants as "botanical elders".[4] The notion of 'plant teachers', which casts natural psychedelics as intelligent and purposeful, is a commonplace belief in the psychedelic community. But it is not often met with the counter-narrative: the view that natural psychedelics are non-purposeful, albeit still potentially transformative. This is a view, I believe, that tries not to rely on unfounded or faulty assumptions. While the ecological messages in (certain) psychedelic experiences can *appear* planned, this may not be the most parsimonious or logical explanation for why they arise.

Yet we should ensure that we are not being overly sceptical in these matters, as this can lead to a premature and unjustified rejection of psychedelic teleology. What I am proposing is an open form of scepticism that takes this subject seriously — an approach that avoids knee-jerk dismissiveness, which is unduly confident and intellectually lazy. This is a subject that calls for epistemic humility.

I should also point out that the teleological view of psychedelics is not purely ecological in nature. Many people also believe that psychedelics, as plant teachers, are trying to deliver lessons that have interpersonal and societal value: these might be lessons about being more prosocial and positively impactful in the world. This is another aspect of the teleological perspective that I will examine.

## The Panpsychist Position

An assumption that the teleological view of psychedelics depends on is the notion that plants have consciousness, sentience, or intelligence. For a plant to have wisdom or knowledge and an intention to impart messages to humans, there would first have to be some sort of consciousness from which these states and behaviours arise.

One way to frame the idea of psychedelic plant teleology — and the plant consciousness that underlies it — is in terms of metaphysics, rather than biology (the latter is how 'plant neurobiologists' make the case for plant consciousness, which is a controversial position, causing much debate and disagreement in the scientific community).[5][6]

According to panpsychism, mind or consciousness is a fundamental feature of the universe and is inherent in all things.[7] It is often related to Russellian monism — the metaphysics of mind defended by Bertrand Russell — which is a form of neutral monism (matter and mind are aspects of a neutral foundation of reality). Some Russellian monists view consciousness as an intrinsic property of matter, whereas others think in terms of proto-conscious, proto-experiential, or proto-phenomenal properties: this means there is an original and rudimentary form of consciousness out of which more complex consciousness evolves.[8] These views fall under the conceptual umbrella of monism because their defenders believe a single reality (consciousness) underlies both mind and matter. Russellian monism differs from the dualistic perspective that places mind and matter in two fundamentally different categories of substance, and it differs too from physicalism: the view that the universe is fundamentally physical in nature. Russellian monism promises to avoid the weaknesses of both dualism and physicalism.

Proponents of panpsychism argue this metaphysical position helps to resolve the *hard problem of consciousness*, a term derived from the philosopher of mind David Chalmers. This is the conundrum of how and why physical states are conscious rather than non-conscious, why certain brain states are correlated with consciousness, or how physical processes in the brain give rise to subjective experience. No laws have been identified that explain the relationship between brain activity and phenomenal experiences.[9] The panpsychist solution is that through the adding up of rudimentary forms of consciousness, found in atoms and fundamental particles, the more complex phenomena of consciousness are created.

If we are to take on board the panpsychist way of seeing things, then we can imagine that complex plant consciousness is made up of combinations of rudimentary proto-conscious properties. So-called 'plant teachers', then, may be the unique assortment of plant and fungal species whose chemical makeup allows humans access to — or dialogue with — their consciousness. While non-psychedelic plants may have a similar level of consciousness, because they do not have psychoactive chemistry, we become experientially closed off from the particular sort of mind they have. This is one way to defend psychedelic teleology, but it falls prey to various criticisms. One such criticism relates to panpsychism more generally, known as the *combination problem*.[10]

On the panpsychist account of the world, consciousness — in humans, animals, perhaps even plants — emerges from billions of subatomic forms of consciousness all combining together. The combination problem refers to the question of how these tiny consciousnesses combine: how the move is made from many tiny subjects of experience to a single, unified, and large conscious subject. What are the forces, laws, and processes allowing microexperiences to come together to create more complex macroexperiences? As the philosopher Keith Frankish writes in an article for *Aeon*,

We understand how particles combine to make atoms, molecules and larger structures, but what parallel story can we tell on the phenomenal side? How do the micro-experiences of billions of subatomic particles in my brain combine to form the twinge of pain I'm feeling in my knee? If billions of humans organized themselves to form a giant brain, each person simulating a single neuron and sending signals to the others using mobile phones, it seems unlikely that their consciousnesses would merge to form a single giant consciousness. Why should something similar happen with subatomic particles?[11]

However, the philosopher Angela Mendelovici has argued that the combination problem is a problem for everyone, not just panpsychists.[12] This is because it is unclear how *any* experiences can combine to create a unified experience (which is known as *phenomenal unity*). How do various visual, auditory, and cognitive experiences combine so that they are experienced *together* as a single conscious state?

Still, there are other specific issues associated with a panpsychist account of plant consciousness and teleology. For instance, if humans, non-human animals, and the basic constituents of matter all have their respective levels of consciousness, what kind of consciousness would an intermediary entity have, such as a plant? How can we know that the combined consciousnesses in a plant are sufficient enough to produce the intentionality, wisdom, and purposeful conscious states that some psychedelic users ascribe to plant teachers?

Not only is panpsychist plant teleology subject to the combination problem that all panpsychists face, but this view also has to resolve problems such as whether psychedelic plants have more complex consciousness than non-psychedelic plants, by virtue of their 'teaching power'. If that is the case, then it needs to be explained why a psychedelic compound adds to the complexity of consciousness more than a non-psychedelic compound. On the other hand, if many plants share complex conscious states but only the psychedelics allow access to these states, then the advocate of panpsychist plant teleology would need to describe how this communication between conscious subjects (humans and plants) takes place.

Similarly, the emerging field of plant neurobiology posits that plants, at a biological level, show signs of consciousness, sentience, and intelligence[13] — a conclusion that has been contested by many plant biologists.[14] But even if this conclusion is correct, it is not clear how the consumption of sentient psychedelic plants would lead to communication between the digested plant and the person. Furthermore, the psychedelic experience seems to depend on psychedelic chemicals as opposed to the entire makeup of a plant; so is the chemical itself made up of enough consciousnesses to be intelligent and enable communication with a person?

## Animistic Worldviews

Another metaphysical perspective on natural psychedelics is that they contain a 'plant spirit', which would fall under an animistic belief system. It is possible to think of the term 'spirit' as equivalent to 'mind', but for the sake of clarity, I'll treat the belief in discrete spirits existing in some or all natural things as distinct from the panpsychist worldview.

Panpsychism and animism do share many similarities, but there are some key differences between the two worldviews. Panpsychism focuses on consciousness, and the smallest constituents of consciousness are seen to be similar and non-unique. In animism, conversely, tiny spirits do not aggregate to create a more complex spirit; rather, each natural entity is seen to have a unique, intelligent, and *purposeful* spirit. Animism places great attention on the purposefulness of natural objects. Trees, rivers, and mountains are persons with agency, able to speak to us when in their presence. In this way, animism is probably more closely linked to the belief in literal plant teachers, although a panpsychist could easily be an animist as well or view nature as purposeful even without invoking the existence of spirits.

Animism is the oldest form of religious belief and is common to many indigenous cultures around the world.[15] I believe an evolutionary perspective on animism holds explanatory power; it can explain, in part, why this worldview is so pervasive and enduring. This is a perspective I will address in part two of this essay (Chapter 8), but for the time being, I would like to hone in on the metaphysical aspect — the nature of the spirits that animistic belief systems refer to.

A potential metaphysical distinction between panpsychism and animistic worldviews is that the latter often postulate the existence of supernatural, immaterial spirits or souls. There are disagreements among both scientists and philosophers about whether supernatural beliefs are testable[16]; if they are not testable, then the notion of plant spirits cannot gain robust evidential grounding. But even if the existence of plant spirits *is* testable, it is doubtful whether any convincing evidence points to their existence. One possible way to test the existence of these spirits may be to find out whether a psychedelic user gains knowledge they otherwise could not possibly have known. I have not personally come across a persuasive, corroborated account of some idea or piece of knowledge that could only have come from this kind of supernatural source.

From a sceptical perspective, the supernatural component of some forms of animism can be difficult to accept. The supposition of supernatural entities or immaterial souls in objects adds realms and entities to the psychedelic experience that do not necessarily need to be supposed in order to account for the phenomenological character and value of the experience. In this way, the animistic perspective on psychedelics may be the less parsimonious explanation. This would mean it violates Occam's razor, a principle that recommends we should not make more assumptions than we need to. Ultimately, it is a principle that draws a relationship between simplicity and truth, positing that metaphysical theories that multiply entities beyond necessity are less likely to be true. As Isaac Newton prescribes in his *Principia Mathematica* (1687),

> We are to admit no more causes of natural things than such as are both true and sufficient to explain their appearances. To this purpose the philosophers say that Nature does nothing in vain, and more is in vain when less will serve; for Nature is pleased with simplicity, and affects not the pomp of superfluous causes.[17]

Galileo Galilei also propounds this principle in his book *Dialogues Concerning the Two Chief World Systems* (1632): "Nature does not multiply things unnecessarily; that she makes use of the easiest and simplest means for producing her effects; that she does nothing in vain, and the like."[18] To ground Occam's razor, we might draw upon relevant examples in the history of science. For example, when Albert Einstein was trying to incorporate gravity and acceleration into his relativity theory, he eschewed considerations of "beauty and simplicity"[19] and instead favoured *completeness*, which the science author Johnjoe McFadden defines as "the incorporation of the maximum amount of available information into a model".[20] But after a decade of wrestling with complex equations and subsequent failures based on this way of thinking, Einstein returned to the principle of Occam's razor, accepting only the most simple and elegant equations. This led to the formulation of his general theory of relativity in 1915.[21] Thereafter, he became a devout follower of simplicity. As he argued in 1933: "Nature is the realisation of the simplest conceivable mathematical ideas."[22]

However, it is questionable whether any clear connection exists between truth and the elegancy of a theory, a point raised by the science writer Philip Ball:

[A]s a tool for distinguishing between rival theories, Occam's razor is only relevant if the two theories predict identical results but one is simpler than the other — which is to say, it makes fewer assumptions. This is a situation rarely if ever encountered in science. Much more often, theories are distinguished not by making fewer assumptions but *different* ones. It's then not obvious how to weigh them up.[23]

Perhaps an important clarification to make here, though, is that Ball is referring to *scientific* theories. Therefore, if animism and the concept of plant teachers and spirits fall outside the purview of science, then perhaps these ideas should not even be counted alongside competing scientific theories that try to explain how plants supposedly impart wisdom to us.

Yet Occam's razor can apply to non-scientific theories, too, such as philosophical ones, including the aforementioned propositions about plant spirits. For example, the philosopher Darren Bradley has argued that the arguments Michael Huemer marshals "for preferring simpler theories in science can also be applied in philosophy,"[24][25] adding that

there are no principled reasons to think that appealing to simplicity in philosophy is any more problematic than appealing to simplicity in science; there are only practical differences that make it difficult to apply simplicity-based arguments in philosophy. These practical issues differ from one case to another.[26]

The justifications for adopting Occam's razor are manifold. There are *a priori* justifications. The philosopher of religion Richard Swinburne, for instance, contends that

other things being equal — the simplest hypothesis proposed as an explanation of phenomena is more likely to be the true one than is any other available hypothesis, that its predictions are more likely to be true than those of any other available hypothesis, and that it is an ultimate *a priori* epistemic principle that simplicity is evidence for truth.[27]

A theological slant on such as an *a priori* justification comes from J.J.C. Smart who points to the theological notion that "we expect God to have created a beautiful universe," to which a beautiful (i.e. simple) theory should correspond.[28] The philosopher David Lewis justifies the simplicity principle — with respect to *qualitative* parsimony (the number of types of a thing postulated) rather than *quantitative* parsimony (the number of individual things postulated) — on the grounds that it is prima facie a theoretical virtue.[29] One could view it as having intrinsic value as a theoretical goal. Others may see simplicity as valuable for aesthetic reasons, which would make Occam's razor preferable in a methodological rather than epistemic sense. It is also possible to defend Occam's razor on the basis that it follows principles of rationality: by minimising the number of entities and mechanisms postulated, Occam's razor can be seen as a form of general epistemic caution, which some might view as characteristic of rational inquiry.

One glaring issue with these *a priori* justifications is that it can be difficult to know if they present an *a priori* defence or no defence at all. The virtue of simplicity may be invoked as self-evident, without any further justifications or elaborations. Can Occam's razor only be justified by the claim that it is intrinsically valuable? Due to this concern, *a posteriori* justifications for simplicity have been proposed.

Rather than supposing that God created an elegant and simple universe, we might argue that the success of relatively simple theories allows us to infer that nature is therefore simple. Einstein used this form of reasoning: he argued that the history of physics justifies the belief that nature is the manifestation of the simplest mathematical ideas.[30] Conversely, many philosophers and scientists resist the idea that nature is simple. As a group of Earth scientists wrote in *Science* in 1994,

> Many scientists accept and apply [Occam's Razor] in their work, even though it is an entirely metaphysical assumption. There is scant empirical evidence that the world is actually simple or that simple accounts are more likely than complex ones to be true. Our commitment to simplicity is largely an inheritance of 17th-century theology.[31]

We do not know if simpler theories are more likely to be true, nor if simpler theories are better confirmed by data than more complex rival theories. Hence, even if animism is a more complex worldview (which is debatable), this may not give us reason to reject it. However, focusing on simplicity and complexity may not be the best way to address animism generally and psychedelic teleology specifically. This is because Occam's razor applies to competing theories that explain phenomena equally well, and with these theories in mind, it recommends we choose the one that invokes the fewest assumptions or entities. In the rest of this essay, I will argue that the plant spirit/teacher explanation of psychedelic effects is not just more complicated; it does not fit the evidence equally as well, and it involves a variety of logical issues.

Another potential problem with some animistic views is that, by virtue of their supernatural claims, they are incompatible with physicalism (the belief that everything is ultimately physical) and naturalism (the belief that all laws, forces, objects, and events are natural). Nonetheless, it is worth bearing in mind the following statement from the philosopher Galen Strawson: "You can't classify anything as supernatural or non-natural until you have a substantive conception of the natural in relation to which something can be classified as non-natural." He goes on to clarify that he believes concrete reality is entirely *physical*.

This view is known as *physicalist naturalism*.[32] On the other hand, the potential incompatibility of animism with physicalism may not be a problem if we have reasons to reject physicalism — and we may do so on the grounds that it is unable to resolve the hard problem of consciousness. In other words, physicalism cannot account for the (self-evident and undeniable) fact of subjective experience: the fact that there is 'something it is like to be conscious'.

Panpsychism, in contrast to supernatural animistic beliefs, is fully compatible with physicalism and naturalism, at least according to philosophers like Strawson.[33] In fact, Strawson has gone so far as to argue that physicalism entails panpsychism[34] (an argument that would deserve a separate, more in-depth discussion). Panpsychism may be metaphysically easier to digest for many people compared to animism, even though the latter is ostensibly in our nature to believe. Yet despite any possible advantages of panpsychism over animism, we are still left with the unresolved issues I raised earlier about panpsychism itself and its relation to the teleological view of psychedelics.

Here it is worth noting that we also do not necessarily have to equate animism with supernatural beliefs. Graham Harvey, a religious studies scholar, points out in his book *Animism: Respecting the Living World* (2005) that animistic cultures differ in their beliefs. These cultures vary in terms of whether particular entities are seen as persons or inanimate objects. Additionally, the belief in disembodied persons is not universal. For this reason, Harvey uses the term "animisms" to properly reflect the plurality of animistic beliefs.[35] Moreover, animism need not assume the existence of supernatural spirits. As Harvey states,

> It may be necessary to note, forcefully, that in the following discussion the terms 'person' and 'other-than-human person' are *not* intended to replace words like 'spirit' or 'deity'. They

are not references to any putative 'greater than human' or 'supernatural' beings unless this is specified in some other way. Animists *may* acknowledge the existence and even presence of deities or discarnate persons (if that is what 'spirit' means), but their personhood is a more general fact.[36]

Animism could be consonant with a naturalistic worldview, depending on how it is formulated. Western anthropologists have sometimes narrowly defined animism as merely the belief that souls, or supernatural beings, inhabit all natural entities and phenomena. (It is important to acknowledge that this definition of animism, now known as 'old animism', has colonial baggage. The Victorian anthropologist E.B. Tylor formulated animism in this way with an attitude of condescension — he wanted to cast indigenous cultures as 'primitive', 'childish', and 'uncivilised'.) We can juxtapose this conception with a form of animism that takes a particular stance towards the natural world and our relationship to it. This is more about a worldview that encourages a certain ethic. As the Australian philosopher Val Plumwood asks in *Environmental Culture: The Ecological Crisis of Reasons* (2002), "is it to be a posture of openness, of welcoming, of invitation, towards earth others, or is it to be a stance of prejudged superiority, of deafness, of closure?"[37]

In her 2009 essay 'Nature in the Active Voice', Plumwood says she is "not talking about inventing fairies at the bottom of the garden. It's a matter of being open to experiences of nature as powerful, agentic and creative, making space in our culture for an animating sensibility and vocabulary".[38] The anthropologist Richard Nelson makes a similar point in *The Island Within* (1989), which details what he learnt from spending time with the Koyukon Indians on an unnamed island in Alaska:

Living with the Koyukon people, I was constantly struck by the wisdom and sensibility of their ways, and I tried — within the limits of my knowledge — to follow their teachings. Of course, their culture is not my own, nor is their way of seeing nature a part of my inheritance. I will never know if animals and plants have spirits, if the tree I stand beside is aware of my presence, if respectful gestures bring hunting luck and protect my well-being. But I am absolutely certain it is wise and responsible to behave as if these things were true.[39]

But again, we should remember that animism — even if it includes mentions of 'spirits' — does not have to conflict with naturalism. Animistic notions of spirits and souls do not always align with Western ideas about these terms. These notions and terms, therefore, may not necessarily presuppose a supernatural category of entities. To better illustrate the animistic worldview, Harvey quotes the Brazilian anthropologist Eduardo Viveiros de Castro: "Body and soul, just like nature and culture, do not correspond to substantives, self-subsistent entities or ontological provinces, but rather to pronouns or phenomenological perspectives."[40]

Animism is even opposed to the ontological category of 'supernatural' since this, by definition, creates a realm that is separate from the 'natural'. Harvey draws attention to

animists' resistance to the notion of 'the supernatural', a domain that appears to transcend everyday reality and hereby dialectically to form another domain called 'nature'. Neither 'nature' nor 'supernature' are necessary in the thinking of animists who understand that many and various persons co-exist and are jointly responsible for the ways the world will evolve next.[41]

(The idea that animists view the natural world as a community of persons is known as 'new animism'. It contrasts with the 'old animism' that focuses on the notion of nature as ensouled.) If a genuine belief in souls and spirits as supernatural entities is not required for an animistic worldview, which we could instead interpret as a normative outlook, can we not then reframe the belief in psychedelic plant spirits in a way that resists appeals to supernaturalism? Undoubtedly we can. This may even encourage people to use psychedelics more respectfully and ethically.[42] However, the belief that one meets or interacts with a 'spirit' in a psychedelic state relies on either supernatural claims or esoteric forms of interspecies communication. Shamanism, for Harvey, involves mediating with other-than-human persons. This view contrasts with two other conceptions: (1) the idea that shamans journey beyond physical embodiment to a non-material realm and (2) the idea that shamans journey to inner worlds rather than outer ones (Mircea Eliade espoused this latter view, which Harvey calls the "psychologisation" of shamanism).[43]

Consequently, if we think about the ingestion of natural psychedelics within a non-supernatural animistic framework (which characterises some animistic cultures), and with Harvey's ideas on shamanism in mind, we could say that users enter into a relationship with an other-than-human person.

In response to this, I would like to raise two points. Firstly, a belief in encounters and interactions with other-than-human persons is not necessary for an animistic ethic, be that towards psychedelic plants and mushrooms specifically or the natural world more generally. Secondly, if one is using the term 'other-than-human persons' in a literal way, and not in a poetic sense, then one needs to clarify the meaning of 'person'. We must surely mean consciousness, awareness, or sentience as a baseline. But normally, these are necessary, not sufficient, conditions for personhood. The idea that plants meet other conditions for personhood needs to be justified. Capacities that constitute personhood — which many psychedelic users feel apply to plant spirits — might include emotionality, rationality, agency, self-awareness, future-directed thinking, and the ability to engage in moral judgements.

Harvey does actually address the topic of psychedelic use in shamanism in his book, which is worth highlighting:

> Some shamans utilise preparations or derivatives of plants that are commonly labelled 'hallucinogenic' in the West. The implication is that what people see and experience with the help of such substances is hallucination: false vision, illusion or delusion. To accept the label is to prejudice everything. Only a little better, perhaps, are words that privilege the internality of the results of ingesting these powerful derivatives and extracts: psychotropics, psychedelics, psycho-actives and even entheogens. Even words that allow the possibility of 'visionary' experiences are problematised by the possible implication that what is seen transcends the mundane world, i.e. that it is not 'real'. The point is, of course, that people who consider themselves helped in this way think what they are enabled to see is really there — the false vision belongs to those who cannot or will not see.[44]

Yet this raises the question: What exactly is the 'spirit' that one meets in the psychedelic state? While Harvey rejects the 'psychologisation' of shamanism, which views altered states in psychological or therapeutic terms, the exclusion of these perspectives may not be helpful. There are legitimate concerns that psychologising animism and shamanism is a way of forcing Western thinking onto indigenous beliefs, a distortion that makes certain experiences and beliefs more comfortable for us. But if we ignore psychological interpretations, then we might miss out on some key aspects of the phenomena we are seeking to understand. If we want to explain encounters with 'spirits' as fully as possible, then we should consider psychological and evolutionary perspectives that seek to clarify the causes and character of these experiences.

This is not to dismiss animism in any respect. Whether naturalised or supernaturalised, animism provides a way of relating to the natural world that is mutually beneficial. This worldview enhances *biophilia* (fondness for nature or the tendency to engage with nature), which feels personally fulfilling and lends itself to an environmental ethic. Nevertheless, making this connection between animism and biophilia does not preclude a further investigation into the ontological status of so-called plant spirits and plant teachers.

There are many reasons to doubt the existence of psychedelic plant spirits, either as other-than-human persons or as supernatural entities. Part of this criticism tackles the teleological status assigned to these supposed entities, which I shall now explore in greater detail.

## The Noetic Quality

It is not just the assumption of plant consciousness that makes the teleological view of psychedelics difficult to accept — there are a number of other logical and philosophical issues involved.

Firstly, not all psychedelic experiences seem to contain meaningful messages, and even when they do, this does not entail that it is the plant itself purposefully imparting wisdom. Turning our attention to the mystical states sometimes induced by psychedelics will be helpful here. In *The Varieties of Religious Experience* (1902), the psychologist William James described — what he believed to be — the four essential components of the mystical experience. The one most relevant to this discussion is the 'noetic quality' of the experience, which James delineates as follows:

> Although so similar to states of feeling, mystical states seem to those who experience them to be also states of knowledge. They are states of insight into depths of truth unplumbed by the discursive intellect. They are illuminations, revelations, full of significance and importance, all inarticulate though they remain; and as a rule they carry with them a curious sense of authority for after-time.[45]

Since this articulation of the mystical experience, other scholars and researchers have come to accept this noetic quality as a key indicator of a mystical experience. For example, when psychedelic researchers want to find out if a participant had a true mystical experience, they might use the Mystical Experience Questionnaire (MEQ30), a 30-item checklist, to compare the participant's subjective experience against classic markers of mystical states.[46] This checklist includes James's noetic quality: "the sense of the experience of truth and reality at a fundamental level", as an article in the *Journal of Psychopharmacology* defines it.[47] Psychedelics certainly can induce such noetic experiences. Whether an individual can actually unearth truths about fundamental reality they otherwise could not have known is another matter. What matters here is whether or not the potential of psychedelic plants to induce noetic states is a sign of purposeful consciousness attributable to the plant.

One issue I see is that noetic states do not accompany all psychedelic experiences and tend to be less likely to occur when taking tiny, low, and medium doses of psychedelics. If the plants were genuinely intelligent teachers, why would they not impart their wisdom in lower-dose experiences? Doing so would ensure as many people as possible become privy to knowledge that will benefit them, others, communities, ecosystems, and the world at large. After all, many people who use psychedelics do not desire high-dose experiences. Some may experiment with a dose that induces a mystical experience and then decide it is not for them — perhaps because the effects feel too intense. Under the assumption of plant intelligence and teleology, I see no sensible reason why high-dose experiences should, by design, be the realm in which insights are most likely to occur.

If psychedelic plants were emissaries whose mission was to rejuvenate the human spirit in the name of psychological, societal, and ecological balance, I would think that every ingestion of such a plant — regardless of dose — should lead to instructive experiences. Otherwise, the pedagogical ability of psychedelics would be dose-dependent, or the plants have an intention to only reward high-dose users with such lessons. These reasons, however, seem to indicate a deficit in intelligence or purpose, especially given how urgent the ecological situation is. Then there is the fact that not all high-dose or mystical psychedelic experiences feature important messages or lessons, or a noetic *feeling* is present but actual content may be lost, unremembered, nebulous, hard to articulate, or impossible to express.

## Chemical Animism

It is common to receive avuncular messages after ingesting psychedelic compounds that have been isolated from plants. This throws into question where the so-called 'plant teacher' is located. The pedagogical potential of isolated compounds would seem to suggest that the intelligent plant spirit is, in some sense, dependent on the compound. Hence, it would no longer be accurate to refer to 'plant spirits' or 'plant teachers'; instead, we should use the terms 'chemical spirits' or 'chemical teachers'. This would leave us with a kind of *chemical animism*. Proponents of plant teleology may resist this conclusion if they subscribe to *vegetal animism* (the view that the spirit depends on the whole plant). However, based on the experiences that are possible with synthetic or extracted compounds, accepting chemical animism is unavoidable (if we begin with the assumption of pedagogical spirits operating in the psychedelic experience).

The idea of purposeful plants may be more attractive than the notion of purposeful chemicals, but this is not a logical reason to consider the former more aligned with reality. It could be argued that whole plants and mushrooms offer a more complete pedagogical experience, due to the presence of other alkaloids. But users differ in their opinions regarding this. It is not clear how and to what extent a compound like baeocystin — contained in psilocybin mushrooms — modulates psychedelic effects, if at all.

Many alkaloids in psychedelic plants produce physical effects and only mild psychoactive effects. Take pellotine as a case in point. It is the second most abundant compound in peyote (after mescaline) and it is known to have sedative and hypnotic effects, so it makes you feel drowsy and decreases your desire to move. Since synthetic mescaline contains no pellotine, it is associated with less sedation and more stimulation. Aside from this, the experience will be similar to that of peyote, as mescaline is what is responsible for the psychedelic effects. It is possible, however, that expecting a whole plant to provide a deeper experience than a synthetic or extracted compound could encourage that very effect to occur. Furthermore, even if it is true that whole plants and mushrooms offer more complex experiences, this does not discount the fact that pure compounds can reliably induce spiritual and transformative experiences.

In any case, if someone were to accept a chemical-based version of animism, this still would not avoid the issues associated with plant- and fungal-based animism. We would still be left with the open question of why psychedelic chemicals naturally possess a pedagogical status but not non-psychedelic chemicals.

## The Use of Psychedelics in Maya, Aztec, and Amazonian Societies

It can also be doubted whether certain plant teachers are wise enough to promote prosocial behaviour in all people who use them. Consider the ancient Maya and Aztec populations, for example, who were known to ceremonially ingest psilocybin mushrooms, peyote, and LSA-containing morning glory seeds. The Aztecs referred to *Psilocybe mexicana* as *teonanácatl* (meaning 'flesh of the gods' or 'divine mushroom' in the Aztec Nahuatl language). This pre-Columbian culture certainly recognised this psychedelic, as well as others that they used, as a sort of divine messenger.[48][49]

These cultures also engaged in ceremonial human sacrifice, although the Aztecs did so on a much larger scale than the ancient Maya. The historian Woodrow Borah has estimated that the Aztecs in central Mexico in the fifteenth century sacrificed 250,000 people *per year*, which amounts to 1% of the total population.[50] The ancient Maya had fewer victims, but unlike the Aztecs, they would commonly torture the victim before the act of sacrifice (this might involve beating, scalping, burning, or disembowelling them).[51] To get a sense of the brutality of these ritual sacrifices, consider this account from Bernal Díaz del Castillo's book *The True History of the Conquest of New Spain* (1568), wherein the author and Spanish conquistador recounts his expeditions to Aztec-ruled Mexico:

> They strike open the wretched Indian's chest with flint knives and hastily tear out the palpitating heart which, with the blood, they present to the idols in whose name they have performed the sacrifice. They cut off the arms, thighs and head, eating the arms and thighs at ceremonial banquets. The head they hang up on a beam, and the body of the sacrificed man is not eaten but given to the beasts of prey.[52]

Why did the sacred plants and mushrooms not warn against or impugn these bloody and cruel actions against the innocent? Why did the plant spirits not inform people in their altered states that they did not need to engage in human sacrifice to appease the gods in the name of good fortune? Or should we assume that plant teachers are cultural and moral relativists, or that they speak on some moral issues but not all?

It seems more likely that the plants are not intelligent themselves but can be used intelligently or unintelligently. They can also serve a religious or spiritual function without necessarily imparting prosocial or ecological wisdom all of the time. We can think of psychedelics as 'non-specific amplifiers' of the human psyche (to borrow a term from the Czech psychiatrist and LSD researcher Stanislav Grof).[53] This would mean that in Aztec culture, psilocybin mushrooms simply amplified the belief that the gods need to be appeased through the sacrifice of many human lives. Under this view, psychedelics magnify whatever states are already present in an individual, which would include their beliefs and attitudes. The researchers Neşe Devenot and Brian Pace supported this perspective in a 2021 paper:

> We suggest that the historical record supports the concept of psychedelics as "politically pluripotent," non-specific amplifiers of the political set and setting. Contrary to recent assertions, we show that conservative, hierarchy-based ideologies are able to assimilate psychedelic experiences of interconnection.[54]

When we look at the societies of the ancient Maya and Aztecs, do we find evidence that psychedelics led to progressive social structures? In the case of both societies, we find patriarchy essentially reigned. Early research illustrated that in ancient Maya culture, men were kings and rulers of the city-state as well as the home. Newer studies do not challenge this notion but they do reveal that, during the Classic period (c. 250–900 AD), certain women held power as rulers in their cities and as oracular priestesses at various sacred sites. Pre-colonial Aztec society was also not as male-dominated as previously thought, given that women held positions of status and authority. In general, however, women were subordinate to men and were constrained to serve the traditional role of caring for their households.[55] [56] [57] [58]

While the Aztec civilisation was patriarchal in many ways (men held most of the political, economic, military, and religious power), women were still considered equally important to the whole of society (most notably as mothers). Additionally, both genders were able to hold authoritative positions within the marketplace. There were generally strict binary gender roles, thought to be complementary, so *gender parallelism* was at work: the view that the genders are separate, with different but *equal* roles; neither men's nor women's work are held in higher regard. Indeed, many researchers have challenged the notion of male dominance in Aztec culture.[59] [60] [61] Disagreements about the existence or extent of male dominance in Aztec society mean it is debatable whether psychedelic use in the culture had a positive or negative effect on gender relations, or any such effect at all.

One might still try to argue, nonetheless, that the traditional use of psychedelic plant teachers in Maya and Aztec societies did not help to subvert existing patriarchal ideology and hierarchical social structures. These are structures that many see as antithetical to spiritual psychedelic experiences. Dr Kimberley Hewitt, for instance, has advanced the notion of *psychedelic feminism*: the intersection between psychedelic experiences and female empowerment.[62] Similarly, in *Food of the Gods*, Terence McKenna argues that "encounters with psychedelic plants throw into question the entire world view of the dominator culture," with "dogma, priestcraft, patriarchy, warfare" standing out as "dominator values".[63] Yet these are values that the Aztecs ascribed to (barring perhaps strict patriarchy). The idea that psychedelics are non-specific amplifiers or politically pluripotent means that McKenna's assessment is not necessarily true: psychedelic experiences can accommodate a wide variety of views. The psychedelic researchers Matthew J. Johnson and David B. Yaden have stressed that the available data does not support the commonplace notion that psychedelics change our political beliefs in a particular direction.[64]

In any case, referring to human sacrifice, patriarchy, and warfare in Maya and Aztec cultures as a way to refute psychedelic teleology could be unwarranted if psychedelic use in these pre-Columbian cultures was rare. According to the researcher Martin Fortier-Davy, who documented psychedelic use throughout history and across cultures, only around 5% of indigenous American groups used psychedelics, which he stresses "is probably a very liberal estimate".[65] Still, it is difficult, from an archaeological perspective, to paint an accurate picture of the prevalence of ancient psychedelic use since conditions of climate can degrade traces of substances.

If psychedelic use among Maya and Aztec populations was actually this uncommon, then it is possible that indigenous trips were not widespread enough for the wise and moral messages of the plant spirits to make an impact on cruel practices like torture and human sacrifice. It makes sense that psychedelic use would need to be a cultural norm if it were to make a significant difference to ingrained religious beliefs and cultural practices. These changes might also require that the most powerful and influential in society experience psychedelic consciousness and become personally transformed by it.

Regarding this last point, the cultural anthropologist Marlene Dobkin de Rios suggests that even if psychedelic mushrooms use was widespread at a folk level at some point, in Aztec imperial society, psychedelics were usurped "for priests, nobility, and special guests of the empire", used by specialists for "distinctive social goals".[66] As we have seen, these goals did not include the abandonment of human sacrifice and strict hierarchy. Even when influential religious and political authorities in Mesoamerican societies — such as high priests who were almost totalitarian in power and influence — used psychedelics, society did not become more progressive. Moreover, in Amazon shamanism, where the use of psychedelics is *common*, not rare, we still find rigid social structures. As the writer Jules Evans underscores,

[Y]ou would ... struggle to call the world of Amazon shamanism 'liberal' or 'progressive'. Rather, Amazon indigenous cultures can be highly patriarchal, heteronormative and conservative.

To live well is to live in static harmony with the land, your tribe, your ancestors and the spirit world.[67]

In any case, one could accept the rarity of psychedelic use in Mesoamerican cultures and yet still question whether the psychedelics used by Maya and Aztec peoples are genuine plant teachers. If psychedelic use was rare in these cultures, this might suggest an absence of plant teleology or perhaps an absence of wise or intelligent plant teleology. By this, I mean that the pattern of psychedelic use and its effects (or lack of effects) on indigenous cultures seems contingent — dependent on circumstances — rather than something planned by an autonomous plant spirit. Alternatively, there *could* be a purpose behind the existence of these psychedelics — that they exist *for* the benefit of human society — but they cannot fully achieve this aim. This aim may not be completely realised because these plant teachers are not highly effective. Another line of thought is that the plant teachers are truly wise and intelligent but they are not so purposeful that they can just force themselves into the consciousness of the most influential people in society. After all, people still have to decide to consume these plants and mushrooms.

In addition, it has been doubted that every household in ancient Maya society had access to psychedelics, or as Thomas M. McGuire puts it: "An ordinary Mayan family probably had about as much access to sacred mushrooms as an ordinary family today has to a Catholic priest's holy waters."[68] While psilocybin mushrooms were abundant in Central America and Mexico, "a priestly litany of respect and fear kept the average person from picking them," says McGuire.[69] Instead, as Dobkin de Rios argues, mushrooms were "usurped by hieratic functionaries" to maintain legitimate power.[70] This point is again reiterated by David E. Smith, a psychopharmacology expert, and Dobkin de Rios: "Psychotropic plants ... are denied to commoners ...

access to the plants became part of a reward system ... the Maya restricted psychoactive flora ... restrictions of drug use helped maintain the elite in power."[71] These plants helped legitimise the power and authority of the elite because they supplied the priests — who represented the people — with visions, insights, and contact with the deific forces residing in the plants.

The anthropologist Peter T. Furst, on the other hand, challenges Dobkin de Rios's and Smith's basic premise here: "There is no evidence for a 'usurpation' of any of the hallucinogens employed in Mesoamerica by a priestly elite."[72] This may be true, but there is also no evidence contradicting Dobkin de Rios's and Smith's explanation. It is at least reasonable to assume that folk people would fear and respect priests' assertions that these psychedelics were repositories of divine power and that they carried the risk of insanity, illness, and even death. While the picture of psychedelic use in Mesoamerica is uncertain, use amongst influential figures certainly existed, yet it seems that these plants and mushrooms did not encourage positive social disruption, contrary to an idealistic view of psychedelics.

To heed plant wisdom and manifest may depend on a certain level of pre-existing wisdom and morality in human society. If that is the case, does this indicate a deficit in wisdom on the part of humanity or the plant teachers? Should effective emissaries, diplomats, and teachers not be able to reach and influence all those who are ignorant and misguided, or is there something unsalvageable about human nature? Have we, throughout history, regrettably decided to turn our backs on these allies of the vegetal and fungal worlds? These are open questions, and I can only speculate about the appropriate answers. However, based on the notion that natural psychedelics are *not* teleological in nature, the picture appears simpler and clearer: some human societies have been able to alter their consciousness in a beneficial way — providing the cultural context and setting are appropriate — but these benefits do not depend on plant spirits that have awareness and benevolent motives.

Furthermore, we can look to societies in which psychedelic use is the norm and yet — unless we are moral and cultural relativists — we find that the use of 'plant teachers' supports some quite unpleasant beliefs and practices. *Magical Death* (1973), a documentary by the anthropologist Napoleon Chagnon, offers a particularly illuminating example of this. The documentary is one of the few depictions of indigenous shamans themselves using psychedelics in a sacramental context.

*Magical Death* portrays shamanism among the Yanomami people, an indigenous group constituting approximately 35,000 people who live in the remote rainforest of the Orinoco River basin in southern Venezuela and the northernmost section of the Amazon River basin in northern Brazil. Chagnon's fascinating footage shows a group of shamans snorting a psychedelic snuff made from *Anadenanthera peregrina* (also called *yopo*), which contains bufotenin and small quantities of DMT and 5-MeO-DMT. But why were these shamans consuming this snuff, widely regarded as a plant teacher? It was to better prepare them for an act of war.

First, let's provide some necessary context. In Yanomami society, the shaman plays a crucial role in calling, commanding, and being possessed by spirits, known as *hekura*. Chagnon's documentary focuses on shamans in one particular village called Mishimishi-mabowei-teri. One of the residents in this village is a shaman called Dedeheiwä, who is known even in distant Yanomami villages for his shamanic powers: his ability to manipulate the hekura of the mountains and the hekura that reside in his own body. In 1970, leaders of the village Bisaasi-teri visited Dedeheiwä's village — this was after 20 years of hostilities between the two villages. The purpose of the visit was to establish an alliance. After a conciliatory feast, one of the visitors from the Bisaasi-teri village stayed behind and

Dedeheiwä asked him: "Brother-in-law, do you have any enemies you want us to kill with our hekura?" The visitor replied that those from the Mahekdodo-teri village had killed his older brother and so he asked Dedeheiwä to send hekura to destroy the souls of the children of that village.

For two days following this request, Dedeheiwä led a group of shamans in a shamanic drama, in which they took yopo, enabling them to communicate with — and become — the hekura. And all of this is done for the purposes of essentially killing innocent children. During the shamanic drama, Dedeheiwä called on a "hot and meat-hungry" hekura to devour the souls of the enemy children with fire. Some of the shamans 'became' their victims — writhing like helpless, dying children — in a pile of ashes, with others bending over the ashes, acting like murderous spirits, devouring their souls. Becoming hekura again, the shamans devoured the ashes that represented the dead children.[73]

This kind of psychedelic shamanism is commonplace in Yanomami culture. It is not rare. It also contrasts with the romantic notion that all indigenous peoples are communicating with plant spirits for the sake of psychological healing, moral improvement, and ecological consciousness. The Yanomami, like other indigenous groups, use psychedelics to access supernatural realms and to engage in practices like divination, physical healing, weather change, and evil magic. As Evans writes,

Amazon shamanism can also be rather violent — there is an entire form of magic known as 'battle magic', in which shamans try to kill each other to prove their superiority and steal their foes' spirit-allies. Amazon shamanic culture is not always a culture of emotional openness and sharing, but has been described as a culture of suspicion and vengeance — its model of medicine is based on the idea that illness and misfortune are caused by curses. Psychedelics help you discover who has cursed you and get revenge.[74]

The Yanomami have been a subject of keen interest to anthropologists, including Chagnon, because of their patterns of warfare and revenge (although the nature, extent, and cause of this violence has been a subject of intense and long-standing disagreement within the field of anthropology).[75] [76] It appears that common psychedelic use does not necessarily mitigate the tendency to engage in violent conflict. We should, therefore, abandon the monolithic view of natural psychedelics as noble plant spirits and plant teachers. The actual picture of psychedelics is much more nuanced than this.

Traditions of using psychedelics to battle evil spirits and increase enmity cannot be ignored. Such traditions indicate that the prosocial effects of psychedelics depend very much on cultural context, intention, and integration — that is, these benefits depend on the people using these plants and their relationship with them. There is nothing *innately* wise or benevolent about psychedelics themselves. However, the *potential* of psychedelics to enhance prosocial emotions and behaviours, and reduce violence, is often realised and has been borne out by multiple studies.[77] [78] [79] [80] [81]

## Why Do Plant Teachers Harm the Mental Health of Certain Users?

I would also want to question why supposedly wise plant teachers give some users nihilistic experiences that leave them mentally worse off than before. Some psychedelic advocates may want to push back here and claim that 'psychedelics give you what you need, not what you want' or that 'challenging trips are the most valuable ones'. One could also leverage notions such as the 'dark night of the soul', whereby an initial period of spiritual agony is seen as necessary for personal growth.[82]

However, while many 'bad trips' can offer insights and lead to improvements in well-being, a minority of experiences can be so traumatic, panic-ridden, hellish, and ruinous that it is difficult to see what plant wisdom is at play. Some experiences go beyond what could reasonably be deemed 'tough love'.

It seems inconsistent to treat one group of experiences as demonstrating the plant teachers at work and ignore the (albeit uncommon) set of experiences that lead to long-term difficulties. These extended difficulties can include anxiety, depression, social disconnection, depersonalisation (feeling detached from yourself), derealisation (the feeling that external reality is unreal), and hallucinogen persisting perception disorder (or HPPD: persistent visual disturbances after a trip that cause distress and/or impairment).[83][84][85]

Many factors can influence distressing psychedelic experiences (e.g. current mood, personality traits, pre-existing mental health problems, and the use of other substances). Moreover, we all have an inner darkness that can be magnified during these experiences, and being in a highly vulnerable and sensitive state on psychedelics means it is easier for negative emotions to spiral out of control. However, one can wonder why supposed plant teachers seem to abandon some users during states of abject fear and paranoia. Such distress can become so intense and unmanageable that the use of a pharmacological intervention (for example, a benzodiazepine) may be recommended to bring the person down.

To reiterate, if the wisdom of the plant only appears when the conditions are right, is this truly the most effective way to deliver such wisdom? Could the plants not act more wisely? Furthermore, there is a general consensus that individuals predisposed to schizophrenia (and other types of psychosis) and mania should refrain from using psychedelics.[86] But why would plant teachers cause harm to this group of people? It seems arbitrary and discriminatory from the teleological perspective.

However, it is not out of keeping with a non-teleological outlook, in which we can accept the ability of psychedelic compounds to potentially help some forms of mental distress (e.g. depression) but not others (e.g. schizophrenia).

Robin Carhart-Harris, a pioneering psychedelic researcher, developed his 'entropic brain hypothesis' to explain — at one level — how psychedelics work as mental health treatments. In a 2014 paper, he and other researchers highlighted that psychedelics increase brain entropy, which means they lead to less predictable, more chaotic, and more disordered brain activity. This increase in brain entropy induced by psychedelics is associated with positive and lasting personality changes, such as higher levels of openness and psychological flexibility, and a reduction in neuroticism. Psychedelics act to reverse low entropy brain states, which Carhart-Harris claims are linked to rigid states of mind, including depression and addiction. High entropy brain states, on the other hand, are linked to more flexible states of mind, according to Carhart-Harris, and these would include phenomena such as dreaming, psychedelic experiences, and early psychosis.[87]

Based on Carhart-Harris's model of the entropic brain, it is risky to give psychedelics to people with psychosis or latent psychosis because this will lead to a more entropic brain state. Such a person needs an intervention that leads to less entropy (i.e. more predictable brain states) — and non-psychedelic treatments exist that can achieve this. Psychedelics work for depression, in contrast, because the depressed person is stuck in negative, ruminative, and inflexible patterns of thinking. In the psychedelic experience, less predictability and more disorder mean that an individual can escape their imprisoning thought loops. This individual can thus experience different and healthier patterns of thinking. The entropic brain hypothesis is one useful way of explaining why psychedelics can benefit people with depression but not those with schizophrenia, whereas plant teleology lacks this explanatory power.

## Barriers to Wisdom

If we assume that plants (or the psychedelic compounds in them) are indeed wise, then why have these emissaries not made their lessons more easily reachable and accessible? If these plants and mushrooms truly had the purpose and mission that psychedelic teleologists claim they have, then we might expect certain facts to apply to them: being able to teach through less daunting experiences, being more plentiful throughout the world, evolving to be more physically inviting and palatable, and being physically comfortable to ingest. There is nothing enticing about consuming peyote, San Pedro cactus, or ayahuasca; their preparations often taste unpleasant at best and revolting at worst. Many users describe these as the most challenging plants, teas, and mixtures to consume, owing to their taste.

Then there is the fact that these plants often have to be prepared in a certain way to make their consumption manageable, which means they clearly do not naturally exist in a state that can be easily consumed. In addition, psychedelic plants and mushrooms (especially peyote, San Pedro cactus, and ayahuasca) can result in intense nausea, vomiting, and sometimes diarrhoea. This can put many people off, or it may encourage people seek out techniques to try to minimise the emetic effects (such effects can be difficult to prevent or eliminate completely). These strategies might include taking anti-nausea medication (e.g. dimenhydrinate, sold under the brand name Dramamine), using cannabis, eating nausea-relieving foods like ginger, tripping on an empty stomach, and pre-trip fasting.

All of these gustatory and physical challenges mean that only a subset of the general population will be attracted to — and willing to engage in — experiences with these plants. One could argue that these plants are attempting to add value to these experiences through the struggle of overcoming the unpleasant taste and physical effects, and there is evidence that the purging aspect does indeed have important therapeutic value.[88] Nevertheless, I would still maintain that this would be a net loss in terms of getting psychedelic wisdom out to as many people as possible. If commonly used psychedelic plants and mushrooms tasted and looked like fruit, and were not nausea-inducing, then much larger sections of the general population would be tempted to consume them.

It is also worth keeping in mind that not all cultures that come across natural psychedelics value their mind-altering properties. For instance, some rural inhabitants in Nagano Prefecture, Japan, eat fly agaric mushrooms as a delicacy, but they prepare the mushrooms by pickling them, which removes their psychedelic components (muscimol and ibotenic acid).[89] They consume these mushrooms as food and not, as some indigenous cultures in Siberia do, for their psychoactive effects.[90] In addition, as the anthropologist Manvir Singh underscores: "The Chinese have known about magic mushrooms since at least the 400s AD, yet considered them poisonous."[91] Familiarity with psychedelic plants and mushrooms does not, therefore, entail that people will intentionally use them to induce altered states of consciousness.

It is not surprising to imagine how people, ancient or otherwise, might view psychedelic effects — such as nausea, loss of balance, and confusion — as a sign of poisoning. The first mention of psychedelic mushrooms in the medical literature in Europe helps to get this point across. The *London Medical and Physical Journal*, in 1800, recorded an event, taking place on 3 October the year before, in which a father went to Green Park to gather wild mushrooms to serve as breakfast for his family. He inadvertently picked some *Psilocybe semilanceata* ('liberty cap') mushrooms in the process. The father, his wife, and his four children all consumed them. Once they were in the throes of psychedelia, a doctor named Everard Brande was called to the family's house. The journal notes that the father, referred to as

'J.S.', experienced vertigo and a loss of balance while the rest of the family complained of poisoning, stomach cramps, and their extremities becoming cold. They were all convinced they were dying, except for the eight-year-old son, Edward, who had a large dose of mushrooms and "was attacked with fits of immoderate laughter", which could not be controlled. The array of effects was described as "deleterious".[92]

*Tabernanthe iboga* (or iboga), which contains the psychedelic compound ibogaine, has some unique effects that many people will find intimidating. It is a rainforest shrub native to Central and West Africa. Members of the Bwiti religion — the Punu and Mitsogo people of Gabon, and the Fang people of Gabon and Cameroon — use this plant as part of their religious life. These indigenous peoples ceremonially ingest a high dose of ibogaine, contained in the root bark of the plant, as part of their initiation into the Bwiti spiritual discipline. The aim is to induce a spiritual experience. As well as this rite of passage, members of the Bwiti religion use iboga in smaller doses when performing certain rituals and engaging in tribal dances. In low doses, it acts as a stimulant, so it is also used to aid hunting.[93]

Moreover, Westerners travel to Central West Africa, typically Gabon, to participate in iboga ceremonies, for reasons such as spiritual exploration and therapeutic healing. A common reason Westerners use iboga is to overcome an addiction, with impressive results: reductions in withdrawal symptoms and rates of recovery that exceed what is offered by conventional forms of addiction treatment. This powerful psychedelic is administered not just in Africa but also at retreats and treatment centres all over the world. At treatment centres, it comes in the form of ibogaine, which has been extracted from the root bark. The result is a powder that contains a higher concentration of the alkaloid.

It is common for users to refer to iboga as a plant spirit or plant teacher because of the lessons and healing it can provide.

However, I believe there is a unique issue with this kind of designation. High doses of other natural psychedelics can cause some unpleasant effects, but if you take too much ibogaine, the result could potentially be fatal.[94] For example, there are several case reports describing the ingestion of ibogaine leading to cardiac arrhythmias, heart damage, cardiac arrest, and death.[95] Around one in 400 users suffer a fatal reaction.[96] The reason for this reaction is that ibogaine can both lower the heart rate and interfere with the heart's electrical signals.[97] Research also indicates that iboga can cause heart issues in people without any underlying heart conditions or family history of them.[98] Unlike the use of other natural psychedelics, taking a strong dose of ibogaine — the dose you would take in a ceremonial or therapeutic context — has a much higher risk of physical complications and death. Consequently, it seems strange to associate such a plant (or chemical) with a benevolent, wise, and healing spirit, given that the full experience of this spirit's power carries a non-negligible physical risk.

A more parsimonious interpretation of this effect would be that iboga is not imbued with a spirit that has our well-being in mind; instead, it contains a remedial compound that is, for some individuals suffering from addiction, simply worth the attendant risks. Would a plant spirit that was genuinely benevolent put the health and lives of certain individuals at risk for no apparent reason at all?

Many people will, furthermore, be put off consuming some psychedelics due to the duration of their effects. This is especially the case when it comes to strong doses of the longer-lasting psychedelics, such as the mescaline-containing cacti (with experiences lasting 14 hours or longer) and iboga (with some experiences lasting up to 48 hours). Is it necessary for the supposed plant spirits to put people through such long physical and psychological experiences to deliver profoundly healing and enlightening effects? Apparently, not all plant spirits or plant teachers demand such a time commitment (for example, psilocybin and ayahuasca experiences are up to six hours long). As in the case of iboga's health risks, it seems more parsimonious to argue that the length of an iboga experience is not a chosen pedagogical tool of the immanent plant spirit but rather an unplanned drug effect. If psychedelic plant spirits found in mescaline-containing cacti and iboga were truly intelligent emissaries, then I do not see why they would not offer shorter experiences.

## On the Origins of Ayahuasca

We can see again the faults of teleological thinking when considering one of the main psychedelics that users refer to as a plant teacher: ayahuasca. It seems highly unlikely that ayahuasca was purposefully put here for us, given the unlikelihood of its discovery. When we think about the origins of ayahuasca, we need to keep in mind that the Amazon basin contains around 80,000 plant species,[99] yet the traditional ayahuasca admixture consists of only two plants. These are the DMT-containing leaves of the *Psychotria viridis* shrub (known as *chacruna* in the indigenous Quechua language of the Andes) and the MAOI-containing *Banisteriopsis caapi* vine (referred to as *ayahuasca* in Quechuan, which means 'vine of the soul' or 'vine of the dead'). The monoamine oxidase inhibitors (MAOIs) contained in the *B. caapi* vine make the DMT orally active (DMT is orally inactive on its own because MAO in the body breaks it down — MAOIs prevent this process from occurring).[100]

Of course, any indigenous culture would not necessarily need to experiment with the millions of possible plant combinations before stumbling upon the powerful brew known as ayahuasca — observation, curiosity, and ingenuity could have narrowed down the possible plant combinations available that indigenous people were interested in. Nevertheless, given the plenitude of plant species in the Amazon, such a discovery would still be extremely lucky and surely require a great deal of trial and error.

If the plant spirit or teacher associated with ayahuasca had such vital messages to impart to humans, why would its existence depend on the mixture of two plant species in an environment so abundant with different plant species? Would a wise teacher not manifest in a single plant rather than rely on the low odds of people discovering ayahuasca? The independent scholar Stephan Beyer highlights that many shamans of the Amazon believe the plants themselves taught indigenous populations to combine a DMT-containing plant with an MAOI-containing plant, although he does not find this explanation persuasive.[101]

The claim assumes the independent existence of plant spirits, which we can call into question for a variety of reasons (some of which have been presented already). Furthermore, if we accept this explanation, it would mean that the plant spirits were waiting around a long time before disclosing the secret of the ayahuasca brew to indigenous people. After all, the earliest archaeological evidence of ceremonial ayahuasca use, discovered in southwestern Bolivia, dates back 1,000 years.[102] It is commonly claimed that indigenous people have been using ayahuasca for 5,000 years. Anthropologists such as Jeremy Narby have made this claim,[103] and people who use ayahuasca and who offer the brew at retreats will commonly repeat it, yet there is no solid evidence to support it. There is a decorated stone bowl from Ecuador, dating back to 500 BC, that some speculate was used to prepare ayahuasca (to make the brew, you need to boil the two plants together). But this remains in the realm of speculation, as no residue of ayahuasca has been detected.[104]

Unquestionably, it is possible that the use of ayahuasca spans several thousand years. But the main point here is that even *if* ayahuasca use is 5,000 years old, this would still mean that indigenous populations existed in the Amazon long before the discovery of the brew. Humans have inhabited the Amazon for the past 13,000 years,[105] and the chacruna and *B. caapi* plants were present in the rainforest that whole time. Why, we should ask, was there a gap between human arrival and ayahuasca discovery? What were the plant spirits waiting for? One might want to speculate that plant spirits communicated with humans about the ayahuasca brew when it was deemed wise to do so. Alternatively, one could posit that ayahuasca use is actually as ancient as the human presence in the Amazon. But we do have to question the likelihood of either claim being true. All things considered, there is little support for the notion that ayahuasca was destined for human use and that the plant spirits worked to make this so.

Beyer's more reasonable and simple explanation for why indigenous peoples concocted ayahuasca was that they were experimenting with possible emetics and purgatives. They were looking for ways to induce vomiting, as vomiting is an effective way to rid the body of parasitic illnesses. Both the chacruna plant and *B. caapi* vine have emetic and purgative properties and thus, when combined, these effects are synergised.[106] It was serendipitous that this brew also made DMT orally active. This discovery must have been quite a surprise to whoever first experimented with the brew. Once the psychedelic effects of the brew were discovered, news of it would have spread quickly.

Given the fact that indigenous cultures throughout South America regard ayahuasca as sacred, it is tempting to envision a romantic notion that the brew had a sacred origin (i.e. plant spirits introduced it to humans). But the more likely scenario is that its discovery was fortuitous, based on the search for vomit-inducing concoctions.

## Could a Cartesian Framework Help?

We could try to resolve the above issues by offering a Cartesian dualistic account of animism generally and plant teachers specifically. Under this view, the natural evolution and physical characteristics of the plant could be separate from the plant's spiritual nature. Hence, we can have all the traits of the plant that seem to frustrate its widespread consumption while maintaining that it has a spiritual essence that, through psychedelic ingestion, reveals itself to be a wise teacher. According to the Cartesian dualistic framework, a psychedelic plant teacher consists of two distinct substances: *matter* and *mind*.

This Cartesian perspective contrasts with the metaphysical monism — the view that there is one fundamental type of substance in reality, or there are no fundamental divisions — that some writers believe characterises animism. As the British poet Emma Restall Orr writes in *The Wakeful World: Animism, Mind and Self in Nature*: "Animism is a monist metaphysical stance, based upon the idea that mind and matter are not distinct and separate substances but an integrated reality, rooted in nature."[107] She notes elsewhere, "Nature's essence is minded."[108]

But does the Cartesian dualistic account really help to address the previous criticisms of the teleological view of psychedelics in a way that monism fails to do? If we adopt Orr's view that the essence of nature is minded or that there are many minded things in nature (the latter position being *pluralistic monism*), then it follows that the *essence* of any particular psychedelic plant is a mind of sorts. However, this throws into question if the mind of the plant is destined for an avuncular role, given the various criticisms of this belief that I have so far highlighted. If the fundamental nature of these plants is 'teacher consciousness', then it seems odd they would reside in plants and mushrooms that do not result in widespread consumption. These plant teachers would have had greater success if they were connected to caffeine-containing plants, for example, which are much more appealing and widely used.

On the other hand, if we accept a Cartesian dualistic account of nature, then a psychedelic plant or mushroom evolves physical attributes that are fundamentally distinct from the organism's mind. Yet this invites us to ask: Why would helpful teachers become tied to one physical life form and not another? Why does Mother Ayahuasca originate in the combination of two plant species among many thousands in the Amazon basin and not in the coffee bean? We could also level this criticism against the monist account of psychedelic plant spirits: if the essence of nature is mind, spirit, or personhood, we can query why one plant has a teacher mind but not another.

Irrespective of which metaphysical account we accept, there are still the following questions that need answering: Do particular plant spirits only emerge when plants and mushrooms evolve the production of psychedelic alkaloids? Or do these alkaloids merely allow the already inherent spirit to make its presence known to us? Let us assume that either the first or second scenario is true; it is not clear *how* the spirits of the natural world originate, nor is it clear if (and *how*) their origination and nature are related to the origination and nature of distinct species. Do spirits evolve in tandem with the evolution of species? These are all conundrums for the metaphysical monist, pluralist, or dualist who believes in plant spirits.

It should be reiterated, nonetheless, that animism tends to reject Cartesian dualism. As the anthropologist Tim Ingold wrote of the hunter-gatherers he studied, "They do not see themselves as mindful subjects having to contend with an alien world of physical objects; indeed the separation of mind and nature has no place in their thought or practice."[109] To apply a Cartesian dualistic framework, then, is arguably anti-animistic, although this does not nullify using such a framework to interpret plant spirits. It is possible to believe in plant spirits from a Cartesian point of view.

In any case, I believe the Cartesian perspective fails to offer explanatory advantages. Regardless of whether or not the physical attributes of a psychedelic plant pose limitations to consumption, encounters with the distinct spirit itself seem to be risky for individuals with certain mental health problems or predispositions. Thus, even if we try to separate off the unpleasant aspects of natural psychedelics through Cartesian thinking, we are still left with inconvenient truths about the distinct plant spirit itself.

Next, we have to confront all the various criticisms of Cartesian dualism as a metaphysical position, which we can apply to the case of plant spirits. First, if we grant that nature is divided into two fundamental types of substances, matter and mind, we run into the interaction problem: How do substances of a fundamentally different nature interact with each other? How does a psychedelic plant, as a *physical* organism, interact with the accompanying plant spirit, as a *minded* entity? The problem of interaction, moreover, persists in the context of psychedelic use: How do the effects of a psychedelic compound on the brain — processes in the physical realm — lead to the appearance of plant spirits in the mental or spiritual realm?

I won't detail all the arguments for and against interactionism (or interactionist dualism): the view that two distinct substances causally affect one another. I only present some criticisms here to show the difficulties that arise when one postulates a dualistic worldview. Metaphysical monism or pluralistic monism at least avoids the problem of interaction since all particular things belong to the same fundamental substance. But either position, nevertheless, still runs into the other difficulties I have outlined.

## Endnotes

1. Radford, T. (2019). 'James Lovelock at 100: the Gaia saga continues', *Nature*, 25 June. https://www.nature.com/articles/d41586-019-01969-y

2. Pinchbeck, D. (2009). 'Another Green World: Psychedelics and Ecology', MAPS *Bulletin*, Vol. XIX No 1. https://maps.org/news-letters/v19n1/v19n1-pg59.pdf
3. Ibid.
4. Ibid.
5. Segundo-Ortin, M. and Calvo, P. (2021). 'Consciousness and cognition in plants'. *Wiley Interdisciplinary Reviews: Cognitive Science*, 13(2), Article: e1578.
6. Mallatt, J., Blatt, M.R., Draguhn, A., Robinson, D.G., and Taiz, L. (2021). 'Debunking a myth: plant consciousness'. *Protoplasma*, 258, pp. 459–476.
7. Goff, P., Seager, W., and Allen-Hermanson, S. (2022). 'Panpsychism', *The Stanford Encyclopedia of Philosophy* (Summer 2022 Edition), edited by Zalta, E.N., 13 May. https://plato.stanford.edu/archives/sum2022/entries/panpsychism/
8. Goff, P. and Coleman, S. (2020). Chapter 14: 'Russellian Monism' in *The Oxford Handbook of the Philosophy of Consciousness*, pp. 301–327. Edited by Kriegel, U. Oxford: Oxford University Press.
9. Chalmers, D. (1995). 'Facing Up to the Problem of Consciousness'. *Journal of Consciousness Studies*, 2(3), pp. 200–219.
10. Chalmers, D. (2017). Chapter 7: 'The Combination Problem for Panpsychism' in *Panpsychism: Contemporary Perspectives*, pp. 179–215. Edited by Brüntrup, G. and Jaskolla, L. Oxford: Oxford University Press.
11. Frankish, K. (2016). 'Why panpsychism fails to solve the mystery of consciousness', *Aeon*, 20 September. https://aeon.co/ideas/why-panpsychism-fails-to-solve-the-mystery-of-consciousness
12. Mendelovici, A. (2019). Chapter 25: 'Panpsychism's Combination Problem is a Problem for Everyone' in

*The Routledge Handbook of Panpsychism*, pp. 303–317. Edited by Seager, W. London: Routledge.

13. Gagliano, M. (2017). 'The mind of plants: Thinking the unthinkable'. *Communicative & Integrative Biology*, 10(2), Article: e1288333.

14. Taiz, L., Alkon, D., Draguhn, A., Murphy, A., Blatt, M., Hawes, C., Thiel, G., and Robinson, D.G. (2019). 'Plants Neither Possess nor Require Consciousness'. *Trends in Plant Science*, 24(8), pp. 677–687.

15. Peoples, H.C., Duda, P., and Marlowe, F.W. (2016). 'Hunter-Gatherers and the Origins of Religion'. *Human Nature*, 27(3), pp. 261–282.

16. Fishman, Y.I. (2007). 'Can Science Test Supernatural Worldviews?' *Science & Education*, 18(6-7), pp. 813–837.

17. Newton, I. (1687). *The Mathematical Principles of Natural Philosophy*, p. 384. Translated by Motte, A. New York: Daniel Adee, 1846.

18. Galileo, G. (1632). *Dialogue Concerning the Two Chief World Systems*, p. 397. Translated by Drake, S. Berkeley: University of California Press, 1962.

19. Einstein, A. (1912). *The Collected Papers of Albert Einstein, Volume 5: The Swiss Years: Correspondence, 1902–1914*, Doc. 377, pp. 276–279. Translated by Beck, A. Princeton: Princeton University Press, 1995.

20. McFadden, J. (2021). 'Why simplicity works', *Aeon*, 11 October. https://aeon.co/essays/why-is-simplicity-so-unreasonably-effective-at-scientific-explanation

21. Ibid.

22. Einstein, A. (1934). 'On the Method of Theoretical Physics'. *Philosophy of Science*, 1(2), pp. 163–169.

23. Ball, P. (2016). 'The Tyranny of Simple Explanations', *The Atlantic*, 11 August. https://www.theatlantic.com/science/archive/2016/08/occams-razor/495332/

24. Bradley, D. (2018). 'Philosophers should prefer simpler theories'. *Philosophical Studies*, 75, pp. 3049–3067.

25. Huemer, M. (2009). 'When Is Parsimony a Virtue?' *Philosophical Quarterly*, 59, pp. 216–236.

26. Bradley, D. (2018). 'Philosophers should prefer simpler theories'. *Philosophical Studies*, 75, pp. 3049–3067.

27. Swinburne, R. (1997). *Simplicity as Evidence for Truth*, p. 1. Milwaukee: Marquette University Press.

28. Smart, J.J.C. (1984). 'Occam's Razor' in *Principles of Philosophical Reasoning*, pp. 118–128. Edited by Fetzer, J.H. and Schlesinger, G.N. Lanham: Rowman & Littlefield.

29. Lewis, D. (1973). *Counterfactuals*, p. 87. Oxford: Basil Blackwell.

30. Einstein, A. (1954). *Ideas and Opinions*, p. 322. Translated by Bargmann, S. New York: Crown Publishers, 1982.

31. Oreskes, N., Shrader-Frechette, K., and Belitz, K. (1994). 'Verification, validation, and confirmation of numerical models in the Earth sciences'. *Science*, 263, pp. 641–646.

32. Strawson, G. (2013). 'Real Naturalism', *London Review of Books*, Vol. 35 No. 18, September. https://www.lrb.co.uk/the-paper/v35/n18/galen-strawson/real-naturalism

33. Strawson, G. (2017). Chapter 27: 'Physicalist Panpsychism' in *The Blackwell Companion to Consciousness*, Second Edition, pp. 374–390. Edited by Schneider, S. and Velmans, M. Hoboken: John Wiley & Sons.

34. Strawson, G. (2006). 'Realistic Monism: Why Physicalism Entails Panpsychism'. *Journal of Consciousness Studies*, 13(10-11), pp. 3 31.

35. Harvey, G. (2005). *Animism: Respecting the Living World*, p. 28. Adelaide: Wakefield Press.

36. Ibid., p. xviii.

37. Plumwood, V. (2002). *Environmental Culture: The Ecological Crisis of Reason*, pp. 175-176. New York: Routledge.

38. Plumwood, V. (2009). 'Nature in the Active Voice'. *Australian Humanities Review*, 46, pp. 113–129.
39. Nelson, R. (1997). *Heart and Blood: Living with Deer in America*, p. 286. New York: Alfred A. Knopf.
40. Harvey, G. (2005). *Animism: Respecting the Living World*, p. 136. Adelaide: Wakefield Press. Quoting Viveiros de Castro, E. (1998). 'Cosmological Deixis and Amerindian Perspectivism'. *Journal of the Royal Anthropological Institute*, 4(3), pp. 469–488.
41. Ibid., p. 185.
42. Ferriss, T. (2021). 'An Urgent Plea to Users of Psychedelics: Let's Consider a More Ethical Menu of Plants and Compounds', tim.blog, 21 February. https://tim.blog/2021/02/21/urgent-plea-users-of-psychedelics-ethical-plants-compounds/
43. Harvey, G. (2005). *Animism: Respecting the Living World*, pp. 140–143. Adelaide: Wakefield Press.
44. Ibid., p. 145.
45. James, W. (1902). *The Varieties of Religious Experience: A Study in Human Nature*, p. 380. New York: Longmans, Green & Co.
46. Barrett, F.S., Johnson, M.W., and Griffiths, R.R. (2015). 'Validation of the revised Mystical Experience Questionnaire in experimental sessions with psilocybin'. *Journal of Psychopharmacology*, 29(11), pp. 1182–1190.
47. Ibid.
48. Carod-Artal, F.J. (2015). 'Hallucinogenic drugs in pre-Columbian Mesoamerican cultures'. *Neurología*, 30(1), pp. 42–49.
49. Guzmán, G. (2008). 'Hallucinogenic Mushrooms in Mexico: An Overview'. *Economic Botany*, 62(3), pp. 404–412.
50. Harner, M. (1977). 'The Enigma of Aztec Sacrifice' in *Natural History*, Vol. LXXXVI, April No. 4, p 49.

51. Velinger, J. (2019). 'Human sacrifice in Maya culture'. Charles University website, 4 March. https://cuni.cz/UKEN-943.html

52. Díaz del Castillo, B. (1568). *The Conquest of New Spain*, p. 229. Translated by Cohen JM. London: Penguin Books, 1963.

53. Grof, S. (1980). *LSD Psychotherapy*, p. 108. Pomona: Hunter House.

54. Pace, B.A. and Devenot, N. (2021). 'Right-Wing Psychedelia: Case Studies in Cultural Plasticity and Political Pluripotency'. *Frontiers in Psychology*, 12, Article: 733185.

55. 'Mayans: Overview of the Civilization and History' (2023). History on the Net, 18 February. https://www.historyonthenet.com/mayans-overview-civilization

56. Hewitt, E.A. (1999). 'WHAT'S IN A NAME: Gender, power, and Classic Maya women rulers'. *Ancient Mesoamerica*, 10(2), pp. 251–262.

57. Miller, B. (2012). 'Women central part of pre-colonial Maya society'. *Phys.org*, 1 March. https://phys.org/news/2012-03-women-central-pre-colonial-maya-society.html

58. Schele, L. and Freidel, D. (1990). *A Forest of Kings: The Untold Story of the Ancient Maya*, p. 42. New York: William Morrow and Company.

59. Horne, J. (2018). 'Worlds Collide: Aztec Gender Parallelism and Spanish Patriarchy'. Submitted for History of Art Bachelor of Fine Arts, Massachusetts College of Art and Design.

60. McCafferty, G. (1988). 'Powerful Women and the Myth of Male Dominance in Aztec Society'. *Archaeological Review from Cambridge*, 7(1), pp. 45–59.

61. Pennock, C.D. (2017). Part IV-B, Chapter 26: 'Gender and Aztec Life Cycles' in *The Oxford Handbook of the Aztecs*, pp. 387–398. Edited by Nichols, D.L. and Rodríguez-Alegría, E. Oxford: Oxford University Press.

62. Hewitt, K. (2019). 'Psychedelic Feminism: A Radical Interpretation of Psychedelic Consciousness?' *Journal for the Study of Radicalism*, 13(1), pp. 75–120.

63. McKenna, T. (1992). *Food of the Gods: A Radical History of Plants, Psychedelics and Human Evolution*, pp. xxxv–xxxvi. London: Penguin Random House, 2021.

64. Johnson, M.W. and Yaden, D.B. (2020). 'There's No Good Evidence That Psychedelics Can Change Your Politics or Religion', *Scientific American*, 5 November. https://www.scientificamerican.com/article/theres-no-good-evidence-that-psychedelics-can-change-your-politics-or-religion/

65. Singh, M. (2020). 'Psychedelics Weren't As Common In Ancient Cultures As We Think', *Vice*, 10 December. https://www.vice.com/en/article/4adngq/psychedelic-drug-use-in-ancient-indigenous-cultures

66. Dobkin de Rios, M. (1976). *The Wilderness of Mind: Sacred Plants in Cross-cultural Perspective*, p. 41. Sage Research Papers in the Social Sciences. Beverley Hills: Sage.

67. Evans, J. (n.d.). 'Do psychedelics make you liberal? Not always'. The Psychedelic Society website. https://psychedelicsociety.org.uk/media/bw06yvjnvblq47vwoocv5owchiyf8b

68. McGuire, T.M. (1982). 'Ancient Maya Mushroom Connection: A Transcendental Interaction Model'. *Journal of Psychoactive Drugs*, 14(3), pp. 221–238.

69. Ibid.

70. Dobkin de Rios, M. (1974). 'The influence of psychoactive flora and fauna on Maya religion'. *Current Anthropology*, 2(15), pp. 147–164.

71. Dobkin de Rios, M. and Smith, D.E. (1976). 'Using or abusing? An anthropological approach to the study of psychoactive drugs'. *Journal of Psychedelic Drugs*, 8(3), pp. 263–266.

72. Furst, P.T. (1974). 'Hallucinogens in pre-Columbian art' in *Art and Environment in Native America*, p. 154. Edited by King, M.E. and Traylor, I.R. Lubbock: Texas Tech Press.

73. Chagnon, N. (1973). 'Magical Death'. State College: Pennsylvania State University, Psychological Cinema Register.

74. Evans, J. (n.d.). 'Do psychedelics make you liberal? Not always'. The Psychedelic Society website. https://psychedelicsociety.org. uk/media/bw06yvjnvblq47vwoocv5owchiyf8b

75. Buckner, W. (2018). 'Yanomami Warfare: How Much Did Napoleon Chagnon Get Right?', Traditions of Conflict, 24 May. https://traditionsofconflict.com/blog/2018/5/24/ yanomami-warfare-how-much-did-napoleon-chagnon-get-right

76. Corry, S. (2013). 'The Emperor's New Suit In The Garden Of Eden, and Other Wild Guesses or, Why Can't Napoleon Chagnon Prove Anything?', Truthout, 21 September. https://truthout.org/articles/the-emperors-new-suit-in-the-garden-of-eden-and-other-wild-guesses-or-why-cant-napoleon-chagnon-prove-anything/

77. Jungaberle, H., Thal, S., Zeuch, A., Rougemont-Bücking, A., Von Heyden, M., Aicher, H., and Scheidegger, M. (2018). 'Positive psychology in the investigation of psychedelics and entactogens: A critical review'. Neuropharmacology, 142, pp. 179–199.

78. Noorani, T., Garcia-Romeu, A., Swift, T.C., Griffiths, R.R., and Johnson, M.W. (2018). 'Psychedelic therapy for smoking cessation: Qualitative analysis of participant accounts'. Journal of Psychopharmacology, 32(7), pp. 756–769.

79. Kettner, H., Rosas, F.E., Timmermann, C., Kärtner, L., Carhart-Harris, R.L., and Roseman, L. (2021). 'Psychedelic Communitas: Intersubjective Experience During Group Psychedelic Sessions Predicts Enduring Changes in Psychological Wellbeing and Social Connectedness'. Frontiers in Pharmacology, 12, Article: 623985.

80. Hendricks, P.S., Crawford, M.S., Cropsey, K.L., Copes, H., Sweat, N.W., Walsh, K., and Pavela, G. (2017).

'The relationships of classic psychedelic use with criminal behavior in the United States adult population', 32(1), pp. 37–48.

81. Thiessen, M.S., Walsh, Z., Bird, B.M., and Lafrance, A. (2018). 'Psychedelic use and intimate partner violence: The role of emotion regulation'. *Journal of Psychopharmacology*, 32(7), pp. 749–755.

82. Bache, C.M. (1991). 'Mysticism and Psychedelics: The Case of the Dark Night'. *Journal of Religion and Health*, 30(3), pp. 215–236.

83. Ona, G. (2018). 'Inside bad trips: Exploring extra-pharmacological factors'. *Journal of Psychedelic Studies*, 2(1), pp. 53–60.

84. Evans, J., Robinson, O.C., Argyri, E.K., Suseelan, S., Murphy-Beiner, A., McAlpine, R., Luke, D., Michelle, K., and Prideaux, E. (2023). 'Extended difficulties following the use of psychedelic drugs: A mixed methods study'. *PLoS ONE*, 18(10), Article: e0293349.

85. Prideaux, E. (2023). 'HPPD, 'Flashbacks', and the Problem of Psychedelic Anxiety', Psychedelic Support, 23 February. https://psychedelic.support/resources/hppd-flashbacks-and-the-problem-of-psychedelic-anxiety/

86. Dos Santos, R.G., Bouso, J.C., and Hallak, J.E.C. (2017). 'Ayahuasca, dimethyltryptamine, and psychosis: a systematic review of human studies'. *Therapeutic Advances in Psychopharmacology*, 7(4), pp. 141–157.

87. Carhart-Harris, R.L., Leech, R., Hellyer, P.J., Shanahan, M., Feilding, A., Tagliazucchi, E., Chialvo, D.R., and Nutt, D.J. (2014). 'The entropic brain: a theory of conscious states informed by neuroimaging research with psychedelic drugs'. *Frontiers in Human Neuroscience*, 8(1), Article: 20.

88. Fotiou, E. and Gearin, A.K. (2019). 'Purging and the body in the therapeutic use of ayahuasca'. *Social Science & Medicine*, 239, Article: 112532.

89. Phipps, A.G. (2000). 'Japanese use of Beni-Tengu-Dake (Amanita Muscaria) and the efficacy of traditional detoxification methods'. Master of Science (MS) thesis, Florida International University.

90. Nyberg, H. (1992). 'Religious use of hallucinogenic fungi: A comparison between Siberian and Mesoamerican cultures'. *Karstenia*, 32, pp. 71–80.

91. Singh, M. (2020). 'Psychedelics Weren't As Common In Ancient Cultures As We Think', *Vice*, 10 December. https://www.vice.com/en/article/4adngq/psychedelic-drug-use-in-ancient-indigenous-cultures

92. Brande, E. (1800). 'On a poisonous species of Agaric'. *The London Medical and Physical Journal*, 3, pp. 41–44.

93. Samorini, G. (1997/1998). 'The Initiation Rite in the Bwiti Religion (Ndea Narizanga Sect, Gabon)' in *Yearbook for Ethnomedicine and the Study of Consciousness*, Issue 6–7, pp. 39–55. Edited by Rätsch, C. and Baker, J.R. VWB: Berlin.

94. Oaklander, M. (2021). 'Inside Ibogaine, One of the Most Promising and Perilous Psychedelics for Addiction', *TIME*, 5 April. https://time.com/5951772/ibogaine-drug-treatment-addiction/

95. Meisner, J.A., Wilcox, S.R., and Richards, J.B. (2016). 'Ibogaine-associated cardiac arrest and death: case report and review of the literature'. *Therapeutic Advances in Psychopharmacology*, 6(2), pp. 95–98.

96. Corkery, J.M. (2018). 'Ibogaine as a treatment for substance misuse: Potential benefits and practical dangers'. *Progress in Brain Research*, 242, pp. 217–257.

97. Koenig, X. and Hilber, K. (2015). 'The Anti-Addiction Drug Ibogaine and the Heart: A Delicate Relation'. *Molecules*, 20(2), pp. 2208–2228.

98. Litjens, R.P.W. and Brunt, T.M. (2016). 'How toxic is ibogaine?' *Clinical Toxicology*, 54(4), pp. 1–6.

99. Schultes, R.E. (1990). 'Gifts of the Amazon Flora to the Natural World'. *Arnoldia*, 50(2), pp. 21–33.

100. Malcolm, B.J. and Lee, K.C. (2017). '*Ayahuasca*: An ancient sacrament for treatment of contemporary mental illness?' *Mental Health Clinician*, 7(1), pp. 39–45.

101. Beyer, S. (2012). 'On the Origins of Ayahuasca', Singing to the Plants, 25 April. https://singingtotheplants.com/2012/04/on-origins-of-ayahuasca/

102. Miller, M.J., Albarracin-Jordan, J., Moore, C., and Capriles, J.M. (2019). 'Chemical evidence for the use of multiple psychotropic plants in a 1,000-year-old ritual bundle from South America'. *PNAS*, 116(23), pp. 11207–11212.

103. Narby, J. (1998). *The Cosmic Serpent: DNA and the Origins of Knowledge*, p. 154. London: Weidenfeld & Nicolson.

104. Beyer, S. (2012). 'On the Origins of Ayahuasca', Singing to the Plants, 25 April. https://singingtotheplants.com/2012/04/on-origins-of-ayahuasca/

105. Panko, B. (2017). 'The Supposedly Pristine, Untouched Amazon Rainforest Was Actually Shaped by Humans', *Smithsonian Magazine*, 3 March. https://www.smithsonianmag.com/science-nature/pristine-untouched-amazonian-rainforest-was-actually-shaped-humans-180962378/

106. Beyer, S. (2012). 'On the Origins of Ayahuasca', Singing to the Plants, 25 April. https://singingtotheplants.com/2012/04/on-origins-of-ayahuasca/

107. Orr, E.R. (2012). *The Wakeful World: Animism, Mind and the Self in Nature*, p. 104. Alresford: John Hunt Publishing.

108. Ibid., p. 269.

109. Ingold, T. (1996). Chapter 5: 'Hunting and Gathering as Ways of Perceiving the Environment' in *Redefining Nature: Ecology, Culture and Domestication*, p. 120. Edited by Ellen, R. and Fukui, K. London: Routledge.

## Chapter 8

# On Plant Spirits and Psychedelic Teleology, Part II

An individual taking ayahuasca or psilocybin mushrooms may have visions and deeply emotional experiences connected to the presence of a spirit. That person may feel that the spirit of the plant or mushroom is making itself known and communicating with them. Is it not justified to believe in plant spirits following these profound and convincing visions, which seem to reveal a newfound reality? If you directly feel and see plant spirits, which many indigenous cultures believe in, is this not all the proof you need? To answer questions like these, we need to be able to distinguish between veridical and non-veridical experiences: those that refer to objective reality and those that do not, respectively. There are countless perceptual experiences we would intuitively deem false and not integrate into our beliefs about what the world is like. But how are we to judge which experiences are hallucinatory (occurring in the absence of external stimuli, so lacking a basis in reality)?

It might be tempting to accept an experience of a plant spirit as veridical but not other psychedelic visions or perceptions, based on their relative value and meaningfulness. But is this the correct way to judge the veridicality of psychedelic phenomena? While understandable from a psychological point of view, the attractiveness or beneficial nature of a perception cannot — simply by virtue of being agreeable — grant it any more truthfulness. We could accept that all psychedelic visions are veridical or somewhat veridical in order to be more consistent, but doing so fails to apply a solid truth-testing technique to these visions. The fact that visions of plant spirits and plant teachers are based on perception is not enough to guarantee that these entities are mind-independent — in other words, that they exist in a reality outside of the person's mind.

## Assessing the Belief in Plant Spirits with Criteria of Truth

To test the veridicality of an experience, the philosopher Peter Sjöstedt-Hughes argues that one requires

1. physiological perceptive processes, such as functioning eyes and brain, 2. an external perceived object, such as a lamp. Both 1. and 2. (subject and object) are necessary for an experience of the real. Neither is sufficient, i.e. enough, by itself to yield a real, veridical experience. 1. without 2. would be a hallucination; 2. without 1. would not be an experience at all. We see, therefore, that the criterion for determining an experience as hallucinatory is not merely the existence of neural correlates of the experience — we must also rule out the existence of that which is perceived. Consequently, *merely presenting the neural correlates of psychedelic experience does not imply that the experience is non-veridical, hallucinatory.* In likewise fashion, presenting the neural correlates of a perceived lamp does not imply that the lamp is a hallucination. Neural correlates of psychedelic consciousness neither prove nor disprove that which is experienced — they are *not* a sufficient condition for establishing non-veridicality. Neural correlates would be expected for *both* veridical and non-veridical psychedelic experience.[1]

To rule out the existence of something perceived by the psychedelic user, Sjöstedt-Hughes suggests several criteria that can act as truth-testers:

- *Sensibility*: something that you sense with your five senses. "Sensibility is useful but not sufficient to give us knowledge of what exists," Sjöstedt-Hughes observes. This is because we can know of things not amenable to the senses (e.g. mathematical theorems and logical axioms), and we cannot directly perceive the consciousness of others through the senses (although this may still exist).

- *Shared objects of experience*: if someone sees something but others do not, the veridicality of the experience becomes questionable. However, the psychedelic experience can include shared objects of experience, such as ultimate unity and the unreality of time.

- *Coherence with other beliefs*: if something you perceive through your senses does not cohere with your prior beliefs, it may be rejected as unreal. Sjöstedt-Hughes, nevertheless, says "this is not a strong criterion for veridicality as one's prior beliefs may be false as they are often inculcated rather than developed through reason."

- *Rationality*: if we can present *reasons* for believing in the reality of what we experience on psychedelics, we are more likely to see the experience as veridical. We may have good reasons to doubt the reality or unreality of an object of experience. Furthermore, if objects of experience are logically coherent and not contradictory, as assessed by our rationality, then we at least know their veridicality is possible.[2]

Sjöstedt-Hughes goes on to quote the philosopher C.D. Broad, who remarked, "So far as [mystical experiences] *agree* they should be provisionally accepted as veridical unless there is some positive ground for thinking that they are not."[3] Indeed, Sjöstedt-Hughes gives special emphasis to the criterion of shared objects of experience. He also points out that the 'positive ground' we may advance for doubting the veridicality of psychedelic experiences that have shared objects of experience can be quite shaky. First, we cannot reflexively dismiss these objects just because they are perceived through drug-altered sense perceptions: "chemically-induced correlates of mystical experience cannot per se disprove the objectivity of that which is experienced," states Sjöstedt-Hughes.[4]

Second, if an object of experience does not cohere with one's pre-adopted creed, such as one's religious view (e.g. monotheism) or metaphysics (e.g. physicalism or naturalism), we need to ask ourselves how adequately the creed itself can explain reality. This has to be established before deciding whether or not the coherence of a psychedelic experience with a creed should determine that experience's veridicality. If physicalism or naturalism cannot account for the natural fact of consciousness, then these systems of thought do not provide a full understanding of reality. Based on this, if psychedelic experiences (like the perception of plant spirits and plant teachers) do not cohere with physicalism, this lack of coherence does not necessarily mean the experiences are non-veridical.[5]

However, I think we can doubt the veridicality of a belief in psychedelic plant spirits based on other criteria. Take the criterion of shared objects of experience. Is it true that the perception of plant spirits is a *shared* object of experience? Perhaps it is shared amongst many, but not all. Making contact with 'Mother Ayahuasca' or 'Grandfather Mescaline' is common during ayahuasca and psychedelic cactus experiences, respectively. But for many users, the genders are reversed; people can encounter a masculine presence under the influence of ayahuasca and a feminine presence after ingesting mescaline-containing cacti. Many people also do not encounter presences or spirits at all. And even for those who do have an experience of an external, discarnate presence appearing during the acute psychedelic effects, users can have a rational basis (this ties into the criterion of rationality) for interpreting such a presence as internally based and connected to one's biology. (Animism as an evolved tendency will be discussed in a later section.)

Therefore, if plant spirits are not shared objects of experience, and they conflict with our rationality, then we are in a position to doubt their veridicality.

Moreover, it is not always clear that the plant spirits and plant teachers that psychedelic users link to particular psychedelics are based on sense perception. *Some* of these experiences might be based on such perception. In these cases, you might see visions of such spirits. However, a lot of the time, the presence of these spirits is *felt*. This might be a nebulous way to phrase the experience, but this feeling of presence is dissimilar to the way that objects in everyday reality are seen, heard, felt, touched, or tasted. Additionally, in many cases, the belief in plant spirits is not based on a felt presence but is an interpretation of the experience of receiving wisdom, lessons, messages, comfort, and healing from *somewhere*. During the experience, or after it has passed, this outer source of information may be designated as *someone*. The label of 'spirit' can be tacked onto the *somewhereness* or *someoneness* of the experience as a way to make sense of it. In this way, the belief in plant spirits can be a belief structure based around an object of experience that, at the time, is not directly perceived as a distinct spirit. One paper, looking at the cultural context surrounding ayahuasca ceremonies, found that

> ritual specialists frequently invite participants to consider some aspects of their experience as signs of the presence and influence of protective or malicious supernatural entities. Depending on the comments given to the participants, ritual specialists, who position themselves as the holders of a discernment skill initially denied to the participants, gradually transmit the criteria that will allow the latter to identify the somatic, emotional, and cognitive signs manifesting the presence and nature of supernatural entities. These narrative interactions will therefore have a great influence on the

participant's subsequent ritual experience, which tends, as the previous examples illustrate, to be organized according to the script proposed by ritual specialists.

As illustrated by the previous testimonies, participants frequently categorize their hallucinations, perceptions, and mental states in a dualistic manner, attributing them to supernatural entities with antagonistic intentions. Visions accompanied by fear, guilt, or confusion are thus almost always interpreted as a sign of the presence of malicious entities seeking to disturb the participant, while those accompanied by relief, joy, and appeasement will instead be attributed to the action of benevolent and protective entities such as the spirit of ayahuasca, animal spirits, or entities of the Catholic pantheon.[6]

In any case, it is plausible that the perception of — or belief in — plant spirits is incoherent with prior beliefs that we have a strong reason to believe in. Say, for instance, that you are not a physicalist that restricts consciousness only to certain organisms but a panpsychist, and you believe the latter metaphysical position is more justifiable. You can, as a panpsychist, hold that levels of consciousness, intelligence, and communication are based on levels of complexity and that plants and fungi are not sufficiently complex to possess the kind of (human-like) attributes that some psychedelic users associate with these life forms.

We have to ask ourselves: Do we have any good reasons to interpret the receiving of wisdom (from a felt/perceived spirit) as originating from a literal spirit? Or can other explanations suffice or be more reasonable? I hope the discussion so far, and its continuation, illustrates why we have stronger reasons to lean towards disbelief in the existence of plant spirits. Sjöstedt-Hughes claims that the plausibility of the veridicality of psychedelic experiences depends on their having a shared type of experience, one that is coherent with a rational metaphysics, and which can be further fortified by a concurrent noetic feeling. This is what better determines whether a psychedelic experience is considered revelation or hallucination."[7]

Reflecting on these three criteria together, it is not at all obvious that encounters with plant spirits should count as genuine revelation.

We can compare the supernatural beliefs related to psychedelics — those that are based on first-hand, subjective experience — with other supernatural beliefs we commonly reject based on a lack of evidence. The experiences that lead to or strengthen the former type of belief are often highly valuable for the individual. But as Sjöstedt-Hughes has underscored, arriving at a sense of veridicality requires more than just personal experience. The same applies to religious experiences — do they substantiate the existence of heaven, angels, or a benevolent god?

Additionally, in terms of veracity, there is no strong reason to lean towards the existence of helpful plant spirits but reject beliefs in demonic or evil spirits as delusional. (Similarly, it is often thought that religious experiences provide support for the existence of a benevolent god; however, Asha Lancaster-Thomas has argued that certain religious experiences could also be used to substantiate the existence of an evil god.)[8] People suffering from schizophrenia featuring religious delusions may perceive (auditorily and/or visually) — and then subsequently believe in — demonic or evil spirits.[9] The perception of dark, hostile, and threatening entities can occur on psychedelics too, and they can feel as real as the good-natured entities. A common response to such perceptions and beliefs is that they are not grounded in reality and that if the person experiencing these perceptions could realise this, then they would be less distressed by them. (Of course, even if that person concludes that the experiences are hallucinatory, they can still be highly distressing.)

In contrast, we are less quick to doubt the veracity of a belief in helpful plant spirits. This is partly because you can experience comfort and enhanced well-being if you believe in discarnate, caring entities; yet there is a mental health cost to believing in demons and evil spirits, as research has indicated.[10] The tendency to believe in plant teachers, then, seems to be (partly) linked to the instrumental and psychological benefits associated with them. However, the attractiveness, benefit, or even trendiness of a psychedelic effect or belief does not grant it any more veracity than other psychedelic effects or beliefs that we deem frightening and detrimental.

There is also the issue of how to ascertain the nature of a plant spirit, given that taking a psychedelic can lead to the presence of both benevolent and malevolent entities. Are both types different aspects of the same spirit, appearing in varied ways based on the messages that the individual needs to receive at that time? Or are these distinct spirits — good and evil entities — that a psychedelic can invoke?

One might maintain that the appearance of malevolent spirits or entities is very much the work of one distinct plant teacher and that these disturbing perceptions can be just as instructive and meaningful as the comforting perception of benevolent spirits or entities. On this point, I would respond by saying that this is not a general fact: the psychedelic perception of evil spirits can be just as unnecessarily distressing as non-psychedelic perceptions of demons that persecute and torment people. Indeed, sometimes these powerful plants and mushrooms do not act like teachers at all, especially in cases where the use of them results in ego inflation and delusions of grandeur. We have to confront the fact that psychedelics have the potential to engender or magnify negative mental states in people.

## Exoticisation and the Tourist Gaze

When it comes to the belief in plant spirits, there may be a tendency to exoticise indigenous beliefs and be biased towards them over other religious beliefs one is exposed to or familiar with. This is despite the fact that both types of belief propound supernatural entities. The former belief may seem more trustworthy since it is based on direct, first-hand encounters with so-called plant spirits that everyone can experience. Nonetheless, Christians can also speak of a personal experience of Jesus or God, which might occur during prayer (this is a practice that can very well induce altered states of consciousness). If one is willing to look sceptically upon one set of claims regarding the supernatural but not another, this may signal an inconsistency — a form of cognitive dissonance.

In the exoticisation of indigenous peoples who traditionally use psychedelics, we may (mistakenly) believe that their lives are perfect, harmonious, and pure, with purposeful psychedelic plants acting as the magic glue holding the community together. But this is often simplistic. It is a narrative that sometimes veers into a desired fantasy of an *Avatar*-esque world. The British sociologist John Urry developed the notion of the *tourist gaze*, explicated in his book *The Tourist Gaze* (1990), which is relevant to this discussion. The term tourist gaze is derived from Michel Foucault's idea of the *medical gaze*, referring to the doctor's tendency to modify a patient's story, fitting it into a biomedical paradigm, and filtering out the humanising, non-biomedical material.[11][12]

The 'gaze' is an act of selecting what we consider to be relevant and important, ignoring other information because it suits us. Urry applies this idea of the gaze — having a particular way of seeing — to the activity of tourism. He states that "we gaze at what we encounter. And this gaze is as socially organised and systematised as is the gaze of the medic".[13] As in the case of the medical gaze, the tourist gaze is often about fulfilling the desires of the person doing the gazing.

Tourists who travel to the Amazon basin may, unwittingly, bring a tourist gaze with them. They might want to see psychedelic-using indigenous cultures in a certain way: as idyllic and free from corruptive traits like selfishness, spite, violence, cruelty, misogyny, abusiveness, and dogma. The less palatable aspects of Amazonian shamanism, such as sorcery, are left out of the mainstreaming of ayahuasca in the West.

The result of the tourist gaze, when applied to Amazonian shamanism, can involve an enhanced motivation to take on board the beliefs in plant spirits before, during, or after psychedelic ceremonies. After all, if one links a belief in plant spirits to communal harmony, and one receives lessons after ingesting psychedelic plants, then adopting a belief in plant spirits would appear to make sense. There is also a kind of romanticism to the notion of plant teachers, which can make the belief in them more attractive.

The anthropologist Alice Beck Kehoe argues in *Shamans and Religion* (2000) that the appropriation of shamanic cultures in neoshamanism and the New Age Movement misrepresents or dilutes indigenous practices and ends up subtly reinforcing racist ideas. One such idea is the 'Noble Savage' trope: the notion of the wild and pure human who has not been corrupted by civilisation and who possesses natural goodness.[14] This way of thinking, which is a form of othering, is also known as *romantic primitivism*. It is misguided, however, to think that indigenous peoples fit this image, that they are somehow magically untouched and untainted by the global capitalist system.

The cultural anthropologist Evgenia Fotiou writes, "Like other scholars, what I have observed among Western ayahuasca participants is a tendency to reinforce stereotypes. Indigenous peoples are still perceived as close to nature, wise, and spiritual and their traditions, most importantly, are presented as endangered."[15] This essentialising feeds into an overly positive and fantasised image — a one-dimensional storyline — that indigenous peoples themselves push back against. "It is not true that indigenous peoples are about to die out. We will be around for a long time, fighting for our land, living in this world, and continuing to create our children," remarks David Kopenawa, a Yanomami shaman and activist.[16]

Fotiou adds that "what many westerners who are looking for guidance or direction from indigenous cultures do not realize is that indigenous peoples do not live in some harmonious state with nature but are people embedded in larger struggles and face important challenges".[17] The essentialising of indigenous peoples of the Amazon basin — which we could call *Amazonianism* — can bear a resemblance to Orientalism (the patronising Western attitude towards Middle Eastern, Asian, and North African societies). It is possible for a belief in plant spirits and plant teachers, when framed in a certain way, to fall prey to this kind of romantic primitivism and essentialising.

There may also be an issue with the concept of plant teachers and plant spirits having a certain trendiness in psychedelic circles. Some users might make these terms a part of their vernacular — and beliefs in them a part of their identity — to appear more spiritual. I am aware this could be interpreted as a cynical viewpoint. But I only raise it as a possibility, as the *spiritualised ego* or *psychedelicised ego* (using spiritual or psychedelic experiences to feed the ego) is a potential pitfall of spirituality and psychedelic use.

Of course, various shamans believe in plant spirits and this belief is central to their worldview and practices. As the Colombian anthropologist Luis Eduardo Luna notes from his study of four mestizo shamans from Iquitos in northeastern Peru who have worked with ayahuasca,

> Crucial to shamanic practices is the belief that many plants, if not all plants, each have their own "mother" or spirit. It is with the help of the spirits of some of these plants, which I have called "plant teachers", that the shaman is able to acquire his powers.[18]

Amazonian shamans share the belief that plant spirits are the source of their knowledge, wisdom, and healing powers. But this commonality does not *in and of itself* demonstrate that plant spirits belong to an external, mind-independent reality. Perhaps uncritically accepting shamanic beliefs about spirits is seen as a sign of respect, with a sceptical approach seen as the opposite. However, applying scepticism here comes from a place of curiosity; it is a way of seriously engaging with the claims of shamanism and animism, with a wish to find out what is true or likely to be true. On the other hand, one could argue that the question of literal truth is not as important as the question of how these worldviews positively affect individuals, communities, and the wider world. The social functions of shamans, and the attitudes that animists have towards nature, can support a pragmatic case for their view of reality.

## The Evolutionary Origins of Agency Detection and Animism

One way to help explain the propensity to believe in psychedelic plant spirits is by referring to the evolution of agent (or agency) detection. Agent detection is the tendency that animals, including humans, have to presume the action of a sentient or intelligent agent in situations that may not involve one.[19] The psychologist Justin Barrett also introduced the notion of a hyperactive agency detection device (HADD) to specifically describe the human hypersensitivity to detect intentional agents at a perceptual level. This occurs when the information presented to us is ambiguous (e.g. we hear the sound of a branch breaking in a dark forest).[20]

The reason for this hypersensitivity is that failing to detect these agents may potentially be more harmful (and life-threatening) than incorrectly assuming that these agents are absent. The cost of regular false alarms (i.e. detecting agents when there aren't, in fact, any) is lower than the cost of a single false negative (i.e. failing to detect an agent), as the potential agent could be a predator or a human enemy. Strongly biased systems like the HADD, therefore, entail greater biological fitness than weakly biased ones. Some researchers caution, nevertheless, that the term 'hypersensitive' may be unwarranted, based on experiments in which people did not show a bias towards perceiving agents.[21]

Many scholars within the field of the cognitive science of religion, including Barrett, have proposed that belief in supernatural agents may be undergirded by evolved cognitive biases, one of these being the HADD. Belief in supernatural beings is seen to be a by-product of these adaptive biases. This argument has encouraged debate, however, as it is also possible that supernatural beliefs are not a functionless spillover from the HADD but are evolved mechanisms that had adaptive functions for ancestral humans.[22]

In line with the view that belief in supernatural beings is a by-product of evolution, the anthropologist Stewart Guthrie has suggested an anthropomorphism account of religion. He argues that due to the central importance of humans in our lives, we easily incorrectly infer the presence of humanness (i.e. humans, human minds, and human language) in our perceptions, such as in weather events like thunder, which historically have been attributed to thunder gods (e.g. Wodan, Zeus, Indra, and Perun).[23] Barrett built on these ideas, arguing that we also have a tendency to perceive intentional agents other than humans —

any agent with purposeful and goal-directed behaviour.[24] A plausible explanation for this tendency is that, for ancestral hominins, being hypersensitive to detect the presence of predators and prey would have been advantageous.

Barrett initially proposed this bias as an 'agent' detection device, but thereafter used the term 'agency' instead, to account for the intentional aspects of agents.[25] [26] The HADD involves not just the detection of agents — that is the first step in the activation of the bias — but also the attribution of beliefs, desires, emotions, and intents to these agents. The latter is made possible by Theory of Mind (ToM): the human capacity to ascribe mental states to others. Humans have a highly developed social intelligence because of the importance of knowing what other members of our group — as well as members of any out-group — are thinking and intending to do. While the HADD may be necessary to explain belief in supernatural entities, it may not be sufficient; other cognitive mechanisms, such as ToM, act as other contributing factors. The HADD encourages an assumption of the 'unseen other' while ToM broadens and deepens our impression of this 'other', helping to explain the omnipresence of belief in spirits and gods.

Animism (the perception of a spiritual essence in natural things and phenomena) is widely considered to be the core of the oldest forms of religion or human belief in the supernatural. Animism is said to predate belief in the afterlife and even language, with animistic thinking perhaps arising in early hominin evolution.[27] This culturally universal belief in the supernatural could be attributed to the HADD, ToM, and other cognitive mechanisms. Guthrie's anthropomorphism account of religion also sheds light on animistic thinking, as the spiritual beings inhabiting natural entities take on our own cognitive, social, and emotional characteristics.

The cognitive tendencies that we have to attribute agency to non-agentive entities and, in turn, our inclination to believe in the supernatural and animism, may help to explain the common perception of — and belief in — plant spirits and plant teachers amongst psychedelic users. The anthropologist Michael Winkelman, in a paper on the evolved mechanisms underlying psychedelic experiences, states that "agency detection" and "theory of mind/mind reading" are innate modules — with adaptive functions — activated by psychedelics. Supernatural experiences are a central feature of psychedelic visionary experiences in cultures all over the world, which leads Winkelman to claim, "Parsimony suggests a common biological bases [sic] for the supernatural beliefs found worldwide and the supernatural beliefs stimulated by psychedelics."[28]

Further research from Johns Hopkins Medicine has found that when beliefs change following a psychedelic experience, attributions of consciousness to living and non-living entities tend to increase, an effect greater in those who have a mystical-type experience.[29] Sandeep Nayak, one of the researchers behind the study, said, "It's not clear why, whether that might be an innate drug effect, cultural factors, or whether psychedelics might somehow expose innate cognitive biases that attribute features of the mind to the world."[30] So one possibility is that these substances activate the mechanisms that underlie animistic thinking, particularly in the context of mystical experiences. This would certainly help to explain why many psychedelic-using indigenous groups are deeply animistic in their worldview. I have personally noticed that after a profound psychedelic experience, natural elements (trees in particular) can appear animated — imbued with energy and personality. Features of the natural environment seem to be sentient, communicative, and capable of expressing moods.

But why would psychedelics activate cognitive capacities such as agency detection and ToM? This is an important question. It could be accidental, in that psychedelics just so happen to activate brain regions responsible for the HADD and ToM. Alternatively, perhaps agency detection and mind reading are enhanced — contributing to the perception of bodiless spirits and teachers — because the perceptual effects are ambiguous. Indeed, much of the psychedelic visionary experience has a degree of ambiguity. Plants and trees look normal in one sense but also unusual in another sense: they are moving; they have become more *alive*. This perceptual ambiguity or unclearness of what is being perceived may enhance the HADD, which is more likely to be triggered in ambiguous situations. Furthermore, with everything in the altered field of perception moving and in flux, the HADD may be activated since movement is one way it can be triggered. With objects moving in a wild manner, it is not surprising that the mind would attach agency and intention to these objects. It is quite common — and this comes back to the anthropomorphism account of religion — to find trees waving and gesturing with emotionality and intentionality. These natural entities become personified.

It should be emphasised that while these cognitive mechanisms serve to alert us to possible threatening actors in the world, they clearly do not just turn every ambiguous perception into a threat. If that were the case, then the HADD and ToM would not engender beliefs in friendly and loving supernatural entities (or at least entities with these capacities).

The character of the intentional agent, in normal and altered consciousness, often depends on the level of threat we feel. Lightning and thunder can be fear inducing, especially for ancestral humans who had little understanding of these natural phenomena, and so it makes sense that the thunder gods have been associated with anger and wrath. On the other hand, when you perceive yourself to be safe, such as when you are enjoying a psychedelic experience and know that you are not in any real danger, then the sentient bushes can exude joy, welcome, and invitations. The flipside of this is that if you experience anxiety and fear in this altered state, those very same bushes can become unpleasant — even monstrous looking.

However, it is not just objects that people perceive as being sentient, intentional, and having a spiritual essence. As mentioned earlier, there can also be a sense in which a spirit is simply *present* during the psychedelic experience, which some users believe is the spirit or teacher contained in the plant. This spirit can be felt to be distinct and separate from the user, perhaps situated above or even inside them. This spirit, such as Mother Ayahuasca or Grandfather Mescaline, will appear to talk, teach, soothe, heal, and forgive. This presence, force, entity, or spiritual essence is not necessarily experienced in a visual or auditory way, although it may still be felt to be feminine or masculine. It is the 'unseen other', often framed in supernatural terms.

Other times, individuals may encounter seemingly autonomous entities — particularly during DMT and ayahuasca experiences — that seem to possess intelligence and agency. These entities are commonly described as 'beings', 'spirits', 'guides', 'aliens', 'helpers', 'angels', 'elves', and 'plant spirits'.[31] Such entities are typically human-like in some way, either in their form or capacities, which is consistent with the anthropomorphism account of religion. One may insist that these entities are super-human — *beyond* our capacities — and therefore godly, which makes them incomparable to us. But do such entities truly reveal anything that is outside the realm of human knowledge and wisdom? Typically, the emotions, desires, and intentions of these entities are palpably human in nature. As Winkelman writes in another paper,

> Projection of a concept of a human-like entity is an inevitable part of how humans conceptualize the unknown. We project human characteristics and an expectation of human-like entities, an inevitable aspect of default human cognitive function derived from adaptations to conditions in which we benefited from knowing the expectations of human

others and their thoughts and attitudes about us that we internalized as scripts for our self.[32]

Applying the HADD to the perception of psychedelic entities, we can suppose that the visual effects of the DMT experience, for instance, are ambiguous — highly ambiguous, in fact. The swirling mass of colours, patterns, and geometry, all changing with a high degree of speed and transformation, may trigger the HADD as well as other mechanisms like pareidolia (perceiving meaningful patterns, such as faces, in meaningless visual noise). This may lead to the perception of fast-moving, fast-acting entities. Winkelman supports this line of reasoning: "We are hyper-tuned to detect an active intentional agent where information is ambiguous or incomplete, and the perception of entities during psychedelic experiences would be a clear example of such decision-making."[33] It also makes sense that the DMT entities often act *on* the user, rather than act disinterestedly *around* them. This is because the detection of agents and agency is always seen as being relevant to the life and interests of the individual.

Yet sometimes, to reiterate, the perception of the spirit or teacher of a plant does not materialise as an entity but is felt as a presence or force, an active intelligence that manifests and speaks to the individual, without a visual form. We could interpret this as a clear sign that this is the discarnate spirit of the plant at work, given that, subjectively, this bodiless presence seems to be conscious, intentional, and intelligent. Nevertheless, we should be careful about making such a leap of judgement, especially when other explanations are available. We should remember that our cognitive capacities can lead to the detection of an *unseen* other.

Ilkka Pyysiäinen, in his book *Supernatural Agents: Why We Believe in Souls, Gods, and Buddhas* (2009), proposes that the general dynamic of religious behaviour combines the

HADD with two other operators. These are the "hyperactive understanding of intentionality device", which is "the tendency to postulate mentality and see events as intentionally caused even in the absence of a visible agent", and the "hyperactive teleofunctioning reasoning device", which is the "tendency to see objects as existing for a purpose".[34] These mechanisms further help to explain the perception of disembodied, purposeful spirits and presences felt in psychedelic states as well as the propensity to believe that psychedelic wisdom comes from spirits.

In co-authored research and their book *Why God Won't Go Away: Brain Science and the Biology of Belief* (2001), Andrew Newberg and Eugene D'Aquili note that humans have a 'causal operator': a cognitive mechanism that allows us to perceive cause and effect. It also leads to the perception of supersensible forces and powers as a way to explain cause and effect when direct evidence is lacking. We have a tendency, moreover, to ascribe a causal order to sense perceptions even when their sequence seems random.[35] In psychedelic states, non-ordinary phenomena are often highly meaningful, profound, and awe-inspiring — unlike anything we have experienced in the normal causal chain of sensory experience. So it is understandable, from a cognitive standpoint, that we would attribute these effects to a supersensible cause of a divine or spiritual nature.

It is common for psychedelic spirits to deliver messages about situations, possible futures, and storylines pertaining to one's life, the lives of others, and humanity as a whole. We can interpret this as either the common wisdom of these spirits or the fact that humans have common cognitive capacities. Winkelman observes,

We appear to have an innate tendency to create models of future scenarios into which we project ourselves, and much of it may be more of a wish for phantasy than a likely scenario. A variety of products of the human imagination such as daydreaming, active imagination, fantasies, and dreams and our capacity to produce fiction all reflect common underlying capacities of the human mind. This scenario-constructing process, combined with our intrapersonal and interpersonal intelligences, provides the basis for content of psychedelic entity experiences and spiritual beliefs and experiences.[36]

Winkelman concludes that the properties of psychedelic entities "can be explained in terms of the overstimulation of ordinary innate cognitive processes".[37] It is crucially important to keep in mind, though, that such an explanation does not mean these entities or spirits, and our belief in them, are nothing more than these cognitive processes. Such an explanation does not capture the meaning and value that an individual attaches to these experiences.

We can also raise the question: Could plant spirits be related to evolved cognitive processes *as well as* accurate perceptions? After all, being cognitively primed to presume the activity of gods does not exclude the possibility that gods exist. Nonetheless, based on the myriad weaknesses and criticisms of the psychedelic brand of animism, I think we have a weaker case for extolling psychedelic animism as both an evolved tendency *and* an accurate perception of the world. The non-supernatural and non-teleological view seems less problematic. This case can be made without relying on the added point that psychedelic animism appears to be the less simple and elegant solution. We do not need to invoke Occam's razor. As illustrated in part one of this essay (Chapter 7), the question of Occam's razor's validity is a complicated one. This principle of parsimony could *potentially* add a further reason to reject psychedelic animism, but it is difficult to confidently make that argument.

Even if cognitive processes explain our tendency to anthropomorphise nature, or endow natural entities with human traits, this does not mean we should adopt a dismissive stance towards such tendencies, experiences, and beliefs. Personally, I am attracted to the animistic worldview because this way of seeing can be highly aesthetic, poetic, sensuous, absorbing, participatory, reciprocal, appreciative, and respectful. But this mode of perception and way of relating to the world does not necessitate the belief that unique souls or spirits inhabit some or all natural things. Psychedelics can imbue the natural world with novel aliveness and beauty without radically changing our metaphysical beliefs. We can call this position *soft animism*: a naturalistic form of animism that retains the animistic sensibility and ethic but which denies the existence of supernatural forces, powers, and beings.

## Does Symbiosis Have More Explanatory Power Than Teleology?

We know, to a certain extent, *how* psychedelics are psychoactive, in terms of their binding to serotonin 5-HT2A receptors. The classic psychedelics are structurally similar to serotonin and so can bind to the same receptors that serotonin binds to, which is how their effects are produced.[38] But even if we can offer a cogent and sensible explanation as to why psychedelics can often deliver restorative messages, why are these compounds so similar to brain chemistry in the first place?

Physically, psilocybin, psilocin (the active metabolite of psilocybin), and DMT are some of the least toxic drugs that exist, and they have a close affinity to serotonin. When DMT is administered, our body rapidly metabolises and clears the compound.[39] This is why the experience is so short. It may appear, at first glance, that psilocybin and DMT are so similar to serotonin because they evolved for human consumption and experience. Symbiotic relationships do, of course, exist in the natural world. Psychedelic plants and mushrooms could have evolved psychoactive compounds so that humans would consume them and receive the insights and call to action necessary to sustain the existence of these organisms. These plants and mushrooms would ultimately encourage us to protect them by imbuing us with an ecological mindset. This is an alternative way of explaining psychedelic wisdom. We could accept it without appealing to the idea of plant spirits that have a 'plan' for us.

The symbiosis argument, like psychedelic teleology, is an attractive proposal. The human-plant symbiosis narrative neatly diagnoses the root of our collective misstep (the forgetting and disrespecting of our birthright to engage with plant wisdom) and prescribes the solution (to re-engage with this wisdom). From an evolutionary perspective, nevertheless, I would argue that the symbiosis argument is dubious. Normally, members of species who are in a symbiotic relationship confer benefits to each other so long as each species continues to reciprocate. Humans destroy and threaten populations of psychedelic-containing plants (e.g. peyote and others through deforestation), yet these plants keep producing their psychoactive compounds. A possible counterargument here could be that our destructive habits are too recent for our plant allies to cease producing these compounds that benefit us.

Another possibility is that it would be risky on an environmental and planetary level to stop making these compounds, especially in the face of potential ecological collapse. However, this argument would no longer be centred on symbiosis. It also implies these plants have a drive to protect an ecological niche and the environment at large, which is incongruent with the view that organisms ultimately seek to maximise the spread of their genetic material. Indeed, the Gaia hypothesis — the view that the Earth itself is a living organism, the parts of which work together to achieve homeostasis (balance or stability) — is seen to conflict with natural selection. As critics of the Gaia hypothesis have argued, individuals compete for reproductive success; evolution has no 'goal' to make Earth a better place for life; and Earth was not produced by natural selection, therefore it is not alive.[40]

You could argue that certain features (i.e. psychedelic compounds) that lend themselves to protecting the environment end up helping individual organisms propagate their genes, by enabling them to survive in the first place. But this still presupposes that plants, like humans, possess ecological or planetary awareness — a claim that seems to lack adequate justification.

Returning to the symbiosis argument: If we imagine a world without human-caused destruction of habitats, what would humans provide that benefits these plants? Simply coexisting in an eco-friendly way cannot be such a benefit because that is a given for most species. That is not strictly symbiosis. Living in harmony with the natural world does not count as a special benefit. If we take a look at an example of symbiosis in the natural world, this can help clarify the point.

Clownfish, for instance, use their bright colours to lure fish into sea anemones, they fertilise the anemone with their faeces, and they feed on small invertebrates that would otherwise harm the anemone. In return, clownfish are protected from predators by the sea anemone's stinging cells (which clownfish are immune to) and they eat food scraps provided by the anemone.[41][42] There are also many examples of cleaning symbiosis, whereby an individual from one species removes and eats parasites and materials from the body surface of an individual from another species.[43] The relationship is mutualistic. It is difficult to see how our relationship with psychedelic plants and mushrooms is comparable.

One might argue that we benefit psychedelic plants and mushrooms by cultivating them and moving their seeds and spores around the world, as this spreads their genetic material far and wide. Nonetheless, they cannot have made their favourable compounds to promote a symbiotic relationship — in which humans like the effects of these plants and fungi and so decide to spread and grow them — because they were producing psychedelics long before humans even existed.

Moreover, the barriers to the psychedelic experience mentioned earlier (e.g. foul taste and nausea) do not suggest that symbiosis is a plausible explanation. As I will now argue, certain plants and mushrooms may produce psychedelic compounds for reasons that have nothing to do with humans.

## Why Do Psychedelic Compounds Exist in Nature?

We are still left with the question of why psychedelic compounds are found in nature. Why do some plants contain compounds that can transform reality; induce feelings of ecstasy; enhance creativity; and provide personal, philosophical, existential, and ecological insights? These plants also allow us to have profound mystical experiences, involving strange phenomena, such as a sense of ineffability, contact with a 'divine intelligence', ego dissolution, and a feeling of becoming one with all of reality. In light of these effects, psychedelic teleology or symbiosis is an attractive proposal. Nonetheless, there are other possible reasons why so many plants contain these compounds, namely, evolutionary reasons.

One of the ways that plants ward off predators is through chemical defences, with other forms of defence being nutritional (making metabolism of the plant difficult for insects) and physical (having characteristics such as thorns). Many plants have developed chemical defences to avoid being consumed by insects. These chemicals achieve this by creating adverse physiological effects in the insect, such as foul taste or poisoning. For example, nicotine, contained in the tobacco plant, kills insects rapidly; it acts on the central nervous system and causes uncontrollable muscular twitching, convulsions, paralysis, and eventually death.[44] It would do the same for humans if the concentration were high enough. Another example would be cocaine, contained in the coca plant, which deters feeding by insects (it suppresses their appetite) and kills them.[45] Again, a similar hunger-inhibiting effect is well established in humans, but the effect is not fatal, unless, of course, doses are high or frequently administered.

While these compounds can induce elation, euphoria, and other subjective effects in humans, they serve completely different functions for the plant. Thus, psychedelic drugs could be accidentally psychoactive for humans. The compounds are essentially part of the plant's mechanism for protection and survival. In some cases, these compounds act as insecticides, but in many cases, there is no known function of the substance.

It may be the case that psychedelic alkaloids in mushrooms and plants are toxic for insects and other small animals when metabolised but for humans are not harmful. This may be because psychoactive doses for humans — at least the range of psychoactive doses we find desirable — are not high enough to produce toxic effects. Another possibility is simply that these particular organisms did not evolve chemical defences to ward off humans. Some plants have chemical defence mechanisms that ward off some animals (including humans) but not others. Poison ivy, for example, contains urushiol, the oily resin in the plant that causes that infuriating rash. But for some animals, urushiol does not cause these undesirable effects — deer, goats, horses, cows, and beetles can happily eat poison ivy and experience no ill effects.

It is worth bearing in mind that mescaline — the most abundant alkaloid in psychedelic cacti like peyote — is bitter tasting. So as soon as an animal bites into a mescaline-containing cactus, they will be put off consuming it and know to avoid it in the future. This would make mescaline (and perhaps some other psychedelics) an *allelochemical* or a 'secondary metabolite': a chemical that is not needed for the plant's basic metabolism but which in many cases serves to counter non-biological and biological stressors. Psychedelics, as allelochemicals, could affect predatory organisms in ways that benefit the plant or mushroom's biological fitness: they increase the likelihood that the organism will live long enough to pass on its genetic material to its offspring. L.G. Nicholas and Kerry Ogamé describe the potential functions of psilocybin in their *Psilocybin Mushroom Handbook*:

> Perhaps these chemicals kill or inhibit the growth of snails, slugs, or worms. It is also possible that they have antibiotic properties, helping to keep bacteria or other fungi from attacking the fungus. The fact that they are produced in much greater concentrations in the fruitbodies than in the naked mycelium lends support to the idea that they serve a defensive function: if the goal of the mushroom life cycle is to produce and release as many spores as possible, it is the fruits that require the greatest protection from attack.[46]

An additional possibility is that psychedelic alkaloids are psychoactive for many other animals, but these altered states are undesirable for them. For example, since water is such a scarce resource in the desert, the peyote cactus may have developed mescaline as a defence mechanism to protect its precious water supply. When an animal consumes mescaline, the disorientation and altered sensory perception may not only be unpleasant (leading the animal to avoid the cactus in the future), but it can also, of course, make the animal more vulnerable to attack by predators. Psilocybin and other psychedelic compounds may produce similar undesirable effects for non-human animals. The fact that some plants have desirable properties for us does not mean that they evolved these properties for us.

This last point applies to many medicinal plants. For example, the bark of willow trees contains salicylic acid, which is known for its ability to ease aches and pains and reduce fever — hence why it was used in the synthesis of aspirin (or acetylsalicylic acid). This chemical also has anti-inflammatory properties (which is why it is used in acne creams) and anti-cancer properties.[47] But the willow tree did not evolve to produce salicylic acid so that humans could use it medicinally. The willow tree does not benefit by having its bark stripped away. Salicylic acid is a plant hormone with multiple functions, including the activation of plant pathogen defence systems.

In short, some plants have medicinal and psychoactive properties, not because we evolved symbiotically with them, but because we stumbled upon active ingredients in the plants that were desirable, so we continued to use them, either for medicinal or exploratory purposes. We may have simply been fortunate in our discovery that — at a certain dosage and in the right context — psychedelic compounds can have positive and advantageous effects (and since humanity is largely removed from the risks of predation, tripping is not so life-threatening).

The ability of these psychedelic compounds to bind to our serotonin and dopamine receptors and produce psychoactive effects could be accidental but not coincidental, as Nicholas and Ogamé suggest:

> [H]uman beings evolved in the same environment as worms, bacteria, and fungi, and are made up from the same basic chemical and biological building blocks. Many organisms have tryptamine-like molecules in them; though they are closely related chemically, the functions they serve are often as diverse as the organisms themselves. Biologists like to use the lock-and-key metaphor to describe the activity of chemicals on biological systems: when the key (the chemical) is inserted into the lock (the receptors on or inside the cells of the organism), some effect occurs. Because all organisms evolved from a common ancestor, the number of such "keys" is limited, while their effects are not. What happens when you put psilocybin into a slug or into a human depends upon the location and the function of the receptors with which it interacts.[48]

However, due to the human tendency to look for patterns where there aren't any (known as *apophenia* or *patternicity*), it may feel like there must be a deeper reason at play. Indeed, the idea that psychedelic effects are accidental can be hard to accept. The 'blandness' or contingent nature of this explanation could lead some people to immediately dismiss it — although this is not in itself a valid refutation.

## Alternative Explanations for Psychedelic Wisdom

There are alternate ways to account for psychedelic wisdom. The messages in the psychedelic state do not have to be gifted from an outside source, arriving from a realm or being that is beyond the self. I propose that the dampening of the ego structure, the dissolving of boundaries, and the deconditioning process can go some way in explaining the tendency for fresh and healthy messages to flood awareness during psychedelic experiences.

The ego can be thought of as the gatekeeper of consciousness. It corresponds to what Aldous Huxley called the 'reducing valve': the mechanism that limits the information that reaches our conscious awareness.[49] This is a survival mechanism. We simply would not survive or function well in the world if the ego were removed; if this occurred, we would be inundated with all kinds of content in our minds that would disrupt the everyday tasks we need to attend to. The ego is thus a necessity in our lives. But what is necessary for survival and functioning in the world does not always align with becoming wiser, happier people. The fortunate gift of psychedelics is that they can give us some reprieve from the unsatisfying wants and insecurities of the ego. And as the gatekeeper leaves its post and the neurotic chatter fades, novel and healthier ways of thinking then become possible.

The default mode network (DMN) — a brain network most active when a person is not focused on the outside world (e.g. when daydreaming) — has been identified as the neural correlate of the reducing valve. This is because it constrains our experience of the world. It has also been described, and popularised, as the neural correlate of the ego — the sense of ourselves as a separate, bounded identity — and the dampening of its activity has been associated with the subjective experience of ego dissolution.[50] However, other brain networks have been found to contribute to our sense of self, such as the salience network, with alterations to it tied to ego dissolution.[51] Researchers have also linked this loss of subjective identity to brain changes involving enhanced connections within and between brain networks[52] rather than decreased activity in one network. The DMN-ego narrative, therefore, appears to be simplistic and inaccurate.[53]

In any case, through the weakening of the ego structure, we gain greater access to the unconscious mind, which we can think of as a reservoir of untapped wisdom. By dampening or dissolving the ego and, subsequently, the boundary between the ego and the unconscious, we open ourselves up to feelings, thoughts, urges, and memories that have sat outside of conscious awareness. Some of these unconscious mental contents are unacceptable or unpleasant to us, such as anxiety, emotional pain, and feelings of unworthiness, and hence they are forced into darkness. Psychedelics can shine a spotlight on these contents as well as change our relationship with them; troubling habits of thought and feeling that were previously unknown and uncared for can then be known and cared for.

As a growing body of evidence suggests, psychedelics may partly drive therapeutic outcomes by reconnecting patients with their emotions.[54] This increased connectedness (on both the neural and psychological level), associated with the muting of the ego, can be seen to underpin the growth of wisdom following psychedelic use. Subjects who participated in a clinical trial of psilocybin for treatment-resistant depression identified two main changes after the treatment: a move from disconnection (from self, others, and world) to connection, and a shift from avoidance (of emotion) to acceptance. A third theme concerned how patients regarded this treatment compared to conventional treatments (medications and short-term talking therapies): they said the latter tended to reinforce their sense of disconnection and avoidance, whereas psilocybin had the opposite effect.[55]

When the ego is dampened or has been completely dissolved, there is an opportunity for wiser attitudes to manifest. The increased connectedness seen in the aforementioned clinical trial can be linked to different perspectives on oneself, one's relationships, humanity as a whole, and the world — perspectives that involve positive emotions like compassion, kindness, and gratitude. Indeed, many patients reported experiencing a number of valuable and therapeutic insights during their psilocybin sessions. But these insights can be seen as originating from *within* the person and their natural, inherent capacity for wisdom and self-healing, rather than viewed as arriving from an outside source.

As well as dissolving boundaries within ourselves and between ourselves and others, psychedelics can remove our felt separateness from the natural environment. This is where ecological wisdom comes in. The natural world is interconnected and interdependent, and we are very much embedded in this system, not specially excluded from it. This realisation is a particularly common aspect of the psychedelic experience. (Here we can notice the theme of connection again.)

The ecologist and researcher Sam Gandy has suggested that psychedelics are biophilia-enhancing agents, which has been borne out by research.[56][57] Biophilia refers to an innate fondness humans have for nature, proposed by the biologist E.O. Wilson. It makes sense when you consider that we have spent most of our existence living in natural environments, to which our physiology and psychology are adapted. Psychedelics can enhance connection to nature (or *nature relatedness*)[58] and biophilia, which, in altered states of consciousness, may be experienced as visions and feelings related to human destruction of ecosystems and the planet. These experiences typically feature the connected impulse to appreciate and protect the natural world. In these states, ecological and ethical wisdom can come from various realisations: our dependence on the environment; how we are connected to and unified with nature (e.g. through the sentience we share with other creatures and the fact that there is a common precious home called Earth); and the aesthetic and life-enhancing qualities of being present in natural environments.

The position of soft animism, or *naturalistic animism*, still places great value on the phenomenological reality of our experiences in nature. By giving primacy to perception — direct, immediate, pre-conceptual experience — we can see the natural world, not as inert and passive, but as active and dynamic. Both during and after a psychedelic experience, the landscape can appear as a sensuous field, with ourselves as but one point of view or way of being which reciprocates, and expressively communicates, with other points of view or ways of being in the ever-shifting landscape. We can think of ourselves as intertwined with these other entities and 'presences'. Psychedelics can put us in touch with the 'truthfulness' of animistic thinking, which stands for the right kind of relationship with the more-than-human world. The philosopher and ecologist David Abram makes this case in *The Spell of the Sensuous* (1996):

> Ecologically considered, it is not primarily our verbal statements that are "true" or "false," but rather the kind of relations that we sustain with the rest of nature. A human community that lives in a mutually beneficial relation with the surrounding earth is a community, we might say, that lives in truth. The ways of speaking common to that community — the claims and beliefs that enable such reciprocity to

perpetuate itself — are, in this important sense, *true*. They are in accord with a right relation between these people and their world. Statements and beliefs, meanwhile, that foster violence toward the land, ways of speaking that enable the impairment or ruination of the surrounding field of beings, can be described as *false* ways of speaking —ways that encourage an unsustainable relation with the encompassing earth. A civilization that relentlessly destroys the living land it inhabits is not well acquainted with *truth*, regardless of how many supposed facts it has amassed regarding the calculable properties of its world.

Hence I am less concerned with the "literal" truth of the assertions that I have made in this work than I am concerned with the kind of relationships that they make possible.[59]

Albert Hofmann, the Swiss chemist who discovered LSD, underscored the dangers of being disconnected from nature as well as the potential of psychedelics to promote ecological consciousness:

Alienation from nature and the loss of the experience of being part of the living creation is the greatest tragedy of our materialistic era. It is the causative reason for ecological devastation and climate change. Therefore I attribute absolute highest importance to consciousness change. I regard psychedelics as catalyzers for this. They are tools which are guiding our perception toward other deeper areas of our human existence, so that we again become aware of our spiritual essence. Psychedelic experiences in a safe setting can help our consciousness open up to this sensation of connection and of being one with nature.[60]

We have been conditioned, both physically and culturally, to feel separate from nature. By living in modern cities, nature becomes atypical and alien to us — much to our detriment. However, psychedelics can dismantle this conditioned separateness and open us up to the vitalising, biophilic attitude, which we are all capable of having and benefiting from but which modern living has stymied.

I would argue, nonetheless, that none of these effects necessarily rely on the teleological view; they are consistent with the non-teleological outlook. The latter outlook also better reflects the nuanced, messy, and multifaceted nature of psychedelics. The non-teleological view relies on fewer assumptions and resists the deification of psychedelic plants and mushrooms. It can be tempting to assign a divine or supernatural status to these organisms, based on the influx of wisdom and healing they engender, but doing so is arguably hasty and unfounded. The teleological view is often simplistic and overzealous; it ignores how the messages in the psychedelic state may, at times, be unwise.

Huxley was perhaps correct when he referred to psychedelics as a gratuitous grace, "not necessary to salvation but potentially helpful and to be accepted thankfully, if made available".[61] With this stance in mind, we are not doomed without psychedelics, but they are nonetheless fortuitous tools — fungal and botanical gifts — that allow us to acquire or deepen wisdom. They are not, as Huxley emphasises, the sole or necessary means for better looking after ourselves, others, and the wider world. But the fact of their existence calls for our gratitude as much as if they were associated with spirits and teleology.

Pinchbeck claims that psychoactive plants and mushrooms are here to help put us on the right path. By "communing with our botanical elders",[62] as he puts it, we can look at the world with the kind of eyes that are necessary to avoid the imminent threats posed by environmental destruction. However, as I have tried to show, it is possible to explain the valuable insights provided by psychoactive plants without depending on the assumption that these life forms are wise emissaries, here to teach us something vital.

These profound insights always have the potential to be realised, but they either lay dormant or they are not sufficiently animated to be truly experienced as high priorities. What psychedelic compounds can do is alter what thoughts and ideas take priority in our space of immediate awareness. But this leaves something unexplained: Why do our priorities drastically change, so that everyday concerns become trivial or non-existent, and what inhabits our full attention instead are wider and more pressing matters, such as the need for connection?

Under Pinchbeck's assumption, this would be because psychedelic compounds exist in various plants as messengers of truth — they are there to deliver messages to us. Yet we can also take a different approach, without presuming a teleological view of nature. We can posit that psychedelics work with pre-existing and latent material in our minds and raise it to the forefront of consciousness because this is always a possibility in altered states. The messages are also received in an emotionally charged way, so that the weight of ecological destruction and human suffering is *felt* as well as intellectually understood. Perhaps this is because, as the psychonaut and lecturer Terence McKenna often stressed, psychedelics are boundary-dissolving drugs.[63] They can temporarily remove the boundaries and rigid thinking created by cultural conditioning, giving intuitive understanding some room to breathe. This makes sense, given that the insights elicited by psychedelics are often universal — they are also expressed in cultures that do not have a tradition of using these compounds.

Accordingly, psychedelics may help us to remember what we have learned to forget, rather than impart lessons that would otherwise seem totally amiss. The kinds of revelations experienced in the psychedelic state can also be had — with varying flavours and degrees of intensity — in other altered states, as well as in sober waking life. Does this, therefore, mean that every profound experience has a purpose? Potentially. These experiences only have the kind of purpose that we, as purpose-creating creatures, assign them.

Ultimately, it is not really the plant that teaches but oneself; the psychedelic is more like the assistant — the chemical counsellor — who opens us up to more aspects of ourselves as well as alternative modes of seeing and relating. But like all helpful relationships, personal growth does not come from dependence on the counsellor but from the internalisation of that relationship, so that one can apply wisdom whenever it is called for in everyday life. In other words, while psychedelics may not be *inherently* wise and purposeful, we can still use them in wise and purposeful ways.

## Endnotes

1. Sjöstedt-Hughes, P. (2021). *Modes of Sentience: Psychedelics, Metaphysics, Panpsychism*, pp. 58–59. London: Psychedelic Press.
2. Ibid., pp. 59–60.
3. Ibid., p. 60.
4. Ibid.
5. Ibid., pp. 60–61.
6. Dupuis, D. (2021). 'The socialization of hallucinations: Cultural priors, social interactions, and contextual factors in the use of psychedelics'. *Transcultural Psychiatry*, 59(5), pp. 625–637.
7. Ibid., p. 62.
8. Lancaster-Thomas, A. (2020). 'Encountering Evil: The Evil-god Challenge from Religious Experience'. *European Journal for Philosophy of Religion*, 12(3), pp. 137–161.
9. Pietkiewicz, I.J., Kłosińska, U., and Tomalski, R. (2021). 'Delusions of Possession and Religious Coping in

Schizophrenia: A Qualitative Study of Four Cases'. *Frontiers in Psychology*, 12, Article: 628925.

10. Nie, F. and Olson, D.V.A. (2017). 'Demonic Influence: The Negative Mental Health Effects of Belief in Demons'. *Journal for the Scientific Study of Religion*, 55(3), pp. 498–515.

11. Urry, J. (1990). *The Tourist Gaze*, pp. 1–16. 2nd ed. London: SAGE Publications, 2002.

12. Foucault, M. (1963). *The Birth of the Clinic*, p. 89. London: Routledge, 1973.

13. Urry, J. (1990). *The Tourist Gaze*, p. 1. 2nd ed. London: SAGE Publications, 2002.

14. Kehoe, A.B. (2000). *Shamans and Religion: An Anthropological Exploration in Critical Thinking*, pp. 85–81. Longrove, IL: Waveland Press.

15. Fotiou, E. (2016). 'The Globalization of Ayahuasca Shamanism and the Erasure of Indigenous Shamanism'. *Anthropology of Consciousness*, 27(2), pp. 151–179.

16. Ibid.

17. Ibid.

18. Luna, L.E. (1983). 'The Concept of Plants as Teachers among four Mestizo Shamans of Iquitos, Northeastern Perú'. *Journal of Ethnopharmacology*, 11(2), pp. 135–156.

19. Guthrie, S. (2002). 'Animal Animism: Evolutionary Roots of Religious Behavior' in *Current Approaches in the Cognitive Science of Religion*, edited by Pyysiäinen, I. and Anttonen, V., pp. 38–67. London: Continuum.

20. Barrett, J.L. and Zahl, B.P. (2013). 'Cognition, Evolution, and Religion' in *APA Handbook of Psychology, Religion, and Spirituality (Vol. 1): Context, Theory, and Research*, edited by Pargament, K.I., Exline, J., and Jones, J.W., pp. 221–238. Washington, DC: American Psychological Association.

21. Maij, D.L.R., van Schie, H.T., and van Elk, M. (2017). 'The boundary conditions of the hypersensitive agency detection device: an empirical investigation of agency detection in

threatening situations'. *Religion, Brain & Behavior*, 9(4), pp. 1–29.

22. Ibid.

23. Guthrie, S.E. (1993). 'Religion as Anthropomorphism' in *Faces in the Clouds: A New Theory of Religion*, pp. 177–205. Oxford: Oxford University Press.

24. Barrett, J.L. and Zahl, B.P. (2013). 'Cognition, Evolution, and Religion' in *APA Handbook of Psychology, Religion, and Spirituality (Vol. 1): Context, Theory, and Research*, edited by Pargament, K.I., Exline, J., and Jones, J.W., pp. 221–238. Washington, DC: American Psychological Association.

25. Barrett, J.L. (2000). 'Exploring the natural foundations of religion'. *Trends in Cognitive Sciences*, 4(1), pp. 29–34.

26. Barrett, J.L. (2004). *Why Would Anyone Believe in God?*, p. 4. Lanham, MD: AltaMira Press.

27. Peoples, H.C., Duda, P., and Marlowe, F.W. (2016). 'Hunter-Gatherers and the Origins of Religion'. *Human Nature*, 27(3), pp. 261–268.

28. Winkelman, M.J. (2017). 'The Mechanisms of Psychedelic Visionary Experiences: Hypotheses from Evolutionary Psychology'. *Frontiers in Neuroscience*, 11, Article: 539.

29. Nayak, S.M. and Griffiths, R.R. (2022). 'A Single Belief-Changing Psychedelic Experience Is Associated With Increased Attribution of Consciousness to Living and Non-Living Entities'. *Frontiers in Psychology*, 13, Article: 852248.

30. Johns Hopkins Medicine (2022). 'New study explores relationship between psychedelics and consciousness', *ScienceDaily*, 31 March. https://www.sciencedaily.com/releases/2022/03/220331134240.htm

31. Lutkajtis, A. (2021). 'Entity encounters and the therapeutic effect of the psychedelic mystical experience'. *Journal of Psychedelic Studies*, 4(3), pp. 171–178.

32. Winkelman, M.J. (2018). 'An ontology of psychedelic entity experiences in evolutionary psychology and

neurophenomenology'. *Journal of Psychedelic Studies*, 2(1), pp. 5–23.

33. Ibid.

34. Pyysiäinen, I. (2009). *Supernatural Agents: Why We Believe in Souls, Gods, and Buddhas*, p. 13. Oxford: Oxford University Press.

35. D'Aquili, E.G. and Newberg, A.B. (1998). 'The Neuropsychological Basis of Religions, or Why God Won't Go Away'. *Zygon*, 33(2), pp. 187–201.

36. Winkelman, M.J. (2018). 'An ontology of psychedelic entity experiences in evolutionary psychology and neurophenomenology'. *Journal of Psychedelic Studies*, 2(1), pp. 5–23.

37. Ibid.

38. Becker, A.M., Klaiber, A., Holze, F., Istampoulouoglou, I., Duthaler, U., Varghese, N., Eckert, A., and Liechti, M.E. (2023). *International Journal of Neuropsychopharmacology*, 26(2), pp. 97–106.

39. Barker, S.A. (2018). 'N, N-Dimethyltryptamine (DMT), an Endogenous Hallucinogen: Past, Present, and Future Research to Determine Its Role and Function'. *Frontiers in Neuroscience*, 12, Article: 536.

40. Ruse, M. (2013). 'Earth's holy fool?', *Aeon*, 14 January. https://aeon.co/essays/gaia-why-some-scientists-think-its-a-nonsensical-fantasy

41. Fautin, D. (1991). 'The anemonefish symbiosis: what is known as what is not'. *Symbiosis*, 10, pp. 23–46.

42. Titus, B.M., Laroche, R., Rodríguez, E., Wirshing, H., and Meyer, C.P. (2020). 'Host identity and symbiotic association affects the taxonomic and functional diversity of the clownfish-hosting sea anemone microbiome'. *Biology Letters*, 16(2), Article: 20190738.

43. Poulin, R. and Grutter, A.S. (1996). 'Cleaning Symbioses: Proximate and Adaptive Explanations'. *BioScience*, 46(7), pp. 512–517.

44. O'Brien, R.D. (1967). Chapter 8: 'Nicotinoids' in *Insecticides: Action and Metabolism*, pp. 148–158. Cambridge, MA: Academic Press.

45. Nathanson, J.A., Hunnicutt, E.J., Kantham, L., and Scavone, C. (1993). 'Cocaine as a naturally occurring insecticide'. *PNAS*, 90(20), pp. 9645–9648.

46. Nicholas, L.G. and Ogamé, K. (2006). *Psilocybin Mushroom Handbook: Easy Indoor & Outdoor Cultivation*, p. 157. Piedmont, CA: Quick American Publishing.

47. Desborough, M.J.R. and Keeling, D.M. (2017). 'The aspirin story — from willow to wonder drug'. *British Journal of Haemotology*, 177(5), pp. 674–683.

48. Nicholas, L.G. and Ogamé, K. (2006). *Psilocybin Mushroom Handbook: Easy Indoor & Outdoor Cultivation*, p. 157. Piedmont, CA: Quick American Publishing.

49. Huxley, A. (1954). *The Doors of Perception.* https://maps.org/images/pdf/books/HuxleyA1954TheDoorsOfPerception.pdf

50. Carhart-Harris, R.L., Leech, R., Hellyer, R.J., Shanahan, M., Feilding, A., Tagliazucchi, E. Chialvo, D.R., and Nutt, D. (2014). 'The entropic brain: a theory of conscious states informed by neuroimaging research with psychedelic drugs'. *Frontiers in Human Neuroscience*, 8, Article: 20.

51. Stoliker, D., Novelli, L., Vollenweider, F.X., Egan, G.F., Preller, K.H., and Razi, A. (2023). 'Effective Connectivity of Functionally Anticorrelated Networks Under Lysergic Acid Diethylamide'. *Biological Psychiatry*, 93(3), pp. 224–232.

52. Tagliazucchi, E., Roseman, L., Kaelen, M., Orban, C., Muthukumaraswamy, S.D., Murphy, K., Laufs, H., Leech, R., McGonigle, J., Crossley, N., Bullmore, E., Williams, T., Bolstridge, M., Feilding, A., Nutt, D.J., and Carhart-Harris, R. (2016). 'Increased Global Functional Connectivity Correlates with LSD-Induced Ego Dissolution'. *Current Biology*, 26, pp. 1043–1050.

53. Briggs, S. (2021). 'Dissolving Ego Dissolution'. MIND Foundation, 14 May. https://mind-foundation.org/ego-dissolution/

54. Roseman, L., Demetriou, L., Wall, M.B., Nutt, D.J., and Carhart-Harris, R.L. (2018). 'Increased amygdala responses to emotional faces after psilocybin for treatment-resistant depression'. *Neuropharmacology*, 142, pp. 263–269.

55. Watts, R., Krzanowski, J., Nutt, D., and Carhart-Harris, R. (2017). 'Patients' accounts of increased "connectedness" and "acceptance" after psilocybin for treatment-resistant depression'. *Journal of Humanistic Psychology*, 57(5), pp. 520–564.

56. Gandy, S. (2019). 'Bridging the Divide: Psychedelic Biophilia & Human Nature Connection', Medium, 1 August. https://medium.com/@sgandy2512/bridging-the-divide-psychedelic-biophilia-human-nature-connection-4bcc5ea99c3

57. Irvine, A., Luke, D., Harrild, F., Gandy, S., and Watts, S. (2023). 'Transpersonal Ecodelia: Surveying Psychedelically Induced Biophilia'. *Psychoactives*, 2(2), pp. 174–193.

58. Kettner, H., Gandy, S., Haijen, E.C.H.M, and Carhart-Harris, R.L. (2019). 'From Egoism to Ecoism: Psychedelics Increase Nature Relatedness in a State-Mediated and Context-Dependent Manner'. *International Journal of Environmental Research and Public Health*, 16(24), Article: 5174.

59. Abram, D. (1996). *The Spell of the Sensuous*, p. 264. New York: Pantheon Books.

60. Hofmann, A. (2013). *LSD and the Divine Scientist: The Final Thoughts and Reflections of Albert Hofmann*, p. 101. Rochester, VT: Inner Traditions.

61. Huxley, A. (1954). *The Doors of Perception*. https://maps.org/images/pdf/books/HuxleyA1954TheDoorsOfPerception.pdf

62. Pinchbeck, D. (2009). 'Another Green World: Psychedelics and Ecology', MAPS *Bulletin*, Vol XIX No 1. https://maps. org/news-letters/v19n1/v19n1-pg59.pdf

63. McKenna, T. (1989). 'The Evolution of a Psychedelic Thinker', organism.earth. https://www.organism.earth/ library/document/evolution-of-a-psychedelic-thinker

# Chapter 9

# A Profound Feeling of Familiarity: Bergson, Déjà Vu, and DMT

Most people experience the strange phenomenon of déjà vu on multiple occasions during their lifetime. Yet it often passes us by without piquing our curiosity, much like many dreams we have. Both our dreams and the experience of déjà vu may feel odd and eerie, but typically, we do not give much thought to the origin and meaning (if any) of their content.

When considering what déjà vu is, we can provide essentially two types of description: a phenomenological one and an ultimate one. The former relates to what the direct, subjective experience of déjà vu is like, while the latter presents an explanation of *why* déjà vu occurs. We will generally be much more familiar with the phenomenological perspective than the ultimate one.

Briefly defined, déjà vu, from the French, means 'already seen'; it is the uncanny sense of having already experienced the present situation at some other time. It is considered an illusion of re-experiencing an event, a scene, or a particular train of thought, *exactly* as it has occurred before, hence the feeling of uncanny familiarity. It is as if we know what we are going to think, say, or do next.

Déjà vu is an illusion that most of us recognise as such, although some will ascribe to it a mystical quality, owing to the sense of gaining spontaneous insight or the feeling of having the exact same experience again. Such an impulse follows from rare and unusual coincidences, too, which are likewise felt to be signposts for something individually meaningful and important.

According to the French philosopher Henri Bergson, the *reason* why déjà vu occurs has to do with the nature of memory and perception, which he saw as interrelated in quite a novel way. I wish to expound on Bergson's views on this phenomenon, as I believe it offers a unique way to interpret the profound sense of déjà vu that often occurs when people use the potent psychedelic compound DMT. While mysterious, déjà vu does not have to be confined to the sphere of supernatural interpretation. However, even if Bergson's explanation of the *re-experienced* is not the correct one — or is in some way incomplete — there are still other explanations that shed light on why this experience occurs, including in the DMT state.

## Bergson's Theory of Déjà Vu

In an intriguing essay titled 'Memory of the Present and False Recognition' (1908), Bergson proposes that déjà vu is the result of memory and perception becoming intertwined in the present moment. This is based on his supposition that memory and perception — the past and the present — occur simultaneously. The British philosopher Keith Ansell-Pearson, who has translated Bergson's work, writes,

Bergson's claim is that at every moment of our lives we are presented with two aspects, even though the virtual aspect may be imperceptible owing to the very nature of the operations of perception. It is because the past does not simply follow the present but coexists with it that we can develop an explanation of paramnesia or the illusion of déjà-vu, in which there is a recollection of the present contemporaneous with the present itself. The illusion is generated from thinking that we are actually undergoing an experience we have already lived through when in fact what is taking place is the perception of the duplication we do not normally perceive, namely, of time into the two aspects of actual and virtual. There is a memory of the present in the actual moment itself. I cannot actually predict what is going to happen but I feel as if I can: what I foresee is that I am going to have known it — I experience a 'recognition to come'. I gain insight into the formation of a memory of the present…[1]

In Bergson's own words,

As we witness an event or participate in a conversation, there suddenly arises the conviction that we have already seen what we are seeing, already heard what we are hearing, and already said what is being said … in sum, we are reliving down to the last detail an instant of our own past life. The illusion is sometimes so strong that in each moment, as long as this illusion lasts, we believe ourselves to be at the point of predicting what is about to happen: how could we not know already, if we feel that soon we will know that we knew it?[2]

If we attend to the felt subjective quality of déjà vu, this does, indeed, ring true. When this experience lasts beyond a split second of uncanny familiarity, and a chain of thoughts is unfolding (usually for no longer than a matter of seconds), there is this sense that you know that the next detail will be familiar, and you are close to predicting it. This is like when you are trying to remember something that is on the tip of your tongue. During the déjà vu experience, you do not actually predict in the moment what the next detail will be, but when it does come, there is an immediate sense that you *knew* this would occur.

Bergson argues that this phenomenon of 'experiencing again' involves a duplication of the present — and, according to him, this results in the strange feeling of simultaneously both acting in and spectating on our lives. Bergson calls this a 'false recognition': you become a person "looking on at his own movements, thoughts and actions". Essentially, you are split into two people: one of whom is "an actor playing a part" and another person who is spectating.[3] This duplication can occur because of the way that memory functions.

Bergson was trying to dispel the illusion, which we do not commonly recognise as such, that a memory is only formed *after* a perception has taken place. He posits that "the formation of memory is never posterior to the formation of perception, it is contemporaneous with it".[4] The illusion that memory follows perception is "generated by the requirements of perception itself, which is always focused on the needs of a present," writes Ansell-Pearson.[5] Or as Bergson states,

> But the forward-springing one, which we call perception, is that alone which interests us. We have no need of the memory of things whilst we hold the things themselves. Practical consciousness, throwing this memory aside as useless, theoretical reflection holds it to be non-existent. Thus the illusion is born that memory *succeeds* perception.[6]

Memory formation is an unconscious process because becoming conscious of this process, which occurs simultaneously with perception, does not serve us in a practical sense. Information from the unconscious is typically only actualised if it serves a useful cognitive function (except, of course, in cases like the illusion of déjà vu, which does not appear to possess any utility). The idea that normal perception is strategically restrictive, due to practical concerns, is a common feature in Bergson's thought. For example, he advanced a view — later accepted by Aldous Huxley in *The Doors of Perception* — that the mind acts as a reducing valve, only letting information enter our conscious awareness that benefits our survival.[7] If we were flooded by all the contents of the mind, conversely, we would be overwhelmed and less likely to achieve self-preservation.

The unconscious, for Bergson, is a vast repository of 'pure' or 'virtual' memory, which is only accessed when it helps to make sense of the present. Pure or virtual memories — which Bergson first described in his text *Matter and Memory* (1896) — are those that have not yet mixed with present perceptions, while pure perceptions are, equally, those that have not yet been mingled with memories. Unrevealed pure memories in the unconscious are primed to combine with new perceptions in the present as and when it is deemed necessary and useful. This is a dynamic relationship between memory and perception, yet with the two formulated as having a 'pure' form, memory and perception are also fundamentally divided in the mind.[8]

This division means that we can see the difference between memory and perception as one of kind and not merely degree or intensity. Memory is not just a weakened or diluted form of perception (with the images we recall being hazier and less vivid images of the actual perception they pertain to). Rather, the recollection of an image is more like a concentrated act of intellectual effort. Memory is also a highly creative act, prone to embellishment and all other kinds of colouring and biases. As Bergson insisted, "To *picture* is not to *remember*."[9]

Returning to the 'false recognition' that is déjà vu, Bergson uses the analogy of our shadow:

Step by step, as perception is created, it is profiled in memory, which is beside it like a shadow is next to a body. But, in the normal condition, there is no consciousness of it, just as we should be unconscious of our shadow were our eyes to throw light on it each time it turned in that direction.[10]

Lynne Pearce explains Bergson's theory of déjà vu as follows: "these presentiments are, in fact, things we have *already* thought — but only just. They belong, as it were, to our shadow-*present* and, rather than waiting to be actualised years later, come into being a heart beat after they have been formed."[11]

Are there any issues with Bergson's exposition? One possibility — which does not necessarily nullify Bergson's account — is that some instances of what we call déjà vu do not involve consciously experiencing the simultaneity of perception and memory formation but instead come from an actual re-experiencing. So, the reason why some experiences feel so uncanny is that they have, in fact, occurred in an identical, near identical, or similar way before. One has had this very thought, or chain of thoughts, before — or one has had a conversation that feels repeated. Certainly, it is difficult to tease apart such instances from the déjà vu Bergson has in mind. It may be that the scenarios I allude to illustrate just how powerful the illusion of déjà vu is: nothing truly repeats; any feeling of spooky repetition simply involves a glitch in the functioning of perception and memory.

I wonder, too, whether some other instances of déjà vu are actually instances of remembering dreams. On this account, some present perceptions may be so similar to a forgotten segment of a dream scenario that one's immediate reality takes on this oneiric quality. We may think that dreams become rapidly erased from our memory upon waking, but many dream memories may be lodged in our unconscious. They are not typically brought to light because from the perspective of practical consciousness (where we are aware of only what is deemed useful: a sliver of reality), dream content can have little utility in our lives. However, it is not unheard of for elements of our dreams to percolate to the surface of conscious awareness. Perhaps this remembering is context-dependent: when a certain context manifests, the memory is triggered. Consequently, when waking life shares the context of a dream — be that a place, thought, feeling, or conversation — we may be struck by an eerie feeling, a sense of déjà vu, influenced by a previous dream that did not disappear into the void after all. (*Déjà rêvé*, meaning 'already dreamed', is the specific term denoting the re-experiencing of a dream but as a real-life event, as if the dream were a premonition. It is distinct from déjà vu.)

In *Matter and Memory*, Bergson argues that *pure memory* is, by its very nature, virtual. It is not located in our brains, or anywhere physical, in fact. Instead, he thought of pure memory as the non-actual repository of all past events, the contents of which will be actualised at different times, depending on our current needs and concerns. Pure memory is the totality of memories existing, eternally, in a virtual state.[12] Recollection, then, is the actualisation of a memory-image from this virtual place, becoming a memory-image in the present. This move from the virtual to the actual, as the lecturer Stamatis Zografos points out, creates "the illusion that memory-images are *archived* somewhere in the brain".[13]

Pure memory records all of our experiences, which of course, then, includes all of our dreams. Bergson's philosophy of memory could help explain why we can recall long-forgotten dreams in the present, which can lead to a sense of déjà vu (or more specifically, déjà rêvé). But the cause of this feeling in this case is not recollecting the present as we experience it. Instead, it is being aware of a dream memory-image that has gone from virtualised to actualised *at the same time* as having a present perception that in some way accords with that memory-image.

One criticism of this take on déjà rêvé, nevertheless, is that it assumes the existence of a virtual realm. The virtual, according to Bergson, is real (unlike the possible) but it is not actual or physical. So how would we establish the existence of this realm — some 'place' of infinite potentiality[14] — as an ontological reality? Postulating such a realm could unnecessarily complicate our explanations of strange memory-related phenomena, especially if we can explain something like déjà rêvé through empirical research.[15]

There may also be a gap or incompleteness in Bergson's explanation of déjà vu since if this phenomenon does involve a glitch in the normal functioning of the mind, we should then ask, *why* does this glitch occur? Is the glitch merely a random malfunctioning that happens, expected in an organism as much as a computer? Or is there an underlying pattern or reason that helps explain why déjà vu occurs in specific instances and so rarely? Later on in the essay, I will explore some more modern, scientific accounts of déjà vu as a way to provide some answers, as this may also shed light on why this feeling is experienced in the DMT state.

For now, I will turn to the profound déjà vu that many people experience under the influence of DMT and relate this subjective effect to Bergson's philosophy.

## A Bergsonian Account of DMT-Induced Déjà Vu

During the DMT trance, there can be an extremely powerful feeling of déjà vu. The realm is strangely familiar, *strangely* so because this familiar realm is, at the same time, utterly *alien*. This world is alien in two senses: it is unlike anything in waking consensus reality and it appears to be a futuristic, hi-tech alien civilisation, populated by intelligent entities. According to research from Christopher Cott and Adam J. Rock, a sense of familiarity is one of the consistent themes of the DMT state.[16] A separate study found that DMT users found many aspects of the experience familiar, including feeling, emotion, knowledge, the space visited, transcendent features, entity encounters, and the act of going through the experience. However, no participants referenced a previous experience with DMT or another psychedelic as the source of that familiarity.[17]

DMT-induced déjà vu is both intense and seems to be extended — it lasts much longer than a standard déjà vu experience will last (which could very well be over in a matter of seconds). Under the influence of DMT, a strong feeling of familiarity — the definite sense that you have been to this realm before or have 'returned home' — can persist throughout the trip. This feeling can be so powerful that it may turn into the conviction that the DMT world is a real place and one's true home (even if the contents of the experience, like those of déjà vu, are hard to remember).

The psychonaut, lecturer, and DMT enthusiast Terence McKenna attempted to describe the DMT experience, in all its stages, as best he could in his lectures. These descriptions have enthralled listeners and users of this compound, and certain snippets and phrases now sit firmly within the public imagination. At about a minute or two into a DMT trip, McKenna said that one may burst through a chrysanthemum-like mandala and find "[t]here's a whole bunch of entities waiting on the other side, saying 'How wonderful that you're here! You come so rarely! We're so delighted to see you!'"[18] He has famously called these entities "jewelled self-dribbling basketballs",[19] who offer objects to you that look like "Fabergé eggs",[20] "elf gifts",[21] or "celestial toys",[22] the sort of objects you would find "scattered around the nursery inside a U.F.O.".[23] What is relevant to this discussion, though, is McKenna's following description:

> We're now at minute 4.5 [of the trip] and you speak in a kind of glossolalia. There is a spontaneous outpouring of syntax unaccompanied by what is normally called "meaning".... After a minute or so of this the whole thing begins to collapse in on itself and they [the entities] begin to physically move away from you. And usually their final shot is they actually wave goodbye and they say "Déjà vu! Déjà vu!".[24]

Of course, it may not be that they actually *say* déjà vu during the experience since their form of communication often feels to be telepathic in nature: an expression of definite meaning without words. Moreover, the entities may not necessarily try to get across to the user that he or she has had this experience before (be that at the tail-end of the experience, in McKenna's case, or at any other point). Instead, déjà vu can simply permeate the experience. The feeling, the space, the entities, or the messages may be imbued with the uncanny quality of 'already experienced'.

Connecting this phenomenological quality to Bergson's theory, it could be that the co-experiencing of memory formation of the present and perception of the present — this glitch — is prolonged in the DMT state. If this is what is happening, DMT's ability to induce a protracted state of déjà vu is enigmatic: Why would this chemical, in particular, have such a tendency? Nonetheless, other substances can elicit déjà vu and sometimes extend it — nitrous oxide is also known to commonly have this effect. But even if DMT is not special in this regard, the peculiar fact that any particular compound will bring on, magnify, or lengthen déjà vu requires an explanation.

DMT and nitrous oxide — both fast-acting, short-lasting compounds — do not only share the effect of déjà vu in common. Perhaps due to the rapid onset of intense effects and equally quick return to sobriety, the DMT and nitrous oxide experiences are also characterised by an intense *noetic* quality. This is the sense of gaining direct knowledge about something of immense value, something that was previously mysterious. Then, as the effects fade, so too does the insight, escaping like liquid gold through one's fingertips. The shining light of illumination turns into the darkness of the unremembered, leaving one puzzled. One may even mourn the loss. The reason I bring up these further similarities — the noetic quality and loss of insight — is that they could be related to psychedelic déjà vu.

Déjà vu, after all, can be imbued with a sense of revelation and illumination. Like the noetic experiences of mystical states, it features this 'Aha!' moment of clear understanding. One believes that the experience is not arbitrary; there is an impression that the content of the re-experience is meaningful, that it is recurring *for a reason* and providing genuine insight.

But again, as the déjà vu fades, as it always does, so too does the noetic quality. This is not to say that the déjà vu is necessary for the noetic quality to appear: many, if not most, mystical states have the feeling of insightfulness and knowing without déjà vu. My point is simply that déjà vu itself often has the noetic quality. Furthermore, these two qualities may entwine in a unique way in the DMT experience. Mingling with the additional qualities of heightened emotions and impressive visions, this kind of déjà vu can be very special indeed.

In the DMT state, awareness of both the memory formation of the visions and the perception of those visions may be what is giving the user that common feeling of having been to this realm before. Moreover, if this déjà vu is intensified, extended, and mixed in with the feelings of awe, reverence, insight, and profound joy that are characteristic of mystical states, it makes sense that such déjà vu will be felt as authoritative in a way that sober experiences of déjà vu are not. There can be the conviction, persisting long after the experience, that one has been to this place before. Someone might believe that, owing to the mind/reality-modulating effects of DMT, this familiar dimension is ever-present but normally hidden or that this realm is where we came from and where we shall return (after our physical death).

Arguably, Bergson's theory of déjà vu could more parsimoniously explain the experience of familiarity than the idea that there are hidden realms only accessible with the help of chemicals. Others may find it hard to accept the notion that our consciousness will survive physical death. These kinds of convictions involve many assumptions. On the other hand, Bergson's theory is not the only (or necessarily best) way of explaining déjà vu. Since the time of his writing on this matter, our scientific understanding of this phenomenon has developed, which may be relevant to the DMT experience.

(Before turning to the science of déjà vu, I would just like to highlight the possibility that the 'eerie feeling' one gets in the DMT state is not — or at least, is *not always* — related to déjà vu. It could be a feeling of *jamais vu*: the phenomenon of experiencing a situation that one recognises in some way but which nonetheless still seems unfamiliar and novel. The experience of jamais vu could equally account for both the feelings of familiarity and unfamiliarity that may arise during a DMT experience.)

## Scientific Explanations of Déjà Vu — and Their Relation to the DMT State

Scientists, in a similar vein to Bergson, have proposed that déjà vu is a phenomenon related to memory, but they explain it differently. The cognitive psychologist Anne Cleary has, through her collaborative research, found that déjà vu occurs when someone encounters a scenario that resembles an actual memory but they fail to recall that memory. This *implicit memory* is essentially what leads to that odd feeling of familiarity. If you could recall the memory in question, you would be able to link the two events, therefore déjà vu would not occur.

Cleary and other researchers demonstrated that déjà vu can be prompted by a visual scene that is spatially similar to a prior one. She and her team created virtual reality scenarios using the Sims virtual world video game. To induce the feeling of déjà vu, the researchers had the participants move through scenes that were spatially mapped to previous ones but which were different in some ways. For example, all of the bushes of a virtual garden were replaced with piles of rubbish, creating a scrapyard with the same layout. Subjects were more likely to report déjà vu among scenes that matched previous ones they were unable to recall.[25]

In further experiments, Cleary created dynamic video scenes in which participants were taken through a series of turns. Later, they were taken through scenes that spatially mapped previous ones to induce déjà vu. The researchers paused the navigation before the final turn in a scene and asked participants what the last turn would be. In those moments, the participants reported whether they were experiencing déjà vu and whether they knew the direction of the next turn. About half of the respondents felt a strong sense of premonition during déjà vu — as if they knew what was going to happen next — but they were no more likely to give the correct answer than if they were to choose randomly. The authors of this research state,

> Building on research showing that déjà vu can be driven by an unrecalled memory of a past experience that relates to the current situation, we sought evidence of memory-based predictive ability during déjà vu states. Déjà vu did not lead to above-chance ability to predict the next turn in a navigational path resembling a previously experienced but unrecalled path (although such resemblance increased reports of déjà vu). However, déjà vu states were accompanied by increased feelings of knowing the direction of the next turn. The results suggest that feelings of premonition or precognition during déjà vu occur and can be illusory.[26]

This feeling of precognition also seems to be interwoven with the déjà vu of psychedelic states, particularly at the peak of DMT and nitrous oxide experiences. As the emotionally and visually rich experience unfolds, there may be a sense of building up to a crescendo of revealed truth, some grand illumination right around the corner. You are about to cross the threshold from unknowing to the clear light of knowing. *Presque vu* — French for 'almost seen' — refers to this intense feeling of being on the brink of an epiphany. It is as if one holds — somewhere, secretly — what is about-to-be-known, but it cannot quite be recalled. This is very much like when you are trying to remember the name of something or someone; the answer is on the tip of your tongue. Likewise, when traversing DMT hyperspace — gliding, turning, and shooting through the cosmic corridors — there is not only déjà vu but, as with many instances of déjà vu, there is a premonitory quality. You have been here before and you know what is going to happen next. The noetic is on the horizon.

Perhaps this feeling of premonition is, in line with Cleary's research, related to the different 'levels' or 'rooms' of hyperspace being similar but different. If so, this would mean that as you transition from one place to the next, which seems to occur at lightning speed, you become overwhelmed with a sense of foreknowing. However, these premonitory feelings associated with déjà vu may, as Cleary and others suggest, be illusory.

Déjà vu, more generally, can be thought of as a memory phenomenon in which we encounter situations similar to an actual memory, but we cannot fully recall that memory. Our brain recognises similarities between a current experience and one from the past, leaving us with a feeling of familiarity *that we cannot place.*

While the DMT realm is often referred to as ineffable, users will nonetheless attach certain descriptions to the idiosyncratic space they find themselves in. This space can resemble a temple, mosque, circus, casino, carnival, or futuristic room. The déjà vu may result from entering these spaces, which are similar to actual memories. If we fail to recall those memories in the DMT state (due to the altered state being markedly different from them), then this could be why déjà vu easily manifests.

Yet as with Bergson's account, the question arises: *Why* does déjà vu occur in certain instances? There are several theories. According to the theory of split perception, déjà vu happens when you see something two different times; the first time you see it, you may see it out of the corner of your eye or while distracted. Your brain begins forming a memory with the limited information available — with a brief glance, you may take in more than you realise. Then, if you look at this scene while paying attention, your brain recalls the previous perception, even though you lacked total awareness when that perception took place. Since you did not give your full attention to the scene the first time, it feels like two different events (despite it being one continuous perception) — hence the déjà vu.[27]

Relating this to the DMT experience, we might say that given its rapidity of change, it is not conducive to full attention. A visionary scene may appear so quickly that we do not have time to focus on it. Yet when we do try to pay attention, it may seem as if we have experienced this before. McKenna said of the experience: "you're being presented with thousands of details per second and you can't get a hold on [them] … and these things [the entities] are saying 'Don't abandon yourself to amazement', which is exactly what you want to do. You want to go nuts with how crazy this is. They say 'Don't do that…. Pay attention. Pay attention to what we're doing.'"[28]

Another theory is that déjà vu is just a glitch occurring in the brain. It may arise when there is a brief electrical malfunction, similar to what happens during an epileptic seizure. Some patients with temporal lobe epilepsy experience déjà vu before an epileptic seizure, as if it is a kind of warning.[29] During this glitch, the part of your brain that tracks present perceptions and the part that recalls memories could become active at the same time. This would lead you to falsely perceive the present as a memory, as something that has already happened. The Bergsonian account, nevertheless, would not necessarily consider this a *false* perception since, under this view, the past is concurrent with the present: we can experience an event as both a memory and a perception *at the same time*.

An additional brain malfunction that could explain déjà vu relates to the distinct functions of short- and long-term memory. When your brain absorbs information, it will generally follow a path from short-term memory storage to long-term memory storage. However, a brain malfunction (or glitch) may result in short-term memories taking a shortcut to long-term memory storage. This can give you the feeling that you are retrieving an old memory rather than information from an event that occurred in the last second.[30]

If any of these brain glitch accounts are true, it implies that DMT and other psychedelics — for some unknown reason — have a tendency to cause these glitches. In terms of particular brain regions implicated in déjà vu, the rhinal cortex — the area of the brain responsible for signalling that something is familiar[31] — could be involved. Experiments have at least demonstrated that stimulating this brain region can induce déjà vu.[32] The activation of the rhinal cortex during a DMT experience might explain the powerful, overwhelming, and continuous déjà vu that is felt. We can confirm (or refute) such an explanation, however, by carrying out brain scans of people under the influence of DMT and observing if the rhinal cortex is particularly activated and if such activity correlates with reports of déjà vu.

The Bergsonian account of DMT-induced déjà vu is, as we can see, not the only viable explanation at our disposal. But what Bergson's theory might correctly place emphasis on, which these main scientific explanations also do, is that déjà vu is a phenomenon of memory. These explanations are also in keeping with Bergson's idea that déjà vu is an interruption in the normal operations of the mind (the natural interplay between perception and memory). Bergson does not, as many people do, assign a supernatural or esoteric status to déjà vu. We do not have to view this feeling of repetition as a clear sign that we live in a simulation (as it is in the 1999 film *The Matrix*, when Neo sees the same scene play out twice). There is also little reason to interpret déjà vu as a meaningful message from a higher reality or being.

Déjà vu, especially in the DMT state, can feel imposing and revelatory. And it is, in a sense, revelatory — although not in the way that is often assumed. It is more likely that this feeling reveals to us how the operations of memory and perception can be altered to produce strange, extraordinary experiences. It is a form of insight into how memory and perception work. We need not jump to the conclusion that déjà vu provides us with the power of precognition or insight into a transcendent reality.

## Endnotes

1. Ansell-Pearson, K. (2018). 'Bergson on the Time of Memory', Centre for Philosophy of Time, 7 March. https://www.centreforphilosophyoftime.it/2018/03/07/keith-ansell-bergson/

2. Bergson, H. (1908). 'Memory of the Present and False Recognition'. *Revue Philosophique de la France et de l'Etranger*, 66, pp. 561–593.

3. Bergson, H. (1908). 'Memory of the Present and False Recognition' in *Henri Bergson: Key Writings*, p. 150. Edited by Ansell-Pearson, K. and Mullarkey, J. London: Continuum, 2002.

4. Bergson, H. (1920). *Mind-Energy*, p. 128. Translated by Carr, H.W. London: Macmillan.

5. Ansell-Pearson, K. (2018). 'Bergson on the Time of Memory', Centre for Philosophy of Time, 7 March. https://www.centreforphilosophyoftime.it/2018/03/07/keith-ansell-bergson/

6. Bergson, H. (1908). 'Memory of the Present and False Recognition' in *Time and the Instant: Essays in the Physics and Philosophy of Time*, pp. 36–63. Edited by Durie, R. Manchester: Clinamen, 2000.

7. Huxley, A. (1954). *The Doors of Perception*. https://maps.org/images/pdf/books/HuxleyA1954TheDoorsOfPerception.pdf

8. Pearce, L. (2016). *Drivetime: Literary Excursions in Automotive Consciousness*, p. 16. Edinburgh: Edinburgh University Press.

9. Bergson, H. (1896). *Matter and Memory*, p. 173. Translated by Paul, N.M. and Palmer, W.S. New York: Dover Publications.

10. Bergson, H. (1908). 'Memory of the Present and False Recognition' in *Time and the Instant: Essays in the Physics and Philosophy of Time*, pp. 36–47. Edited by Durie, R. Manchester: Clinamen, 2000.

11. Pearce, L. (2016). *Drivetime: Literary Excursions in Automotive Consciousness*, p. 17. Edinburgh: Edinburgh University Press.

12. Bluemink, M. (2020). 'On Virtuality: Deleuze, Bergson, Simondon'. Epoché Magazine, Issue 36, December. https://epochemagazine.org/36/on-virtuality-deleuze-bergson-simondon/

13. Zografos, S. (2019). *Architecture and Fire: A Psychoanalytic Approach to Conservation*, p. 83. London: UCL Press.

14. O'Sullivan, S. (2013). Chapter 10: 'A Diagram of the Finite-Infinite Relation: Towards a Bergsonian Production of Subjectivity' in *Bergson and the Art of Immanence: Painting, Photography, Film*, pp. 165–186. Edited by Mullarkey, J. and De Mille, C. Edinburgh: Edinburgh University Press.

15. Curot, J., Valton, L., Denuelle, M., Vignal, J., Maillard, L., Pariente, J., Trébuchon, A., Bartolomei, F., and Barbeau, E.J. (2018). 'Déjà-rêvé: Prior dreams induced by direct electrical brain stimulation'. *Brain Stimulation*, 11(4), pp. 875–885.

16. Cott, C. and Rock, A.J. (2008). 'Phenomenology of N,N-Dimethyltryptamine Use: A Thematic Analysis'. *Journal of Scientific Exploration*, 22(3), pp. 359–370.

17. Lawrence, D.W., DiBattista, A.P., and Timmermann, C. (2023). 'N, N-Dimethyltryptamine (DMT)-Occasioned Familiarity and the Sense of Familiarity (SOF-Q)'. *Journal of Psychoactive Drugs*, DOI: 10.1080/02791072.2023.2230568

18. Gallimore, A. (2013). 'Building Alien Worlds — The Neuropsychological and Evolutionary Implications of the Astonishing Psychoactive Effects of N,N-Dimethyltryptamine (DMT)'. *Journal of Scientific Exploration*, 27(3), pp. 455–503.

19. Ibid.
20. McKenna, T. (1990). 'Time and Mind', Erowid. https://erowid.org/culture/characters/mckenna_terence/mckenna_terence_time_mind.shtml
21. Lin, T. (2014). 'DMT: You Cannot Imagine a Stranger Drug or a Stranger Experience', *Vice*, 5 August. https://www.vice.com/en/article/5gkkpd/dmt-you-cannot-imagine-a-stranger-drug-or-a-stranger-experience-365
22. Ibid.
23. Drone Dimension. 'The DMT Experience - Terence McKenna'. 27 July, 2021. YouTube video, 10:07. https://www.youtube.com/watch?v=tj63oEteQmE
24. Ibid.
25. Cleary, A.M., Brown, A.S., Sawyer, B.D., Nomi, J.S., Ajoku, A.C., and Ryals, A.J. (2012). 'Familiarity from the configuration of objects in 3-dimensional space and its relation to déjà vu: a virtual reality investigation'. *Consciousness and Cognition*, 21(2), pp. 969–975.
26. Cleary, A.M. and Claxton, A.B. (2018). 'Déjà Vu: An Illusion of Prediction'. *Psychological Science*, 29(4), pp. 635–644.
27. Brown, A.S. and Marsh, E.J. (2010). Chapter 2: 'Digging into Déjà Vu: Recent Research on Possible Mechanisms' in *The Psychology of Learning and Motivation*, Volume 53, pp. 33–62. Edited by Ross, B.H. San Diego: Elsevier Academic Press.
28. Drone Dimension. 'The DMT Experience - Terence McKenna'. 27 July, 2021. YouTube video, 10:07. https://www.youtube.com/watch?v=tj63oEteQmE
29. Texas A&M University (2016). 'What causes déjà vu?', ScienceDaily, 13 April. https://www.sciencedaily.com/releases/2016/04/160413113530.htm
30. Ibid.

31. Raslau, F.D., Mark, I.T., Klein, A.P., Ulmer, J.L., Matthews, V., and Mark, L.P. (2015). 'Memory Part 2: The Role of the Medial Temporal Lobe'. *American Journal of Neuroradiology*, 36(5), pp. 846–849.

32. Bartolomei, F., Barbeau, E., Gavaret, M., Guye, M., McGonigal, A., Régis, J., and Chauvel, P. (2004). 'Cortical stimulation study of the role of rhinal cortex in déjà vu and reminiscence of memories'. *Neurology*, 63(5), pp. 858–864.

# Chapter 10

# Catalysts for Existential Joy

In many discussions surrounding psychedelics, there can be a tendency to focus on how these compounds alleviate various ills, instead of what they can positively *add* to people's lives. This speaks to a more general theme in the psychological field, where there is a preference for trying to resolve the negative and maladaptive aspects of human experience while ignoring or undervaluing the promotion of positive thoughts, feelings, and behaviours. The latter is seen as secondary. This is why the approach of *positive psychology* originally emerged — it aimed to complement (not replace) psychology's negative bias.

Helping individuals to function well and overcome emotional suffering should, of course, be prioritised, but human drives go well beyond functioning well and simply being *free* from suffering. People also have a strong desire for happiness, joy, inspiration, love, gratitude, resilience, and compassion. Positive psychology is the scientific study of how we can best help people to cultivate these mental states — in a nutshell, how to help people flourish.

It is uplifting to see how effective psychedelic therapy is in treating numerous conditions that are often difficult to treat, chronic, severe, and debilitating.[1] However, psychedelics also have the potential to increase the kinds of positive mental states already mentioned. By supplementing a positive psychological approach when discussing the benefits of psychedelics, we can see that many of these substances are helpful in terms of building strengths and enhancing life satisfaction. This applies both to people who are experiencing emotional distress and to those who are more or less feeling well and not in need of mental health treatment.

One particular positive state that psychedelics seem to elicit is existential joy. This mental state can feel highly pronounced and meaningful during the experience, as well as remain, to some degree, for weeks, months, and years following the experience — perhaps even lasting a lifetime.

This essay will first describe what existential joy is and then elucidate how psychedelics can catalyse or manifest the various aspects of this particular kind of joy. I will draw on the ideas of Irvin Yalom, Martin Buber, and Friedrich Nietzsche with this aim in mind, and then present a concept that I call the *will to novelty*: the fundamental drive that humans have for the new and the different, which ties into psychedelic states. I will also connect this drive to psychological research and the metaphysics of Alfred North Whitehead, which can be called a *philosophy of creativity*: the view that the creation of novelty is the essential characteristic of the universe.

## What Is Existential Joy?

Existential joy is joy related to the human condition, similar to how existential depression or existential anxiety involves depressive or anxiety symptoms, respectively, that follow from what Yalom describes as our four ultimate concerns in life: death, freedom, isolation, and meaninglessness. Each of these concerns, individually or in combination, can become a source of what we would call the classic feelings of depression or anxiety. These concerns are often related as well: knowledge of one's mortality can be linked to feelings of meaninglessness, for instance, since the finality of death can make all our striving and efforts seem futile.

We can struggle with emotional distress due to a sense of fundamental isolation (we cannot bridge the gap between our mind and that of another) or because of our inescapable freedom, described by existentialists like Jean-Paul Sartre (as he put it, "man is condemned to be free.")[2] Moreover, involved in our essential freedom is always the choice to be true to ourselves or not, with inauthenticity being a source of what Yalom calls *existential guilt*.

Ordinary joy, like ordinary sadness and worry, has specific triggers, such as a personal achievement, being in a new relationship, or exploring a new country. Existential joy, conversely, is not so much related to life events as *life itself*: it tends to be more of an underlying and longer-lasting joy that flows from a different, clearer, or fuller appreciation of the human condition. Of course, situations in one's life can catalyse this feeling since it is in the particularities of day-to-day living that we confront our fundamental concerns.

For example, being reminded of the finality of death can make one's existence — and that of others — seem incredibly precious (and therefore joy-inducing). There can be a joy in using one's innate freedom, each day, to be true to oneself. There is joy in the opposite of isolation: the intimate connection that comes with compassion and unconditional love. And lastly, strong feelings of joy can accompany the attainment of personal meaning, whether that be in one's interpersonal life, work, projects, acts of kindness, or a cause one is dedicated to. One may experience existential joy after grappling with, and overcoming, psychological distress or a crisis state related to one's ultimate concerns. Alternatively, it may come after dealing with depression or anxiety that is non-existential in nature. It can also arise when one feels mentally well. Whatever the circumstances might be, the very fact of one's existence and the tapestry of experience this entails can be a source of joy.

## Buber's Philosophy of Dialogue
Existential joy is a component of Buber's philosophy of dialogue (a version of dialogical existentialism). In this form of existentialism, based on dialogue, Buber places primacy on

what he terms the 'I-You' relationship. This is "an essential act of pure relation",[3] characterised by mutuality, reciprocity, and directness — and in these moments of connection, one is a whole unique being addressing another whole unique being. Buber contrasts this kind of relation with the (unfortunately) more common type: the 'I-It' relationship, which is based on conceptualisation, utilisation, manipulation, and accumulation. 'What can you do for me?' would be the sort of attitude one would bring to an I-It relationship.

We can have I-You relationships with many sorts of entities: other human beings, non-human animals, the natural world, and God. When we encounter God in an I-You relationship, we encounter the 'Eternal You', which for Buber can never become an It. Moreover, any other I-You relationship — with another person, say — gives us an intimation or glimpse of the Eternal You, so in this way, relation becomes a form of mysticism.

For Buber, I-You relationships make life "heavy with meaning",[4] which when experienced eliminate the question about the meaning of life since it has been discovered. He emphasises this is an ineffable meaning which "we lack any image or formula for", but it is nonetheless "more certain for you than the sensations of your senses".[5] I-It relationships, on the other hand, do not provide our lives with meaning; instead, they are sources of alienation. A life concentrated with these latter relationships is one burdened with meaninglessness and oppressiveness.

I-You relationships — in contradistinction to I-It relationships — are our deepest desire and they are what lead to our greatest happiness, joy, and peace. The emptiness of I-It relationships comes from our inability to satisfy what we long for the most. What we need for a truly joyful existence is more desire, just with the right object in mind: the more we say You, the greater our desire for the You becomes, which puts ourselves in a better position to experience joy-inducing relationships.

This is relevant to the psychedelic experience because a common theme in these states is connection.[6] The vital importance of one's relations can be emphasised — in the I-You sense, not the I-It sense. *Meaningful* connection with others and the natural world may be such a common theme because it is so common to feel alienated. What psychedelics do, then, is amplify the deep-seated desire for the opposite — pure and direct connections with others. As 'non-specific amplifiers', psychedelics can bring to the surface whatever is latent but unexpressed. If the need for I-You relationships is one such latent feature, ignored and suppressed much to our detriment, these compounds may allow us to recognise and appreciate this great longing.

If psychedelics help to highlight this desire, magnify it, and increase the frequency of I-You connections, this could be one essential reason why people's sense of meaningfulness and joyfulness is enhanced following psychedelic use. This is relevant in the context of psychedelic-assisted therapy because the relational therapeutic approach — which emphasises how our emotional well-being is dependent on the interpersonal dimension — is not the dominant model that is applied. If Buber's analysis of the human condition is correct, then failing to integrate the relational approach into psychedelic therapy could make meaningful and sustained change difficult to achieve.

## The Nietzschean Affirmation of Life

For Nietzsche, the correct response to the trials, tribulations, and tragedies of life was one of embrace: a yes-saying attitude. This has since become known as the *Nietzschean affirmation of life*, and we can juxtapose it with the Schopenhauerian rejection of life: a no-saying to suffering.

Nietzsche championed "Saying yes to life even in its strangest and hardest problems", as he writes in *Twilight of the Idols* (1889).[7] This attitude was based on his belief that being a yes-sayer — affirming everything in the past, present, and future — encourages health, vitality, strength, and power. In *Ecce Homo* (1908), he states, "My formula for greatness in men is *amor fati*: that one wants nothing to be different, not forward, not backward, not in all eternity. Not merely bear what is necessary, still less conceal it ... but love it."[8]

Nietzsche saw the opposite (saying no to life) — rejection, turning away, resignation — as weak, unhealthy, and unnatural. This disgust towards life was pathological, a kind of sickness, he insisted. Nietzsche, moreover, disdained the outcomes of the Schopenhauerian rejection of life, these being self-denial and pity, which he viewed as central to the Christian ethic — an ethic that degrades the human spirit.

To be fully alive and human, according to Nietzsche, is to fully embrace all that life has to offer, no matter how stinging, harsh, and outrageous these offerings may be. As well as encouraging health, Nietzsche thought you cannot say yes to the pleasant without also affirming the unpleasant: "Have you ever said Yes to one joy? Oh my friends, then you also said Yes to *all* pain. All things are enchained, entwined, enamored."[9]

Furthermore, for Nietzsche, suffering is deeply valuable, with our interpretation of it being what provides meaning to our lives. Our pain and hardship test our true worth and shape us into better people. Aligning himself with the ancient Greek attitude towards pain, Nietzsche opined in *Twilight of the Idols*, "In the teachings of the [Greek] mysteries, pain is declared holy; the 'pangs of the childbearer' make pain in general holy—all becoming and growth, everything that vouches for the future requires pain."[10] To achieve psychological growth, health, and resilience, we have to experience and overcome resistance and pain, as we are meant to — and the greatest, most admirable people, Nietzsche argues, are those who can endure the greatest suffering.

The Nietzschean affirmation of life, this saying yes to everything, can sometimes find its expression in the psychedelic experience. This can happen, I believe, in two different ways. Firstly, in a psychedelic state, one can be overcome by a renewed (or new) zest for life. There is a yes-saying that gets evoked, an inner and jubilant welcoming of the whole tapestry of human experience. In these moments of psychedelic yes-saying, the affirmation is loud, clear, and complete, and any sense of rejection is absent.

The second manner in which yes-saying might occur is in the confrontation with struggle. Psychedelics can present us with moments, sometimes prolonged stages, of mental discomfort and distress. It is normal and habitual to reject these feelings through resistance and the wish to abolish them. Common psychedelic wisdom states that resistance is likely to just prolong that mental suffering or worsen it.

A Nietzschean approach to difficult psychedelic experiences, however, involves saying yes to them: this means accepting, approving, and even thanking what is happening. When affirmed, difficult experiences become zestful; they can enliven us, viscerally unlocking a reserve of energy and joy. While thinking about the Nietzschean affirmation of life and its application to psychedelics, I was reminded of Rumi's brilliant poem 'The Guest House':

> This being human is a guest house.
> Every morning a new arrival.
>
> A joy, a depression, a meanness,
> some momentary awareness comes
> as an unexpected visitor.
>
> Welcome and entertain them all!
> Even if they're a crowd of sorrows,
> who violently sweep your house

empty of its furniture,
still, treat each guest honorably.
He may be clearing you out
for some new delight.

The dark thought, the shame, the malice,
meet them at the door laughing,
and invite them in.

Be grateful for whoever comes,
because each has been sent
as a guide from beyond.[11]

This very much fits in with Nietzsche's conception of sorrow:
we should not shy away from it or reject it, because it may
elevate us towards a mountain peak of joy.

Psychedelic experiences are like dramatic plays in which the
Nietzschean affirmation of life is put to the test: difficult feelings
we wrestle with in the everyday — such as anxiety and being
overwhelmed — may be intensified and placed on the centre
stage in an altered state, becoming so loud so as to demand a
response. And how do we respond? To put it simply, we can be
a yes-sayer or a no-sayer in such moments.

When the yes-saying attitude is adopted and everything
uncomfortable is embraced, the whole character of the
experience can change; it becomes perfect, in a sense. Nietzsche
too makes this point in *The Antichrist* (1895): "*The world is perfect*
— thus says the instinct of the most spiritual, the Yes-saying
instinct."[12] This instinct allows enthusiasm to replace anxiety.
Nietzsche's use of the term 'perfect' may seem inappropriate,
as it can appear to excuse or justify tragedies, injustices, and
atrocities in the world. However, it is intended to refer to the
recognition that nothing can be separated from anything else —
everything fits together; nothing is out of place.

But if one has had the experience of yes-saying during a psychedelic experience and discovered the way it transforms suffering, this is not a lesson that applies only to this experience and no others. These states can be seen as the training ground for the trials and obstacles we will inevitably run up against in everyday life. When you reflect on the zest for life or affirmation of negative experiences felt in a psychedelic state — and remind yourself of the subjective changes that followed — you may come to see that *every* experience is susceptible to this attitude and the improvement that follows.

Yes-saying is often a common feature of the psychedelic experience, helping to benefit both the experience itself and its long-term effects on an individual's attitudes. To integrate profound moments of yes-saying under the influence of psychedelics, it might be useful to absorb what Nietzsche has to say about yes-saying and apply this attitude to everything, no matter how painful or ugly the situation may be. Doing so makes the world and all of one's life take on a kind of beauty that was previously absent. We can also think of yes-saying as an animating force, vivifying a mind that perhaps for far too long has been demoralised.

## The Will to Novelty

Another way in which psychedelics may intersect with existential concerns is through the generation of novelty. If at least one of our fundamental drives is to experience what is new, then psychedelics can serve this drive — and in turn our depths of satisfaction — through the proliferation of novelty that these substances offer. They lead to states of thinking, perception, and feeling never before experienced. These reserves of novelty can appear unlimited, with new kinds and degrees of experience manifesting with every new traversing of the psychedelic mindscapes.

Philosophers and psychologists throughout history have tried to define the human species by referring to certain basic drives that we all share. Sigmund Freud, for instance, proposed that all people possess a *will to pleasure*: we instinctually seek out pleasure and avoid pain, in order to satisfy our basic needs. (In his 1920 essay 'Beyond the Pleasure Principle', Freud revised his position and argued that humans also have an opposite motivation, a *death drive*: we are driven towards destruction; or as he famously declared, "The aim of all life is death.")[13]

Nietzsche thought that the main driving force in humans, as in the rest of the cosmos, was the *will to power*. As he put it, "This world is the will to power — and nothing besides!"[14] He believed that deep down we all have our minds set on strength, growth, expansion, advancement, and self-mastery. These are expressions of the will to power, which is the drive to seek and overcome resistance in the world and within ourselves. 'Power' is the feeling of overcoming resistance. Both Nietzsche and Freud were influenced by the German philosopher Arthur Schopenhauer, who in his works developed the notion of the *will to live*. This desire for self-preservation is a blind, unconscious force that is present in all living organisms.[15]

In contrast, the psychiatrist Viktor Frankl focused on a motive that seems to be distinctly human. This is the *will to meaning*. He developed his own type of therapy called *logotherapy*, which follows from the assumption that our main motivation for living is our will to find meaning in life. It is tricky to try to define what 'meaning' actually is. But we can all denote certain human activities and aspects of our lives as 'meaningful', such as being of service to others or overcoming a personal challenge. Frankl posited that

we can discover this meaning in life in three different ways: (1) by creating a work or doing a deed; (2) by experiencing something or encountering someone; and (3) by the attitude we take toward unavoidable suffering.[16]

Meaning is what is most significant and fulfilling in our lives. From an objective standpoint, or the point of view of the universe, the action in question may be meaningless (a position known as *cosmic nihilism*). But from the human perspective, alleviating the suffering of another person *means* something more than the basic fact of doing something so that someone is in less pain than they otherwise would be. *Terrestrial meaning* is possible, even if *cosmic meaning* is not. Meaning, as it is experienced, is like this extra layer of more or less inexpressible significance that comes wrapped up with particular thoughts, actions, people, and events. It seems less clear that other animals lead what could rightly be called 'meaningful' lives.

The will to novelty — the desire to seek out what is new and different — may be an additional core drive we have. While the way that we seek novelty may be unique to humans (since we *produce* new forms — be they cultural or technological — and we amass greater knowledge over time), the basis for our novelty-seeking tendencies appears to be shared by other species. Animal studies have shown that levels of dopamine increase in the context of novelty.[17] The release of dopamine motivates us to act,[18] rather than being a reward in itself. (Dopamine is not a 'feel-good chemical', 'pleasure chemical', or 'reward chemical', as it is commonly — and mistakenly — called.)[19] Thus, the brain responds to novelty with the release of dopamine, which motivates us to explore in order to find a reward.

The researchers Nico Bunzeck and Emrah Düzel carried out experiments to shed light on how novelty motivates us.[20] Düzel concluded that

When we see something new, we see it has a potential for rewarding us in some way. This potential that lies in new things motivates us to explore our environment for rewards. The brain learns that the stimulus, once familiar, has no reward associated with it and so it loses its potential. For this reason, only completely new objects activate the midbrain area and increase our levels of dopamine.[21]

A 2013 paper highlights that dopamine activations in the context of exploration "are generated when an animal perceives novel states and ... serve the function of increasing the animal's tendency to explore the environment, thus augmenting the probability that the animal finds rewards".[22] However, the human penchant for novelty is quite unique. Since leaving the African savanna, humans have spent tens of thousands of years venturing into new landscapes all over the world; so it makes evolutionary sense that we would be primed to react positively to novelty. As the neuroscientist Robert Sapolsky observes in *Behave: The Biology of Humans at Our Best and Worst*, "A high incidence of [the gene] 7R, associated with impulsivity and novelty seeking, is the legacy of humans who made the greatest migrations in human history."[23]

As the most nomadic species on the planet, we are motivated to seek out new terrain as a potential source of new rewards. We are also unique as a species because we have the capacity to innovate in manifold ways and at an exponential rate. Relative to the rest of the animal kingdom, we seem to possess a special kind of curiosity that perpetually propels us towards novelty. Perhaps, then, we can refer to our species as *Homo philonovitas* (derived from the Greek *philo* for 'love' and the Latin *novitas* for 'freshness' or 'novelty'). We are the novelty-loving animal. Our behaviour indicates that we are *experiential omnivores*.

Individuals who are adventurous and curious enjoy many advantages. But it is, nonetheless, normal to see variations in the novelty seeking personality trait. In the words of the journalist Winifred Gallagher, "Although we're a neophilic [novelty-loving] species, as individuals we differ in our reactions to novelty, because a population's survival is enhanced by some adventurers who explore for new resources and worriers who are attuned to the risks involved."[24] Indeed, there are some people who are neophobic, who have an aversion to novelty and change.

The lecturer and psychedelic writer Terence McKenna often discussed novelty, although he believed that the universe becomes more novel (more complex or advanced) over time.[25] In support of this idea, which was inspired by his psychedelic experiences, he cites "the emergence of more and more complex forms, languages, organisms, technologies, always building on the previously achieved levels of complexity".[26] In this respect, it would be uncontroversial to say that over the course of time, technologies have certainly become more novel. Our hunger for the new and the innovative — and our ability to make our imagination a reality — have taken us from crude stone tools to artificial intelligence.

We might also have a desire for *ultimate novelty* or *maximal novelty*: an apogee of novelty that is the final, unfathomable destination of human development. McKenna argued this is a point of infinite novelty (or complexity) and he referred to it as the "concrescence" (a term borrowed from Whitehead), the "strange attractor", or "the transcendental object at the end of time".[27] He believed this to be the endpoint of the universe's natural trajectory towards interconnection, novelty, and complexity. In his view, the universe is being pulled through time towards this attractor.

Yet while the idea of moving towards a state of ultimate, maximal, or infinite novelty is enticing, it is not at all clear that the cosmos is heading in that direction. Because we inhabit a novelty-producing world, it may seem like there is always something unique being formed; so perhaps it is understandable to conclude that this is a universal law. But such a view may be mistaken if the universe is becoming increasingly disorganised over time (although physicists disagree about this).[28] McKenna's novelty theory may also invite criticism because it presupposes that nature is teleological. The notion that the universe has a goal or purpose is, of course, not unique to McKenna's theory, but it does require justification. On the other hand, it is possible that the universe is like this in its fundamental nature — this is a metaphysics also proposed by Whitehead, who influenced McKenna's ideas on novelty.

Whitehead essentially presents a philosophy of creativity or process philosophy, which emphasises becoming and change over static being. "The ultimate metaphysical principle is the advance from disjunction to conjunction, creating a novel entity other than the entities given in disjunction," says Whitehead.[29] This 'creative advance into novelty', as he calls it, is the fundamental nature of reality. The philosopher Peter Sjöstedt-Hughes explains this idea in his book *Noumenautics* as follows: "For Whitehead, the universe is constantly creating novelty rather than running a determined path. The universe creates a path in its stead; it does not drive along an already created track. It is in this sense more plane than train, more thrust than rail."[30] Under Whiteheadian metaphysics, "the universe is potentially infinite in its creative capacity," writes Sjöstedt-Hughes.[31]

Whitehead also includes God in his metaphysics in a way that makes his philosophy *panentheistic*: he believes God and the world to be interrelated but, unlike the pantheist, he makes an ontological distinction between the divine and the non-divine. Pantheism posits, in contrast, that God and the universe are identical. For the panentheist, the universe is in God and God is in the universe, but God is ultimately greater than the universe. In *Process and Reality* (1929), Whitehead describes God as having, like all entities (including us), an aim of achieving "some maximum depth of intensity of feeling"[32] or "depth of satisfaction".[33] Novelty allows us to achieve this aim. Whitehead also claims that "God is the organ of novelty"[34] and adds, "Apart from the intervention of God, there could be nothing new in the world."[35] Novelty, therefore, is divine.

While Whitehead himself does not use the term 'will' with respect to novelty as I do, novelty is, nonetheless, key to his metaphysics, and so this has implications for our psychology. If everything tends towards novelty, then so do we. I believe that both the urge to have a psychedelic experience and the levels of satisfaction it provides us with can at least partly be explained by the will to novelty. This is an optimistic interpretation of how psychedelic-induced novelty affects our well-being. A more pessimistic angle is also possible. I would now like to consider both of these perspectives, either one of which could be true under Whiteheadian metaphysics. I will begin by examining the pessimistic point of view.

Firstly, the trait of novelty seeking has been tied to impulsivity and attention deficit hyperactivity disorder (ADHD). We should keep in mind, however, that a short attention span is also a sign of natural variability in the gene pool, with its strengths and weaknesses depending on the environmental context, as with any other genetic variation. A 2008 study discovered that an ADHD-associated version of the gene DRD4 is associated with better health in nomadic tribesmen in Kenya, but it can cause malnourishment in their settled cousins.[36] Dan Eisenberg, the lead author of the study, explains,

> The DRD4/7R allele has been linked to greater food and drug cravings, novelty-seeking, and ADHD symptoms. It is possible that in the nomadic setting, a boy with this allele might be able to more effectively defend livestock against raiders or locate food and water sources, but that the same tendencies might not be as beneficial in settled pursuits such as focusing in school, farming or selling goods.[37]

Indeed, it is no coincidence that people with high levels of novelty seeking are prone to risk-taking and various addictions.[38] Moreover, novelty *itself* may become a kind of addiction. If novelty increases dopamine, as other drugs do, this can motivate us to seek out more novelty. A 2014 study on monkeys found that "dopamine enhances novelty-driven value", implying that "excessive novelty seeking—characteristic of impulsivity and behavioral addictions—might be caused by increases in dopamine, stemming from less reuptake".[39] So not only does novelty excite our dopamine neurons, but dopamine may also spur us on to seek out novelty.

Novelty 'addiction' may follow the path of other behavioural addictions: being exposed to novelty excites us, encouraging us to seek out more novelty to reanimate that positive feeling. But as with any addiction, we become sensitised to the initial pleasurable feelings triggered by the first exposure; in other words, our tolerance for novelty increases. We desire an even more intense experience, which leads us to seek out a higher degree of novelty. We fall into a *novelty trap* when we are not only dissatisfied with familiarity but with novel situations that do not feel novel enough.

It is easy to fall into a pattern of pursuing one pleasure after another. The *hedonic treadmill* is a metaphor that is often used to explain this behaviour. It refers to the tendency to return to a baseline level of happiness after each positive event, a baseline that encourages us again to seek out a new pleasure — a spike in positive mood. Perhaps novelty seeking can also fit the pattern of the hedonic treadmill. If so, one can be continually exposed to novelty and yet always return to a baseline state (an uncomfortable craving for novelty that only passes once something different and unusual is experienced).

According to the Romanian philosopher Emil Cioran, the tendency to become bored is part of the human condition. In *The Trouble with Being Born* (1973), he claims that non-human animals crave monotony and only want it to continue, whereas we flee from it. Cioran writes,

A zoologist who observed gorillas in their native habitat was amazed by the uniformity of their life and their vast idleness.

Hours and hours without doing anything. Was boredom unknown to them? This is indeed a question raised by a human, a busy ape. Far from fleeing monotony, animals crave it, and what they most dread is to see it end. For it ends, only to be replaced by fear, the cause of all activity. Inaction is divine; yet it is against inaction that man has rebelled. Man alone, in nature, is incapable of enduring monotony, man alone wants something to happen at all costs — something, anything.... Thereby he shows himself unworthy of his ancestor: the need for novelty is the characteristic of an alienated gorilla.[40]

Contrary to Whitehead, then, it is not novelty that is divine for Cioran but monotony. Our striving for novelty could be at the heart of much of our discontent. We can think of this analysis as a combination of Whitehead's metaphysics and Schopenhauer's pessimism (the latter sees dissatisfaction as an inevitable consequence of our constant striving). By being unable to sit with monotony and reiteration, we are destined to be the restless ape. We are *Homo inquietus* ('restless human').

In Schopenhauerian metaphysics, the *will* is the fundamental level of reality.[41] This metaphysical will is a blind striving that manifests in different forms and degrees, such as physical objects following the laws of motion and gravity, plants growing towards the sunlight, and animals acting on instinct.[42] Everything is, in a sense, alive: all behaviour in the universe is dictated by the blind and futile force of the will. (One could argue that this makes Schopenhauer a panpsychist.) In humans, the will manifests as the will to live — the desire to carry on and further life through procreation. All of our other desires (including our personal goals and desire for romantic love), in Schopenhauer's worldview, are subsumed under the will to live.[43] Schopenhauer's pessimism arises from his belief that, as in Buddhism, desire is the root of suffering. Ultimately, desire can never be fully sated, so dissatisfaction is unavoidable.[44]

Incorporating Whiteheadian metaphysics here, we could say that the desire for novelty can never be fully satisfied. We crave something new, we get a brief experience of enjoyment when we find it, and then we are stuck again with this craving. Furthermore, as with other desires, there are innumerable novel things we could experience or obtain, so no matter how much novelty we have in our lives, we know — as finite beings — we will only ever experience a fraction of what is possible. Additionally, since the desire for novelty — like other desires — often goes unfulfilled, we are bound to feel frustrated a lot of the time.

This is just one way of modifying Whitehead's metaphysics. Adopting the more optimistic angle, I have wondered, too, whether his philosophy of creativity could be combined with Nietzsche's philosophy, which states that living in accordance with the will (in this case, the will to power) provides us with strength, vitality, and healthfulness. By satisfying the will to novelty and living in harmony with the natural order of the universe (which is, for Whitehead, novelty), we will experience the boon of this harmonious relationship: the 'intensity of feeling' and 'depth of satisfaction' that Whitehead describes. With a Nietzschean outlook included, we can say that embracing novelty is also a source of strength and a way of saying 'yes' to life. This could be why novelty seeking so often makes us feel more fully alive and human, providing us with joys and memories we cherish, not choices we come to regret.

Sjöstedt-Hughes argues that the psychedelic experience can be one way to achieve unique novel states, allowing us to "access the infinite bank of possibility that conditions the advance of creativity in the universe".[45] He adds, "The common ineffability of these experiences indicate their novelty: words are not created for phenomena that are never considered."[46] Consequently, seeking out highly novel states, like those occasioned by psychedelics, can be seen as part of the divine or cosmic order, resulting in extraordinary depths of satisfaction and joy. Our yearning for intense or maximal novelty — something that truly shocks our system into a state of awe and reverence — can be satisfied through otherworldly psychedelic experiences, particularly those induced by DMT.

The relationship between novelty and well-being, nevertheless, is a complicated one. "Novelty-seeking is one of the traits that keeps you healthy and happy and fosters personality growth as you age," says C. Robert Cloninger, the psychiatrist who developed personality tests for measuring this trait.[47] On the other hand, as Gallagher underscores, "Neophilia spurs us to adjust and explore and create technology and art, but at the extreme it can fuel a chronic restlessness and distraction."[48] The target of one's neophilia matters. Seeking out shallow entertainment will probably not feel as fulfilling as deeply exploring subjects and experiences that are truly important to you.

Altered states of consciousness are by no means shallow or trivial entries into the new, the different, and the weird. They expose ourselves to untold heights, depths, and variations of novelty that *immediately and profoundly* instil in us joy, fascination, and awe — and they rejuvenate us through the new details and perspectives gained. It is uncertain whether this is because the ultimate purpose of the universe is to create further and greater instantiations of novelty, as McKenna and Whitehead argued. What is more palpable is the notion that we, at the very least, are driven by novelty, and embarking on a psychedelic journey is a unique way to feed this drive.

## Concluding Thoughts on Psychedelics and Existential Joy

The use of psychedelics, at the right dose and in the right context, can catalyse a spontaneous and profound feeling of existential joy. This might be the very first instance of existential joy in someone's life or at least the most intense manifestation of this feeling. To reiterate, reflecting on the experience of being human can be a cause for joy. Specifically, this joy can relate to the basic fact of being alive and sentient. This includes having the ability to perceive, feel, think, imagine, create, and connect — in other words, the ability to have experiences and so many varieties of experience.

Psychedelics can be useful tools that allow you to view the human condition in this more joyous way. This can occur for a variety of reasons. Psychedelics can reconnect you with your emotions,[49] such as the existential form of joy. They are perspective shifting, allowing you to see the many sides of the human condition, not just its negative side. And they can quiet or dissolve the ego, the part of you that focuses on thoughts, feelings, and behaviours related to your sense of self (e.g. how you stack up against others and the kind of self-image you want to impress the world with). When the ego is dampened or dissolved, your mind is free from these concerns, and what you are left with is raw existence: the ever-present background of pure awareness. This pure awareness is usually unfelt because the noisy ego tends to be in the foreground, taking up your attention. But if the ego dissipates during a psychedelic experience, you can attend to the subjective quality of existence itself, and this can be enough to make you feel exalted and content. This can be a highly valuable experience, both for people struggling with emotional distress or an existential crisis and those who are not.

Psychedelics are promising catalysts for states like existential joy. This contrasts with many people's experiences with traditional antidepressants, which often have a general blunting effect, reducing both negative emotions (sometimes very beneficial) and positive emotions (not so desirable).[50][51]

Psychedelics, on the other hand, can significantly reduce troubling negative emotions while significantly increasing life-affirming positive emotions. This is not to say that anyone feeling empty of positivity should rush into a psychedelic experience. It is crucially important to prepare for the experience by paying attention to 'set and setting' (your current mental state and the kind of environment where you will have the experience). But if sensibly approached, a single psychedelic journey could open someone up to positive mental states never before experienced, both in terms of variety and intensity. This not only has the potential to relieve psychological suffering; it can also serve to promote human flourishing.

## Endnotes

1.  Cavarra, M., Falzone, A., Ramaekers, J.G., Kuypers, K.P.C., and Mento, C. (2022). 'Psychedelic-Assisted Psychotherapy — A Systematic Review of Associated Psychological Interventions'. *Frontiers in Psychology*, 13, Article: 887255.
2.  Sartre, J.P. (1948). *Existentialism is a Humanism*. https://homepages.wmich.edu/~baldner/existentialism.pdf
3.  Buber, M. (1923). *I and Thou*, p. 158. Translated by Kaufmann, W. New York: Charles Scribner's Sons, 1970.
4.  Ibid.
5.  Ibid., p. 159
6.  Watts, R., Kettner, H., Geerts, D., Gandy, S., Kartner, L., Mertens, L., Timmermann, C., Nour, M.N., Kaelen, M., Nutt, D., Carhart-Harris, R., and Roseman, L. (2022). 'The Watts Connectedness Scale: a new scale for measuring a sense of connectedness to self, others, and world'. *Psychopharmacology*, 239, pp. 3461–3483.
7.  Nietzsche, F. (1889). *Twilight of the Idols*, p. 91. Translated by Polt, R. Indianapolis/Cambridge: Hackett Publishing Company, 1997.

8. Nietzsche, F. (1967). *Basic Writings of Nietzsche*, p. 714. Edited and translated by Kaufmann, W. New York: Modern Library.

9. Nietzsche, F. (1883). *Thus Spoke Zarathustra*, p. 263. Edited by Caro, A.D. and Pippin, R.B., and translated by Caro, A.D. Cambridge: Cambridge University Press, 2006.

10. Nietzsche, F. (1889). *Twilight of the Idols*, p. 90. Translated by Polt, R. Indianapolis/Cambridge: Hackett Publishing Company, 1997.

11. Rumi (2004). *Selected Poems*, p. 109. Translated by Barks, C. London: Penguin Classics.

12. Nietzsche, F. (1954). *The Portable Nietzsche*, p. 645. Translated by Kaufmann, W. New York: Viking Press.

13. Freud, S. (1920). 'Beyond the Pleasure Principle', p. 32. Translated and edited by Strachey, J. New York: W.W. Norton & Company, 1961.

14. Nietzsche, F. (1901). *The Will to Power*, p. 550. Translated by Kaufmann, W and Hollingdale, R.J., and edited by Kaufmann, W. New York: Vintage Books, 1968.

15. Schopenhauer, A. (1818). *The World as Will and Representation*, Vol. 1, p. 355. Translated by Haldane, R.B. and Kemp, J. London: Kegan Paul, Trench, Trübner & Co., 1909.

16. Frankl, V. (1946). *Man's Search for Meaning*, p. 115. Massachusetts: Beacon Press.

17. Morrens, J., Aydin, Ç., Rensburg, A.J.B., Rabell, J.E., and Haesler, S. (2022). 'Cue-Evoked Dopamine Promotes Conditioned Responding during Learning'. *Neuron*, 106(1), pp. 142–153.

18. Salamone, J.D. and Correa, M. (2012). 'The Mysterious Motivational Functions of Mesolimbic Dopamine'. *Neuron*, 76(3), pp. 470–485.

19. Chen, A. (2018). 'Please stop calling dopamine the 'pleasure chemical''. *The Verge*, 27 May. https://www.theverge.com/2018/3/27/17169446/dopamine-pleasure-chemical-neuroscience-reward-motivation

20. Cell Press (2006). 'Pure Novelty Spurs the Brain', ScienceDaily, 27 August. https://www.sciencedaily.com/releases/2006/08/060826180547.htm
21. UCL News (2006). 'Novelty aids learning', UCL News, 2 August. https://www.ucl.ac.uk/news/2006/aug/novelty-aids-learning
22. Barto, A., Mirolli, M., and Baldassarre, G. (2013). 'Novelty or Surprise?' *Frontiers in Psychology*, 4, Article 907.
23. Sapolsky, R.M. (2017). *The Biology of Humans at Our Best and Worst*, p. 281. New York: Penguin Books.
24. Tierney, J. (2012). 'What's New? Exuberance for Novelty Has Benefits', *New York Times*, 14 February.
25. Horgan, J. (2012). 'Was Psychedelic Guru Terence McKenna Goofing About 2012 Prophecy?', *Scientific American*, 6 June.
26. Hazard, J. (1998). 'Terence McKenna - Final Earthbound Interview'. YouTube video, uploaded by loadedshaman, 4 October, 2011, 1:03:47. https://www.youtube.com/watch?v=NCaK35DQ4uk
27. McKenna, T. (1991). 'Alchemical Youth on the Edge of the World'. organism.earth. https://www.organism.earth/library/document/alchemical-youth
28. Azarian, B. (2023). 'Life Need Not Ever End', Noema Magazine, 28 February. https://www.noemamag.com/life-need-not-ever-end/
29. Whitehead, A.N. (1929). *Process and Reality*, p. 21. Edited by Griffin, D.R. and Sherburne, D.W. New York: The Free Press, 1978.
30. Sjöstedt-Hughes, P. (2015). *Noumenautics: Metaphysics, Meta-ethics, Psychedelics*, p. 34. Falmouth: Psychedelic Press UK.
31. Ibid.
32. Press, H. (1971). 'Whitehead's Ethic of Feeling'. *Ethics*, 81(2), pp. 161–168.

33. Whitehead, A.N. (1929). *Process and Reality*, p. 105. Edited by Griffin, D.R. and Sherburne, D.W. New York: The Free Press, 1978.
34. Ibid., p. 67
35. Ibid., p. 247
36. Eisenberg, D.T.A., Campbell, B., Gray, P.B., Sorenson, M.D. (2008). 'Dopamine receptor genetic polymorphisms and body composition in undernourished pastoralists: An exploration of nutrition indices among nomadic and recently settled Ariaal men of northern Kenya'. *BMC Evolutionary Biology*, 8(1), Article: 173.
37. BMC Evolutionary Biology (2008). 'Is ADHD An Advantage For Nomadic Tribesmen?', ScienceDaily, 10 June. https://www.sciencedaily.com/releases/2008/06/080609195604.htm
38. Wingo, T., Nesil, T., Choi, J., and Li, M.D. (2016). 'Novelty-Seeking and Drug Addiction in Humans and Animals: From Behavior to Molecules'. *Journal of Neuroimmune Pharmacology*, 11(3), pp. 456–470.
39. Costa, V.D., Tran, V.L., Turchi, J., and Averbeck, B.B. (2014). *Behavioral Neuroscience*, 128(5), pp. 556–566.
40. Cioran, E.M. (1973). *The Trouble with Being Born*, p. 193. New York: Arcade Publishing, 2002.
41. Schopenhauer, A. (1818). *The World as Will and Representation*, Vol. 1, p. 157. Translated by Haldane, R.B. and Kemp, J. London: Kegan Paul, Trench, Trübner & Co., 1909.
42. Ibid., p. 182.
43. Schopenhauer, A. (1818). *The World as Will and Representation*, Vol. 3, pp. 341–344. Translated by Haldane, R.B. and Kemp, J. London: Kegan Paul, Trench, Trübner & Co., 1909.
44. Ibid., Vol. 1, p. 464.
45. Sjöstedt-Hughes, P. (2015). *Noumenautics: Metaphysics, Meta-ethics, Psychedelics*, p. 52. Falmouth: Psychedelic Press UK.

46. Ibid.
47. Tierney, J. (2012). 'What's New? Exuberance for Novelty Has Benefits', *New York Times*, 14 February. https://www.nytimes.com/2012/02/14/science/novelty-seeking-neophilia-can-be-a-predictor-of-well-being.html
48. Ibid.
49. Roseman, L., Demetriou, L., Wall, M.B., Nutt, D.J., and Carhart-Harris, R.L. (2018). 'Increased amygdala responses to emotional faces after psilocybin for treatment-resistant depression'. *Neuropharmacology*, 142, pp. 263–269.
50. Price, J., Cole, V., and Goodwin, G.M. (2009). 'Emotional side effects of selective serotonin reuptake inhibitors: qualitative study'. *British Journal of Psychiatry*, 195(3), pp. 211–217.
51. Langley, C., Armand, S., Luo, Q., Savulich, G., Segerberg, T., Søndergaard, A., Pederson, E.B., Svart, N., Overgaard-Hansen, O., Johansen, A., Borgsted, C., Cardinal, R.N., Robbins, T.W., Stenbæk, D.S., Knudsen, G.M., and Sahakian, B.J. (2023). 'Chronic escitalopram in healthy volunteers has specific effects on reinforcement sensitivity: a double-blind, placebo-controlled semi-randomised study'. *Neuropsychopharmacology*, 48, pp. 664–670.

# Bibliography

Abram, D. (1996). *The Spell of the Sensuous*. New York: Pantheon Books.

Addison, J. (1753). *Remarks on Several Parts of Italy: In the Years 1701, 1702, 1703*. London: J. and R. Tonson and S. Draper.

Adler, G. and Hull, R.F.C. (2014). *The Collected Works of C.G. Jung, Volume 9*, Part 1. 2nd ed. Princeton: Princeton University Press.

Ai, A.L., Wink, P., Paloutzian, R.F., and Harris, K.A. (2020). *Assessing Spirituality in a Diverse World*. New York: Springer Nature.

Ansell-Pearson, K. and Mullarkey, J. (2002). *Henri Bergson: Key Writings*. London: Continuum, 2002.

Baird, F.E. (2010). *Philosophic Classics: From Plato to Derrida, Sixth Edition*. Oxford: Routledge.

Bakhtin, M. (1963). *Problems of Dostoevsky's Poetics*. Minneapolis: University of Minnesota Press, 1984.

Bakhtin, M. (1965). *Rabelais and His World*. Translated by Iswolsky, H. Bloomington, IN: Indiana University Press, 1984.

Barrett, J.L. (2004). *Why Would Anyone Believe in God?*. Lanham, MD: AltaMira Press.

Bassil-Morozow, H. (2011). *The Trickster in Contemporary Film*. London: Routledge.

Bergson, H. (1896). *Matter and Memory*, translated by Paul, N.M. and Palmer, W.S. New York: Dover Publications.

Bergson, H. (1920). *Mind-Energy*. Translated by Carr, H.W. London: Macmillan.

Bisbee, C.C., Bisbee, P., Dyck, E., Farrell, P., Sexton, J., and Spisak, J.W. (2018). *Psychedelic Prophets: The Letters of Aldous Huxley and Humphry Osmond*. Montreal: McGill-Queen's University Press.

Blood, P.B. (1920). *Pluriverse: An Essay in the Philosophy of Pluralism*. Boston: Marshall Jones Company.

Breton, A. (1924). *Manifestoes of Surrealism*. Translated by Seaver, R. and Lane, H.R. Ann Arbor, MI: University of Michigan Press, 1969.

Broad, C.D. (1953). *Religion, Philosophy and Psychical Research*. New York: Harcourt.

Brody, J. (1958). *Boileau and Longinus*. Geneva: Droz.

Brüntrup, G. and Jaskolla, L. (2017). *Panpsychism: Contemporary Perspectives*. Oxford: Oxford University Press.

Buber, M. (1923). *I and Thou*. Translated by Kaufmann, W. New York: Charles Scribner's Sons, 1970.

Burke, E. (1757). *A Philosophical Inquiry into the Origin of Our Ideas of the Sublime and Beautiful*. London: Thomas McLean, 1823.

Campbell, J. (1949). *The Hero with a Thousand Faces*. Novato, CA: New World Library, 2012.

Campbell, J. (1976). *The Portable Jung*. London: Penguin Books.

Carlin, G. (2001). *Napalm and Silly Putty*. New York: Hyperion Books.

Charing, H.G., Cloudsley, P., and Amaringo, P. (2011). *The Ayahuasca Visions of Pablo Amaringo*. Rochester, Vermont: Inner Traditions.

Cioran, E.M. (1973). *The Trouble with Being Born*. New York: Arcade Publishing, 2002.

Davy, H. (1800). *Researches, Chemical and Philosophical; Chiefly Concerning Nitrous Oxide, or Dephlogisticated Nitrous Air, and Its Respiration*. London: Printed for J. Johnson, St. Paul's Church-Yard, by Biggs and Cottle, Bristol.

Dennis, J. (1688). *The Critical Works of John Dennis*, Vol. 1. Edited by Hooker, E.N. Baltimore: Johns Hopkins University Press, 1943.

Dobkin de Rios, M. (1976). *The Wilderness of Mind: Sacred Plants in Cross-cultural Perspective*. Sage Research Papers in the Social Sciences. Beverley Hills: Sage.

Doran, R. (2015). *The Theory of the Sublime from Longinus to Kant*. Cambridge: Cambridge University Press.

Durie, R. (2000). *Time and the Instant: Essays in the Physics and Philosophy of Time*. Manchester: Clinamen.

Díaz del Castillo, B. (1568). *The Conquest of New Spain*. Translated by Cohen, J.M. London: Penguin Books, 1963.

Einstein, A. (1912). *The Collected Papers of Albert Einstein, Volume 5: The Swiss Years: Correspondence, 1902–1914*. Translated by Beck, A. Princeton: Princeton University Press, 1995.

Einstein, A. (1954). *Ideas and Opinions*. Translated by Bargmann, S. New York: Crown Publishers, 1982.

Ellen, R. and Fukui, K. (1996). *Redefining Nature: Ecology, Culture and Domestication*. London: Routledge.

Fetzer, J.H. and Schlesinger, G.N. (1984). *Principles of Philosophical Reasoning*. Lanham: Rowman & Littlefield.

Flournoy, T. (1900). *From India to the Planet Mars: A Case of Multiple Personality with Imaginary Languages*. Princeton: Princeton University Press, 1994.

Flusser, V. (1991). *Gestures*. Translated by Roth, N.A. Minneapolis: University of Minnesota Press, 2014.

Fontana, D. (2006). *Meditating with Mandalas: 52 New Mandalas to Help You Grow in Peace and Awareness*. London: Duncan Baird.

Foucault, M. (1963). *The Birth of the Clinic*. London: Routledge, 1973.

Fowler, R.E. (1979). *The Andreasson Affair: The Documented Investigation of a Woman's Abduction Aboard a UFO*. Englewood Cliffs: Prentice-Hall.

Frankl, V. (1946). *Man's Search for Meaning*. Massachusetts: Beacon Press.

Freud, S. (1900). *The Interpretation of Dreams*. Translated by Brill, A.A. Ware: Wordsworth Editions, 1997.

Freud, S. (1920). 'Beyond the Pleasure Principle'. Translated and edited by Strachey, J. New York: W.W. Norton & Company, 1961.

Galileo, G. (1632). *Dialogue Concerning the Two Chief World Systems*. Translated by Drake, S. Berkeley: University of California Press, 1962.

Grof, S. (1975). *Realms of the Human Unconscious: Observations from LSD Research*. London: Souvenir Press, 1979.

Grof, S. (1980). *LSD Psychotherapy*. Pomona: Hunter House.

Gunaratana, B.H. (2011). *Mindfulness in Plain English*. https://www.vipassana.co.uk/meditation/mindfulness_in_plain_english.html

Guthrie, S.E. (1993). *Faces in the Clouds: A New Theory of Religion*. Oxford: Oxford University Press.

Hancock, G. (2005). *Supernatural: Meetings with the Ancient Teachers of Mankind*. London: Arrow Books.

Harvey, G. (2005). *Animism: Respecting the Living World*. Adelaide: Wakefield Press.

Grønstad, A., Gustafsson, H., and Vågnes, Ø. (2017). *Gestures of Seeing in Film, Video and Drawing*. New York: Routledge.

Hofmann, A. (2013). *LSD and the Divine Scientist: The Final Thoughts and Reflections of Albert Hofmann*. Rochester, VT: Inner Traditions.

Hood, B. (2012). *The Self Illusion: Why There is No 'You' Inside Your Head*. London: Constable.

Hood, R.W., Hill, P.C., and Spilka, B. (2018). *The Psychology of Religion: An Empirical Approach*, Fifth Edition. New York: The Guildford Press.

Hume, D. (1739). *A Treatise of Human Nature*. London: Longmans, Green, and Co., 1874.

Huxley, A. (1945). *The Perennial Philosophy*. London: Chatto & Windus, 1947.

Huxley, A. (1954). *The Doors of Perception*. https://maps.org/images/pdf/books/HuxleyA1954TheDoorsOfPerception.pdf

Hyde, L. (1998). *Trickster Makes This World: How Disruptive Imagination Creates Culture*. Edinburgh: Canongate Books, 2008.

James, W. (1902). *The Varieties of Religious Experience: A Study in Human Nature*. New York: Longmans, Green & Co.

Janik, V.K. (1998). *Fools and Jesters in Literature, Art, and History: A Bio-Bibliographical Sourcebook*. Westport, CT: Greenwood Press.

Jansen, K. (2001). *Ketamine: Dreams and Realities*. Sarasota: Multidisciplinary Association for Psychedelic Studies (MAPS), 2004.

Jung, C.G. (1963). *Memories, Dreams, Reflections* Edited by Jaffé, A. and translated by Winston, R. and Winston, C.B. New York: Vintage Books, 1989.

Jung, C.G. (1964). *Man and His Symbols*. New York: Dell Publishing.

Kant, I. (1781). *Critique of Pure Reason*. Translated and edited by Guyer, P. and Wood, A.W. Cambridge: Cambridge University Press, 1998.

Kant, I. (1790). *Critique of Judgment*. Translated by Bernard, J.H. New York: Cosimo, 2007.

Kehoe, A.B. (2000). *Shamans and Religion: An Anthropological Exploration in Critical Thinking*. Longrove, IL: Waveland Press.

Keown, D. and Prebish, C. (2009). *Encyclopedia of Buddhism*. London: Routledge.

King, M.E. and Traylor, I.R. (1974). *Art and Environment in Native America*. Lubbock: Texas Tech Press.

Kriegel, U. (2020). *The Oxford Handbook of the Philosophy of Consciousness*. Oxford: Oxford University Press.

Leary, M.R. and Tangney, J.P. (2003). *Handbook of Self and Identity*. New York: Guildford Press.

Leitch, V.B. (2001). *The Norton Anthology of Theory and Criticism*. New York: Norton & Co.

Lewis, C.S. (1940). *The Problem of Pain*. New York: The Macmillan Company, 1947.

Lewis, D. (1973). *Counterfactuals*. Oxford: Basil Blackwell.

Mack, J.E. (1994). *Abduction: Human Encounters with Aliens*. New York: Scribner.

Mann, D. (2011). *Understanding Society*. Oxford: Oxford University Press.

McKenna, T. (1992). *Food of the Gods: A Radical History of Plants, Psychedelics and Human Evolution*. London: Penguin Random House, 2021.

Michaux, H. (1951). *Mouvements*. Paris: NRF/Le Point de jur.

Michaux, H. (2001). *Oeuvres Complètes II*. Edited by Bellour, P. Paris: Gallimard.

Michaux, H. (2006). *Stroke by Stroke*. Translated by Sieburth, R. New York: Archipelago Books.

Milton, J. (1667). *Paradise Lost*. Oxford: Oxford University Press, 2005.

Morris, D.B. (1972). *The Religious Sublime: Christian Poetry and Critical Tradition in 18th-Century England*. Lexington, KY: University Press of Kentucky.

Mullarkey, J. and De Mille, C. (2013). *Bergson and the Art of Immanence: Painting, Photography, Film*. Edinburgh: Edinburgh University Press.

Nadler, S. (2020). *Think Least of Death: Spinoza on How to Live and How to Die*. Princeton: Princeton University Press.

Narby, J. (1998). *The Cosmic Serpent: DNA and the Origins of Knowledge*. London: Weidenfeld & Nicolson.

Nelson, R. (1997). *Heart and Blood: Living with Deer in America*. New York: Alfred A. Knopf.

Newton, I. (1687). *The Mathematical Principles of Natural Philosophy*. Translated by Motte, A. New York: Daniel Adee, 1846.

Nichols, D.L. and Rodríguez-Alegría, E. (2017). *The Oxford Handbook of the Aztecs*. Oxford: Oxford University Press.

Nicholas, L.G. and Ogamé, K. (2006). *Psilocybin Mushroom Handbook: Easy Indoor & Outdoor Cultivation*. Piedmont, CA: Quick American Publishing.

Nietzsche, F. (1883). *Thus Spoke Zarathustra*. Edited by Caro, A.D. and Pippin, R.B., and translated by Caro, A.D. Cambridge: Cambridge University Press, 2006.

Nietzsche, F. (1889). *Twilight of the Idols*. Translated by Polt, R. Indianapolis/Cambridge: Hackett Publishing Company, 1997.

Nietzsche, F. (1901). *The Will to Power*. Translated by Kaufmann, W. and Hollingdale, R.J., and edited by Kaufmann, W. New York: Vintage Books, 1968.

Nietzsche, F. (1954). *The Portable Nietzsche*. Translated by Kaufmann, W. New York: Viking Press.

Nietzsche, F. (1967). *Basic Writings of Nietzsche*. Edited and translated by Kaufmann, W. New York: Modern Library.

Noland, C. (2009). *Agency and Embodiment: Performing Gestures/ Producing Culture*. Cambridge, Massachusetts: Harvard University Press.

O'Brien, R.D. (1967). *Insecticides: Action and Metabolism*. Cambridge, MA: Academic Press.

Orr, E.R. (2012). *The Wakeful World: Animism, Mind and the Self in Nature*. Alresford: John Hunt Publishing.

Otto, B.K. (2001). *Fools Are Everywhere: The Court Jester Around the World*. Chicago: University of Chicago Press.

Otto, R. (1917). *The Idea of the Holy*. Translated by Harvey, J.W. London: Oxford University Press, 1923.

Papadopolous, R.K. (2006). *The Handbook of Jungian Psychology: Theory, Practice and Applications*. London: Routledge.

Pearce, L. (2016). *Drivetime: Literary Excursions in Automotive Consciousness*. Edinburgh: Edinburgh University Press.

Pine, R. (2006). *The Heart Sutra*. Berkeley, California: Counterpoint.

Plato (c. 360 BC). *Timaeus*. Translated by Zeyl, D.J. Indianapolis: Hackett Publishing Company, 2000.

Plumwood, V. (2002). *Environmental Culture: The Ecological Crisis of Reason*. New York: Routledge.

Popper, K. (1935/1959). *The Logic of Scientific Discovery*. London: Routledge, 2002.

Pyysiäinen, I. (2009). *Supernatural Agents: Why We Believe in Souls, Gods, and Buddhas*. Oxford: Oxford University Press.

Pyysiäinen, I. and Anttonen, V. (2002). *Current Approaches in the Cognitive Science of Religion*. London: Continuum.

Radin, P. (1956). *The Trickster: A Study in American Indian Mythology*. New York: Greenwood Press.

Rank, O. (1924). *The Trauma of Birth*. London: Kegan Paul & Co., Ltd., 1929.

Ross, B.H. (2010). *The Psychology of Learning and Motivation*, Volume 53. San Diego: Elsevier Academic Press.

Rumi (2004). *Selected Poems*. Translated by Barks, C. London: Penguin Classics.

Russell, B. (1948). *Human Knowledge: Its Scope and Limits*. Reprint, London: George Allen and Unwin.

Sapolsky, R.M. (2017). *The Biology of Humans at Our Best and Worst*. New York: Penguin Books.

Sartre, J.P. (1948). *Existentialism is a Humanism*. https:// homepages.wmich.edu/~baldner/existentialism.pdf

Schele, L. and Freidel, D. (1990). *A Forest of Kings: The Untold Story of the Ancient Maya*. New York: William Morrow and Company.

Schneider, S. and Velmans, M. (2017). *The Blackwell Companion to Consciousness*, Second Edition. Hoboken: John Wiley & Sons.

Schopenhauer, A. (1818). *The World as Will and Representation*, Vol. 1. Translated and edited by Norman, J., Welchman, A., and Janaway, C. Cambridge: Cambridge University Press, 2010.

Schopenhauer, A. (1818). *The World as Will and Representation*, Vol. 1. Translated by Haldane, R.B. and Kemp, J. London: Kegan Paul, Trench, Trübner & Co., 1909.

Schopenhauer, A. (1818). *The World as Will and Representation*, Vol. 2. Translated and edited by Norman, J., Welchman, A., and Janaway, C. Cambridge: Cambridge University Press, 2010.

Schopenhauer, A. (1818). *The World as Will and Representation*, Vol. 3. Translated by Haldane, R.B. and Kemp, J. London: Kegan Paul, Trench, Trübner & Co., 1909.

Schwenger, P. (2019). *Asemic: The Art of Writing*. Minneapolis: University of Minnesota Press.

Seager, W. (2019). *The Routledge Handbook of Panpsychism*. London: Routledge.

Shelburne, W.A. (1988). *Mythos and Logos in the Thought of Carl Jung: The Theory of the Collective Unconscious in Scientific Perspective*. Albany, NY: State University of New York Press.

Sjöstedt-Hughes, P. (2015). *Noumenautics: Metaphysics, Meta-ethics, Psychedelics.* Falmouth: Psychedelic Press UK.

Sjöstedt-Hughes, P. (2021). *Modes of Sentience: Psychedelics, Metaphysics, Panpsychism.* London: Psychedelic Press.

Smith, S.B. (2003). *Spinoza's Book of Life: Freedom and Redemption in the Ethics.* New Haven: Yale University Press.

Spinoza, B. (1677). *Ethics.* Translated by White, W.H. Ware, Hertfordshire: Wordsworth Editions, 2001.

Stace, W.T. (1960). *Mysticism and Philosophy.* London: Macmillan, 1973.

Stapledon, O. (1937). *Star Maker.* https://www.astro.sunysb.edu/fwalter/AST389/TEXTS/StarMaker.pdf

Storr, A. (1998). *The Essential Jung.* Glasgow: Fontana.

Strassman, R. (2001). *DMT: The Spirit Molecule: A Doctor's Revolutionary Research into the Biology of Near-Death and Mystical Experiences.* Rochester, VT: Park Street Press.

Swinburne, R. (1997). *Simplicity as Evidence for Truth.* Milwaukee: Marquette University Press.

Urry, J. (1990). *The Tourist Gaze.* 2nd ed. London: SAGE Publications, 2002.

Vandenabeele, B. (2015). *The Sublime in Schopenhauer's Philosophy.* London: Palgrave Macmillan.

Whitehead, A.N. (1929). *Process and Reality.* Edited by Griffin, D.R. and Sherburne, D.W. New York: The Free Press, 1978.

Woolf, V. (1924). *The Diary of Virginia Woolf, Volume II.* Edited by Bell, A.O. London: Penguin, 1984.

Yalom, I. (1980). *Existential Psychotherapy.* New York: Basic Books.

Zografos, S. (2019). *Architecture and Fire: A Psychoanalytic Approach to Conservation.* London: UCL Press.

# About the Author

Sam Woolfe is a London-based writer and blogger who has been covering philosophical and psychedelic topics for over a decade — both on his blog and for various publications. His writings on philosophy have been published in *Philosophy Now*, the Psychedelic Press journal, and IAI News. He has written about the science of psychedelics for a number of media companies and educational platforms, such as Third Wave, *Lucid News*, Psychedelic Support, and HealingMaps. He is also a bad movie lover and has explored philosophical perspectives on 'so bad they're good' movies for the online film journal *Senses of Cinema*.

You can find more of his work at www.samwoolfe.com.

IFF
BOOKS

## ACADEMIC AND SPECIALIST

Iff Books publishes non-fiction. It aims to work with authors and
titles that augment our understanding of the human condition,
society and civilisation, and the world or universe in which we live.
If you have enjoyed this book, why not tell other readers by
posting a review on your preferred book site.
Recent bestsellers from Iff Books are:

### Why Materialism Is Baloney
How true skeptics know there is no death and fathom answers
to life, the universe, and everything
Bernardo Kastrup
A hard-nosed, logical, and skeptic non-materialist metaphysics,
according to which the body is in mind, not mind in the body.
Paperback: 978-1-78279-362-5 ebook: 978-1-78279-361-8

### The Fall
Steve Taylor
*The Fall* discusses human achievement versus the issues of war,
patriarchy and social inequality.
Paperback: 978-1-78535-804-3 ebook: 978-1-78535-805-0

### Brief Peeks Beyond
Critical essays on metaphysics, neuroscience, free will,
skepticism and culture
Bernardo Kastrup
An incisive, original, compelling alternative to current mainstream
cultural views and assumptions.
Paperback: 978-1-78535-018-4 ebook: 978-1-78535-019-1

## Framespotting

Changing how you look at things changes how
you see them
Laurence & Alison Matthews
A punchy, upbeat guide to framespotting. Spot deceptions and
hidden assumptions; swap growth for growing up. See and be free.
Paperback: 978-1-78279-689-3 ebook: 978-1-78279-822-4

## Is There an Afterlife?

David Fontana
Is there an Afterlife? If so what is it like? How do Western ideas
of the afterlife compare with Eastern? David Fontana presents the
historical and contemporary evidence for survival of
physical death.
Paperback: 978-1-90381-690-5

## Nothing Matters

a book about nothing
Ronald Green
Thinking about Nothing opens the world to everything by
illuminating new angles to old problems and stimulating new
ways of thinking.
Paperback: 978-1-84694-707-0 ebook: 978-1-78099-016-3

## Panpsychism

The Philosophy of the Sensuous Cosmos
Peter Ells
Are free will and mind chimeras? This book, anti-materialistic but
respecting science, answers: No! Mind is foundational
to all existence.
Paperback: 978-1-84694-505-2 ebook: 978-1-78099-018-7

## Punk Science
Inside the Mind of God
Manjir Samanta-Laughton
Many have experienced unexplainable phenomena; God, psychic abilities, extraordinary healing and angelic encounters. Can cutting-edge science actually explain phenomena previously thought of as 'paranormal'?
Paperback: 978-1-90504-793-2

## The Vagabond Spirit of Poetry
Edward Clarke
Spend time with the wisest poets of the modern age and of the past, and let Edward Clarke remind you of the importance of poetry in our industrialized world.
Paperback: 978-1-78279-370-0 ebook: 978-1-78279-369-4


Readers of ebooks can buy or view any of these bestsellers by clicking on the live link in the title. Most titles are published in paperback and as an ebook. Paperbacks are available in traditional bookshops. Both print and ebook formats are available online. Find more titles and sign up to our readers' newsletter at
www.collectiveinkbooks.com/non-fiction
Follow us on Facebook at
www.facebook.com/CINonFiction